T0289940

Event Portfolio Management:
Theory and Methods for Event Management and Tourism

Vladimir Antchak, Vassilios Ziakas and Donald Getz

(G) Goodfellow Publishers Ltd

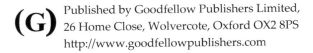

Published by Goodfellow Publishers Limited,
26 Home Close, Wolvercote, Oxford OX2 8PS
http://www.goodfellowpublishers.com

British Library Cataloguing in Publication Data: a catalogue
record for this title is available from the British Library.

Library of Congress Catalog Card Number: on file.

ISBN: 978-1-911396-91-8

The Events Management Theory and Methods Series

Copyright © Vladimir Antchak, Vassilios Ziakas and Donald Getz, 2019

All rights reserved. The text of this publication, or any part thereof,
may not be reproduced or transmitted in any form or by any means,
electronic or mechanical, including photocopying, recording, storage in
an information retrieval system, or otherwise, without prior permission
of the publisher or under licence from the Copyright Licensing
Agency Limited. Further details of such licences (for reprographic
reproduction) may be obtained from the Copyright Licensing Agency
Limited, of Saffron House, 6–10 Kirby Street, London EC1N 8TS.

 Design and typesetting by P.K. McBride, www.macbride.org.uk

Cover design by Cylinder

Printed by Baker and Taylor, www.baker-taylor.com

Contents

List of figures

List of tables

Introduction to the Events Management Theory and Methods Series

Event management as a field of study and professional practice has its textbooks with plenty of models and advice, a body of knowledge (EMBOK), competency standards (MBECS) and professional associations with their codes of conduct. But to what extent is it truly an applied management field? In other words, where is the management theory in event management, how is it being used, and what are the practical applications?

Event tourism is a related field, one that is defined by the roles events play in tourism and economic development. The primary consideration has always been economic, although increasingly events and managed event portfolios meet more diverse goals for cities and countries. While the economic aspects have been well developed, especially economic impact assessment and forecasting, the application of management theory to event tourism has not received adequate attention.

In this book series we launch a process of examining the extent to which mainstream theory is being employed to develop event-specific theory, and to influence the practice of event management and event tourism. This is a very big task, as there are numerous possible theories, models and concepts, and virtually unlimited advice available on the management of firms, small and family businesses, government agencies and not-for-profits. Inevitably, we will have to be selective.

The starting point is theory. Scientific theory must both explain a phenomenon, and be able to predict what will happen. Experiments are the dominant form of classical theory development. But for management, predictive capabilities are usually lacking; it might be wiser to speak of theory in development, or theory fragments. It is often the process of theory development that marks research in management, including the testing of hypotheses and the formulation of propositions. Models, frameworks, concepts and sets of propositions are all part of this development.

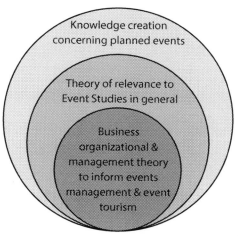

The diagram illustrates this approach. All knowledge creation has potential application to management, as does theory from any discipline or field. The critical factor for this series is how the theory and related methods can be applied. In the core of this diagram are management and business theories which are the most directly pertinent, and they are often derived from foundation disciplines.

All the books in this series will be relatively short, and similarly structured. They are designed to be used by teachers who need theoretical foundations and case studies for their classes, by students in need of reference works, by professionals wanting increased understanding alongside practical methods, and by agencies or associations that want their members and stakeholders to have access to a library of valuable resources. The nature of the series is that as it grows, components can be assembled by request. That is, users can order a book or collection of chapters to exactly suit their needs.

All the books will introduce the theory, show how it is being used in the events sector through a literature review, incorporate examples and case studies written by researchers and/or practitioners, and contain methods that can be used effectively in the real world.

About the authors and contributors

Dr Vladimir Antchak is Senior Lecturer in Applied Management at the University of Derby, UK. His research interests focus on event portfolio design and management, place experience, destination branding and strategic storytelling. He has over 10 years of experience in events management, including organisation of business forums and conferences, cultural exhibitions, international business visits and presentations. The geography of completed projects includes Austria, Germany, Italy, the Netherlands and Russia.

Dr Vassilios Ziakas is Associate Professor at Plymouth Marjon University, UK with a research interest in sport and leisure policy through the lens of an interdisciplinary approach that seeks to create linkages among the sectors of sport, recreation, leisure, tourism and events. His primary emphasis is on strategic planning for obtaining a range of sustainable community benefits. His research has been published in a range of leading journals and is widely cited. He is author of the book *Event Portfolio Planning and Management: A Holistic Approach* (Routledge, 2014) and co-editor of the *Routledge Handbook of Popular Culture and Tourism* (Routledge, 2018).

Professor Donald Getz is a leading international researcher, author and consultant in the fields of tourism and event studies. Dr. Getz is Professor Emeritus, the University of Calgary, where he worked in the Haskayne School of Business from 1991 through 2009. Following his retirement, he held part-time research positions at the University of Queensland (Australia), University of Stavanger (Norway), and the University of Gothenburg (Sweden), and he was Visiting Professor at Linnaeus University in Sweden. Today, he is Visiting Professor at the University of Derby, UK. He has authored a number of relevant books including *Event Management and Event Tourism*, *Event Studies*, *Event Tourism*, *Event Evaluation*, and *Event Impact Assessment*, and co-authored *Event Stakeholders*.

Dr Valentina Gorchakova is Senior Lecturer at the University of Derby, teaching and leading an online business and management programme. She returned to academia after spending more than 10 years working in business, not-for-profit organisations and the UN Development Programme. Her research interests lie within service and arts marketing, branding, place-making, cultural and event tourism. She is also exploring the area of online learning, and learning in adulthood.

Ms Zuzana Vokacova has recently graduated from the University of Derby in MSc Events Management, which she passed with distinction. She has experience organising projects and events including congresses and business conferences, which she gained through working for a Professional Congress Organizer in Prague and interning at the International Congress and Convention Association in Amsterdam. She is passionate about events and traveling and her professional specialisation is in the meetings industry. She is currently working as an event project manager.

Acknowledgements

The authors would like to acknowledge Dr Valentina Gorchakova and Ms. Zuzana Vokacova for contributing Chapter 9 and Chapter 10 respectively to this book. We are grateful to all the practitioners from DMOs and other organisations in Auckland, Canberra, Dunedin, Manchester, Melbourne and Wellington, who shared with us their experience and provided research data for the book. The case study for Chapter 11 was prepared with the assistance of Festivals Edinburgh, and we are grateful for their participation. Special thanks goes to James McVeigh, Head of Marketing and Innovation.

1 Introduction

The increasing use of planned events by cities, regions and countries world-wide to achieve their policy goals and obtain economic, tourism, place-marketing, or broader community benefits has led to the creation of city-wide programmes staging a series of recurring events all year round. The strategic intent of host communities and destinations to manage a calendar of events engenders the development of event portfolios. For example, the cities of Edinburgh (City of Edinburgh Council, 2007), Gold Coast (City of Cold Coast, 2011) and Auckland (ATEED, 2018) have developed, their own strategic portfolios by assembling and coordinating a balanced number of periodic events of different type and scale. Portfolio strategies have also been employed on national level, for example, in Wales (Welsh Government, 2010), Scotland (Visit Scotland, 2015) and New Zealand (Cabinet Office Wellington, 2004).

The endeavour of places to develop event portfolios lies upon the alignment of their event strategies with their policy agendas. In so doing, the underlying rationale is to create a diversified portfolio of events that take place at different times of the year and that appeal to audiences across the span of consumer profiles which a host destination seeks to target (Chalip, 2004; Getz, 2013; Ziakas, 2014). From this standpoint, multiple purposes can be achieved by leveraging the event portfolio and fostering synergies among different events and their stakeholders in order to optimise the overall portfolio benefits and value.

The process of event portfolio development and management is highly complex and can occasionally become challenging. This is mainly because an array of assembled events brings forth a number of stakeholders who have different, or sometimes, antithetical interests, values, perceptions, and worldviews. Within host communities and destinations there are found different organisations with their own strategies representing key constituents from the commercial, non-profit, sport and culture realms, including chambers of commerce, visitor and convention bureaus, public and private sport and entertainment venues, convention and exhibition centres, private event companies, parks and recreation agencies, museums and historical sites, art centres, culture development agencies, and various non-profit health or charitable organisations. Their roles in the event sector often intersect, creating tensions over priorities and goal orientations. As such, collaborative efforts for crafting a comprehensive event portfolio strategy may be constrained with events, hence, not being effectively synergised. The move towards an integrated portfolio approach that strategically uses events as part of a wider policy framework (Richards, 2017a) requires synergy, cooperation as well as coordination of actors, resources and actions. Still, the ability of cities to develop integrated event policies differs widely (Antchak, 2017; Getz, 2017; Smith, 2005, 2012). Consequently, cities adopt different approaches in developing and managing event portfolios, based upon their capabilities (Richards, 2017b).

It is within this context, therefore that the phenomenon of event portfolio as a policy tool has gained acceptance and gradually attracted academic attention. The first explicit empirical study of the phenomenon of event portfolios dated back to 2010 (Ziakas, 2010). The research explored a portfolio of local events in a small rural community in Texas, USA. However, the conceptual origins of strategic event portfolio creation go back much farther. In their seminal paper on the role of events in countering seasonality, Ritchie and Beliveau (1974) made the case for 'hallmark events' as strategic tools in destination tourism planning and development, concluding that more sophisticated consumer research could be employed (p. 19) "...to plan a complementary series of events on a regional basis". In his later article, Ritchie (1984) comprehensively examined the potentially diverse impacts of events and established the basis for a triple-bottom-line approach. In the book *Festivals, Special Events and Tourism* (1991), Getz explained the various roles of events in tourism and community planning and provided a detailed event-tourism strategy that included (p. 171) models of four types of multiple-event packaging for destinations. In the book *Event Management and Event Tourism* (1997), Getz illustrated portfolio planning with a pyramid model, with acknowledgement to the Boston Consulting Group's famous matrix, created in 1970, for product portfolio management. The term 'event portfolio' certainly had been in use in New Zealand earlier than 1995, as Ryan and Bates (1995) referred to a city's 'event portfolio'.

Since Ziakas' 2010 paper, the literature includes portfolio studies on Gainesville, Florida (Gibson, Kaplanidou, & Kang, 2012), Termoli in Italy (Presenza & Sheehan, 2013), London, Ontario (Clark & Misener, 2015), Portimão in Portugal (Pereira, Mascarenhas, Flores, & Pires, 2015), Barcelona (Richards, 2015), Sunshine Coast in Australia (Gration, Raciti, Getz, & Andersson, 2016), Auckland (Antchak, 2017), Berlin (Viol, Todd, Theodoraki, & Anastasiadou, 2018) and Cook Islands (Dickson, Milne, & Werner, 2018). Diverse portfolio approaches, issues and perspectives have also attracted attention of some scholars (Andersson, Getz, & Mykletun, 2013; Andersson, Getz, Gration, & Raciti, 2017; Antchak & Pernecky, 2017; Dragin-Jensen, Schnittka, & Arkil, 2016; Kelly & Fairley, 2018; Taks, Chalip, Green, Kesenne, & Martyn, 2009; Westerbeek & Linley, 2012; Ziakas & Boukas, 2012). However, as Ziakas (2019) posits, "evidently, therefore, the seed has grown but the fruits are thin on the ground and not yet ready for harvesting" (p. 27).

The above number of empirical studies is a rather limited response to the increasing growth of event portfolios, their instrumental value and underlying complexity. Nonetheless, it reveals the diversity of emergent portfolio configurations in different national and urban contexts, their design patterns and implementation strategies. It also sets out a common ground for furthering the progress of event portfolios as a sustainable policy tool and creating a knowledge base for their planning and management. It has now become apparent that conventional wisdom of the past cannot serve portfolio management, but instead, a holistic and strategic approach is needed. This marks a paradigm shift from the predominant focus on single events to a more comprehensive focus on multiple events. The shift under way demands the development of specialist know-how and intelligence mandated to foster synergies among different events, a mindset not previously executed in mainstream event management. Current literature thus is needed to elaborate on portfolio management principles and practices. In response, this book makes a timely addition to the latest body of emerging event portfolio literature.

The overall aim of this book is to provide the readers with a concise introduction to portfolio theory and methods, as well as demonstrate how related approaches can be used and adapted using international case studies. This book provides a comprehensive review of the roles of event portfolios in the contexts of event policy, event strategy and event management. The book offers insights into how city event planners apply different portfolio approaches and what principles govern the realisation of city-wide major event strategies. There is strong evidence presented of the global adoption of an event portfolio approach by cities and destinations, and this trend is certain to continue. To support this increased sophistication, and to encourage long-term sustainability in its fullest sense, the field must develop appropriate theory and methods, some of which will arise from original research and experimentation, and some through adaptation of theory and methods from other fields.

The book is divided in two parts. The first part, 'Theory', explores and evaluates the theoretical underpinnings behind the development, application and evaluation of portfolio strategies. Chapter 2 introduces the event portfolio as a theoretical phenomenon and urban policy tool. The chapter provides a theoretical background to the relationship between contemporary cities and their events. Such concepts as place-making, eventfulness, destination capitals and event populations are introduced and discussed in detail.

Chapter 3 discusses portfolio leveraging strategies. The concept of leveraging is a result of a paradigmatic shift in event studies from short-term impacts to planned long-term leveraged outcomes from events. An event portfolio is introduced as a strategic tool to accumulate different leveraging plans for different events included in the portfolio. Such plans can aim at achieving positive economic, socio-cultural, environmental and political outcomes.

Chapter 4 is focused on inter-organisational relationships and stakeholder networking. A multi-level network approach is pivotal for the integration of portfolios into destination policies and structures. Event portfolios are embedded within wider social networks and their on-going implementation can play a role as social agents in shaping their own environment through systemic and structural effects. A portfolio-level network perspective is discussed and employed to examine the strength of relationships among event-related organisations based on their level of communication and exchange of information, sharing of resources, common programmes or activities, and assistance.

Chapter 5 analyses critical aspects of event portfolio design. The chapter pinpoints differences between organic and formalised portfolios, and introduces the concepts of meta-event and multiple portfolios. Four event portfolio development strategies, including symmetrisation, specialisation, multi-constellation, and macro-expansion are introduced and discussed. A holistic model of event portfolio design is introduced. This consists of two processes of Composing and Synergising. Composing deals with different portfolio assemblage strategies, event roles and design factors. Synergising is responsible for portfolio balancing, timing and leveraging.

Chapter 6 concludes the theoretical part of the book and explores diverse evaluation and assessment strategies. An event portfolio success and overall value are discussed from the perspectives of organisational ecology, theory of change, and financial theory. Several evaluation models and matrices are introduced.

The second part of the book, 'Case Studies', introduces and explores different examples of event portfolio planning, development and implementations in various urban and national contexts. Thus, Chapter 7 reviews a governmental approach to major events in New Zealand. Chapter 8 analyses institutional contexts of portfolio development in three cities in New Zealand, Auckland, Wellington and Dunedin. Chapter 9 provides a thorough investigation into the value of touring exhibitions and their utilisation as part of city portfolio approach in Canberra and Melbourne, Australia. Chapter 10 describes a sector-focused approach to business events in Manchester, UK. Chapter 11 focuses on Edinburgh's portfolio approach to festivals. The purpose of Chapter 12 is to compare 23 cities, the winners of the International Festivals and Events Association's World Festival and Event City award and their event strategies. Finally, Chapter 13 concludes the book by providing a summary and recommendations for further research.

On the whole, this book demonstrates that the emergence of event portfolios, as a new phenomenon, brings forth significant opportunities and equally major challenges. Appropriate responses require concerted attention in order to fully understand the nature of portfolios, carefully define their parameters, and systematically investigate processes for their management. Evidently, event portfolios represent a multi-dimensional phenomenon with a notable complexity due to the multiple events and stakeholders involved. As such, the mindset of a holistic approach on event portfolio planning and management constitutes a novel paradigm for event management with distinctive theory and methods, still to be developed in the next years, informing evidence-based policy and practice. From this perspective, event portfolios are viewed as complex systems, living organisms composed of multiple parts and structures. Their study is currently at the beginning and there is a lot to be learned, as the case studies in the second part of the book illustrate. Learning from the growth of event portfolios sets a critical juncture between theory and practice that shape the logics of this book.

References

Andersson, T. D., Getz, D., Gration, D., & Raciti, M. M. (2017). Event portfolios: Asset value, risk and returns. *International Journal of Event and Festival Management*, **8**(3), 226–243. doi:10.1108/IJEFM-01-2017-0008

Andersson, T. D., Getz, D., & Mykletun, R. (2013). The 'festival size pyramid' in three Norwegian festival populations. *Journal of Convention & Event Tourism*, **14**(2), 81–103. doi:10.1080/15470148.2013.782258

Antchak, V. (2017). Portfolio of major events in Auckland: characteristics, perspectives and issues. *Journal of Policy Research in Tourism, Leisure and Events*, **9**(3). doi:10.1080/19407963.2017.1312421

Antchak, V., & Pernecky, T. (2017). Major events programming in a city: Comparing three approaches to portfolio design. *Event Management*, **21**(5), 545-561. doi:10.3727/152599517X15053272359013

ATEED. (2018). Auckland major event strategy. Retrieved from https://www.aucklandnz.com/sites/build_auckland/files/media-library/documents/Auckland-Major-Events-Strategy-October-2018.pdf

Cabinet Office Wellington. (2004). Government major event strategy. Wellington, New Zealand: Cabinet Economic Development Committee. Retrieved from http://www.med.govt.nz/majorevents/pdf-library/nz-major-events/strategy-documents/major-events-strategy-2004

Chalip, L. (2004). Beyond impact: A general model for sport event leverage. In B. W. Ritchie (Ed.), *Sport Tourism: Interrelationships, impacts and issues* (pp. 226–252). Clevedon, England: Channel View.

City of Cold Coast. (2011). Gold Coast city events strategic plan 2011-2015. Retrieved April 14, 2017, from http://www.eventsgoldcoast.com.au/uploads/file/Gold-Coast-City-Events-Strategic-Plan-2011-2015.pdf

City of Edinburgh Council. (2007). Inspiring events strategy. Edinburgh, Scotland. Retrieved from http://eventsedinburgh.org.uk/files/documents/inspiring-events-strategy.pdf

Clark, R., & Misener, L. (2015). Understanding urban development through a sport events portfolio: A case study of London, Ontario. *Journal of Sport Management*, **29**(1), 11–26. doi:10.1123/jsm.2013-0259

Dickson, G., Milne, S., & Werner, K. (2018). Collaborative capacity to develop an events portfolio within a small island development state: The Cook Islands. *Policy Research in Tourism, Leisure and Events*, **10**(1), 69–89. doi:10.1080/1940796 3.2017.1409751

Dragin-Jensen, C., Schnittka, O., & Arkil, C. (2016). More options do not always create perceived variety in life: Attracting new residents with quality- vs. quantity-oriented event portfolios. *Cities*, **56**, 55–62. doi:10.1016/j.cities.2016.03.004

Getz, D. (1991). *Festivals, Special Events and Tourism*. New York: Van Nostrand Reinhold.

Getz, D. (1997). *Event Management and Event Tourism*. New York: Cognizant Communication Corporation.

Getz, D. (2013). *Event Tourism: Concepts, international case studies, and research*. New York, NY: Cognizant Communication Corporation.

Getz, D. (2017). Developing a framework for sustainable event cities. *Event Management*, **21**(575–591). doi:10.3727/152599517X15053272359031

Gibson, H. J., Kaplanidou, K., & Kang, S. J. (2012). Small-scale event sport tourism: A case study in sustainable tourism. *Sport Management Review*, **15**(2), 160–170. doi:10.1016/j.smr.2011.08.013

Gration, D., Raciti, M., Getz, D., & Andersson, T. D. (2016). Resident valuation of planned events: An event portfolio pilot study. *Event Management*, **20**(4), 607–622. doi:10.3727/152599516X14745497664596

Kelly, D. M., & Fairley, S. (2018). The utility of relationships in the creation and maintenance of an event portfolio. *Marketing Intelligence & Planning*, **36**(2), 260–275. Retrieved from doi:10.1108/MIP-11-2017-0270

Pereira, E. C. S., Mascarenhas, M. V. M., Flores, A. J. G., & Pires, G. M. V. S. (2015). Nautical small-scale sports events portfolio: A strategic leveraging approach. *European Sport Management Quarterly*, **15**(1), 27–47. doi:10.1080/1618 4742.2015.1007883

Presenza, A., & Sheehan, L. (2013). Planning tourism through sporting events. *International Journal of Event and Festival Management*, **4**(2), 125–139. doi:10.1108/17582951311325890

Richards, G. (2015). Events in the network society: The role of pulsar and iterative events. *Event Management*, **19**(4), 553–566. doi:10.3727/1525995 15x14465748512849

Richards, G. (2017a). From place branding to placemaking: The role of events. *International Journal of Event and Festival Management*, **8**(1), 8–23. doi:10.1108/IJEFM-09-2016-0063

Richards, G. (2017b). Emerging models of the eventful city. *Event Management*, **21**(533–543). doi:10.3727/152599517X15053272359004

Ritchie, J.R.B. (1984). Assessing the impact of hallmark events: Conceptual and research issues. *Journal of Travel Research*, **23**(1), 2-11. doi:10.1177/004728758402300101

Ritchie, J.R.B. & Beliveau, D. (1974). Hallmark events: An evaluation of a strategic response to seasonality in the travel market. *Journal of Travel Research*, **13**(2), 14-20. doi:10.1177/004728757401300202

Ryan, C. & Bates, C. (1995). A rose by any other name: The motivations of those opening their gardens for a festival. *Festival Management and Event Tourism*, **3**(1) 59-71.

Smith, A. (2005). Reimaging the city: The value of sport initiatives. *Annals of Tourism Research*, **32**(1), 217–236. doi:10.1016/j.annals.2004.07.007

Smith, A. (2012). *Events and Urban Regeneration: The strategic use of events to revitalise cities*. New York, NY: Routledge.

Taks, M., Chalip, L., Green, B. C., Kesenne, S., & Martyn, S. (2009). Factors affecting repeat visitation and flow-on tourism as sources of event strategy sustainability. *Journal of Sport & Tourism*, **14**(2–3), 121–142. doi:10.1080/14775080902965066

Viol, M., Todd, L., Theodoraki, E., & Anastasiadou, C. (2018). The role of iconic-historic commemorative events in event tourism: Insights from the 20th and 25th anniversaries of the fall of the Berlin Wall. *Tourism Management*, **69**, 246–262. doi:10.1016/j.tourman.2018.06.018

Visit Scotland. (2015). Scotland the perfect stage: Scotland's events strategy 2015-2025. Retrieved from http://www.eventscotland.org/assets/show/4658

Welsh Government. (2010). Event Wales: A major events strategy for Wales 2010-2020. Retrieved from gov.wales/topics/culture-tourism-sport/major-events/event-wales-a-major-events-strategy-for-wales-2010-2020/?lang=en

Westerbeek, H., & Linley, M. (2012). Building city brands through sport events: Theoretical and empirical perspectives. *Journal of Brand Strategy*, **1**(2), 193–205.

Ziakas, V. (2010). Understanding an event portfolio: the Uncovering of interrelationships, synergies, and leveraging opportunities. *Journal of Policy Research in Tourism, Leisure and Events*, **2**(2), 144–164. doi:10.1080/19407963.2010.482274

Ziakas, V. (2014). *Event Portfolio Planning and Management: A holistic approach*. Abingdon, England: Routledge.

Ziakas, V. (2019). Embracing the event portfolio paradigm in academic discourse and scholarship. *Journal of Policy Research in Tourism, Leisure and Events*, **11**(s1), 27–33. doi:10.1080/19407963.2018.1556861

Ziakas, V., & Boukas, N. (2012). A neglected legacy: Examining the challenges and potential for sport tourism development in post-Olympic Athens. *International Journal of Event and Festival Management*, **3**(3), 292–316. doi:10.1108/17582951211262710

Part I: Theory

2 Cities and Events: Introducing Event Portfolios

In this chapter the paradigm of the event portfolio will be introduced and its theoretical underpinnings explained. The emphasis will be placed on the strategic utilisation of planned events in host cities. The concepts of place-making, competitive identity, eventfulness and destination capitals will be presented and discussed. The chapter will outline the different definitions of an event portfolio and analyse the relationship between a portfolio of planned events and an overall population of events in a host destination. This chapter paves the way to an in-depth presentation and analysis of the tenets of event portfolio theory in this book.

Events and places

The origins of events as ritualistic practice and markers of a community's life date back to the archaic times of human history. Social and cultural anthropologists have many records of different events, which have been following the existence and development of a human society, such as 'celebrations', 'rituals', 'ceremonies', 'processions' and 'parades' (Foley, McGillivray, & McPherson, 2012). As Pernecky and Lück (2013, p. 1) note: "They [events] mark important milestones and achievements, they are deployed to celebrate and engage communities, and they are an inherent aspect of many public occasions". Richards (2015a) argues that events represent spaces of social interaction. Such spaces consolidate people by creating a sense of 'togetherness', belonging to a particular subculture or community (Silvanto & Hellman, 2005). Moreover, as spaces of interaction, events influence the formation of a unique place identity, providing points of identification and attachment to a particular location, for example, a host city (Derrett, 2003; McClinchey, 2015). From this perspective, events have been actively engaged in *place-making*. Place-making is a concept that:

> aims to turn public spaces into places; places which engage with those who inhabit them, places through which people do not merely pass, but have reason to 'stop and become involved'; places which offer rich experience and a 'sense of belonging'; places in short, which have meaning, which evoke pleasure or contemplation or reflection and, most importantly, an appreciation of cultural and environmental diversity (Ryan, 1995, p. 7).

Although this concept emerged initially in urban design, it has been actively implemented recently in events studies. Indeed, events play an integral role in creating visibility and attracting attention to cities. Cities have become not just stages for events, but also places that are produced through events (Richards & Rotariu, 2015). Smith (2016) proposes the term *eventalisation* that refers to "the process through which urban space is produced via the staging of events" (p. 37). From this perspective, events can animate venues and open grounds, bring in new people and change the identity of city spaces. In the contemporary world of an 'experience economy' (Pine & Gilmore, 1999) cities try to sustain these temporary space changes and create permanent areas of festivity, leisure and entertainment. Cities aspire to include events into their fibre, marking places, adding life to city streets and redeveloping depressed city zones. Dansero and Puttilli (2010) argue that public events can be seen as an excellent opportunity to create new territories in the city and brand them, using the identity from a successful event.

Events and competitive identity

Place-making is intimately linked to competitive identity (Anholt, 2007, 2010). This concept was proposed as an alternative to a mainstream understanding of place branding, where cities and nations are seen as an equivalent to corporate products and services. A common practice of destination brand promoters is to adopt tactics developed for physical goods. However, such models are unlikely to suit city brands. City brands represent a complexity of tangible and intangible assets that have been developed through the networks of different stakeholders with their own interests and priorities. While branding is a process that mainly occurs in the mind of a receiver or consumer, identity is usually defined by the sender itself (Moilanen & Rainisto, 2009).

Anholt (2007) argues that in order to create a desirable and distinctive place identity, cities need to capitalise on the interplay of factors, including destination policy, destination tourism, destination brands, investment, culture and people. Such complex activities require the coordination of a large number of stakeholders, strategies and functions. The realisation of competitive identity in a city can be achieved by: 1) the things that are done in the city; 2) the things that are made in the city; 3) the way other people talk about the city and; 4) the way the city talks about itself (Anholt, 2007, p. 30). Events play a significant role within this strategic framework. For example, the global awareness of such mega-events, as the Olympic Games or the FIFA World Cup and their close associations with the host cities, significantly contribute to the reputation and image of those destinations. Public large-scale events possess all three properties of a 'competitive identity magnet': they attract visitors, tourists and consumers; they transfer 'magnetism' to other objects (for example, Sydney and Barcelona capitalise on their Olympic history and construct an image of modern and open cities); and they are able to integrate normally disparate or competitive stakeholders around shared purposes and goals (Anholt, 2007).

Eventfulness

A seminal concept exemplifying the emergence of a strategic approach to managing public events in cities is *eventfulness*. The term was coined by Richards and Palmer (2010) to explain the shift in the event policy of cities to develop an annual programme of events. They suggest that eventfulness embodies the integration of events with the other strategies and policies of a city, such as tourism, economic, social and cultural development, urban regeneration and brand promotion. An eventful city purposefully uses a programme of events to strategically and sustainably support long-term policy agendas that enhance the quality of life for all (Richards, 2015b). The concept of eventfulness epitomises a holistic policy approach relating to the coordinated management of a city's calendar of events. From this standpoint, staging single events is insufficient for cities to become eventful, and thereby optimise the benefits of events. Eventfulness entails thinking holistically about events and encompassing a number of complex processes, such as developing an effective stakeholder network, creating a strategic vision, programming the eventful city, marketing events to publics and audiences, monitoring outcomes and ensuring sustainability (Richards & Palmer, 2010).

Eventfulness brings to the fore the relationship between event policy and broader urban policy agendas. The increasing integration of events and urban policy involves a wide range of stakeholders, including civic administrations, commercial companies, the media and national governments. The role of the city therefore has moved from the direct organisation of events towards a more facilitatory role, in line with increasingly neo-liberal policies (Richards & Palmer, 2010). The notion of urban regimes is useful for connecting the development of event strategies to specific types of urban policy and governance. Urban regimes are alliances between local governments and interest groups in the city, such as businesses, social groups or development organisations, which have specific 'agendas' or aims that they come together to support (Stone, 1989). For example, the city of Edmonton, Canada was found to have a progressive regime using sport events to facilitate a wider range of civic goals than the economic development regimes in Manchester and Melbourne, which were focused on using sports events to attract capital and investment (Misener & Mason, 2008, 2009). These examples illustrate that the increasing employment of events for achieving economic goals is not only linked to neo-liberal policies but also tends to be integrated into general urban policies. In this fashion, events have emerged as significant policy tools for the agendas of cities seeking to obtain a wide range of benefits. The integration of events as an important part in the policy agenda of a city creates opportunities to influence the direction of urban policies and structures.

One such strategic opportunity is the development of event portfolios. From a portfolio perspective, the investment of a host city in a series of periodic events creates a permanent structure that can influence general city policies, arrangements and institutions. An event portfolio has the potential to become a space in which existing norms and rationales meet and are discussed, mirrored, and turned upside down in search for creating alternative social structures (Olsen, 2012). In this respect, there is a need for portfolios to allow room for accommodating competing rationales and stakeholder orientations through the array of events. Evidently, this approach echoes an aspiration of integrative mentalities to move towards synthesising disparate events and their stakeholders, associated purposes, and underlying rationales or orientations (Chalip, 2006; Dredge & Whitford, 2010; Quinn, 2010; Whitford, 2009). While urban regimes as they embrace eventfulness and portfolios in their policy agendas create the conditions for a fruitful synthesis, this may also create tensions that inhibit in essence the development of an inclusive and holistic approach.

Eventfulness provides a holistic policy perspective for the effective incorporation of events into the structures of a host community by building conduits that arrange and coordinate the strategy, planning, governance, and policy development for an array of events (Ziakas, 2019). In so doing, the type of strategy employed and the governance arrangements, the skills, knowledge and resources required for effective implementation vary considerably according to particular local conditions and institutional structures. In other words, based on the governance-policy context, an eventful programme will have to meet different aims and objectives, and therefore utilise different performance indicators (Richards & Palmer, 2010).

The cultivation of eventfulness can be operationalised through the inventive design, management and leveraging of event portfolios as adaptive systems, which brings forward the imperative for holistic integration and constant change management. Integration can be achieved by creating systemic structures, and change management competence can be nurtured by building mechanisms that foster adaptability and resilience of system elements. As such, the concept of event portfolios as an adaptive system should be defined and their basic principles as well as relationships with relative perspectives need to be demarcated.

Defining event portfolios

The term *event portfolio* is derived from two well-established lines of theory development: product portfolios, linked to the product life-cycle concept, and modern financial portfolio analysis. Stern and Stalk (1998) compiled papers from the Boston Consulting Group including Bruce Henderson's 1970 articulation of the BCG product portfolio model (variations of this graphical model abound online). It arranges 'products', which could be events within a city or destination portfolio, into four cells defined by 'relative market share' and 'market growth', resulting in categories labelled 'stars, dogs, cash cows and question marks'. Strategic responses to this type of analysis can range from termination of products to extension of their life cycles to maximise profit. Application of this particular portfolio approach to events is made difficult by the fact that market share and growth are better indicators for the private sector than for governments and non-profit organisations.

Event portfolio also borrows from modern financial portfolio theory (Markowitz, 1952, 1991). This theory prescribes decision-making over optimal investment of wealth in financial assets, which differ in regard to their expected return and risk. According to Markowitz, a portfolio is a grouping of financial assets, such as stocks, bonds, and cash equivalents, as well as their mutual, exchange-traded, and closed-fund counterparts. Markowitz's theory refers to households' and firms' allocation of financial assets under uncertainty by analysing how wealth can be optimally invested in assets that differ in regard to their expected return and risk, and thereby assessing how risks can be reduced. This theory stipulates that investors should focus on selecting portfolios based on their overall risk–reward characteristics, instead of merely compiling portfolios from individual securities each holding attractive risk–reward characteristics. Diversification is a key tenet and risk management technique for Markowitz as it dictates to merge a variety of investments within a portfolio based on the rationale that a portfolio comprising different kinds of investments can yield higher returns and pose a lower risk than any individual investment found within the portfolio.

Along these lines, the shared terrain between financial portfolio theory and event portfolios can be delineated by drawing the following analogy: a strategic selection of events can attain more benefits than individual events since the sum of multiple assets is greater than the parts, generating thereby additional value. Furthermore, hosting multiple events increases the diversification of events in a portfolio and can reduce the risks and/or costs, thus helping to achieve the portfolio-level goals (Ziakas, 2014a).

Getz (2013) proposes several 'investment-oriented' approaches to manage event portfolios. These are an 'aggressive event portfolio' with high reward and high risks which are usually related to the staging of one-off mega events; a 'defensive portfolio' which is based on low-risk local festivals and small sporting events; and a 'balanced portfolio' with different kinds of events aimed at different markets during the year.

The above mentioned investment-oriented portfolio concept can be successfully implemented in event tourism and destination brand promotion (e.g., Chalip, 2005; Chalip & Costa, 2005; Getz, 2005, 2008, 2013). However, events are social constructs with a variety of roles, institutional complexity and cultural polysemy. Therefore, they cannot be viewed merely as commercial products or financial assets. That would leave unexploited the opportunity to use different events for sustainable development purposes balancing their economic, social and environmental value (Ziakas, 2019). Consequently, a broader theorisation of event portfolios is needed; conceptualising portfolios in a way that captures their multifaceted social and economic value for host communities. Ziakas and Costa (2011b) call for a new comprehensive interdisciplinary framework to study event portfolios. Such a framework takes into account, first, diverse contexts whereby events can be used to achieve community goals (economic, social, cultural, environmental); and second, a variety of opportunities with respect to utilising event portfolios to establish joint strategies, synergies, and collaboration among different event stakeholders (Ziakas, 2014a). Considering that an event portfolio has the potential to assemble different events, event stakeholders and host community resources in a network and manage an array of community purposes through the implementation of joint strategies, Ziakas (2014a) suggests the following holistic definition:

> An event portfolio is the strategic patterning of disparate but interrelated events taking place during the course of the year in a host community that as a whole is intended to achieve multiple outcomes through the implementation of joint event strategies (p. 14).

This definition highlights the strategic nature of developing an event portfolio. As an act of strategic planning entails the grouping of events, which cover an array of different themes, cater for a range of audiences, and serve multiple community purposes by producing different outcomes (Getz, 2012; Richards & Palmer, 2010; Ziakas, 2014a). This is defined as *multiplicity*, particularly characterising the capacity of an event portfolio to engender and convey multiple meanings and serve multiple purposes (Ziakas, 2013). Accordingly, events included in a portfolio can encompass diverse genres in order to reach a wide range of target audiences. Diversification of events in a portfolio is not an end in itself, but should capitalise on the capacity of each event to maximise the overall value of a particular event portfolio (Ziakas, 2014a). As a result, synergy for overall portfolio multiplicity and relatedness among events should be cultivated. According to Ziakas (2014a, 2014b), relatedness of events may occur through the generation of new and complementary markets, transfer of knowledge, utilisation of event theming based on conceptual continuity and common internal logic of events in a portfolio, mobilisation of sharing of resources, common elements and objectives, as well as volunteer pools that can facilitate the staging of events. Relatedness along with multiplicity, constitute the two foundational concepts that demarcate the event portfolio as a paradigm and as a phenomenon.

Overall, different approaches to event portfolio utilisation (economic goals, socio-cultural objectives) determine the definitional variety and researchers' preferences on how to treat this phenomenon. As a relatively new model, the event portfolio paradigm still needs a comprehensive theoretical examination of its key patterns, properties and characteristics. A range of organisational and managerial contexts, as well as different challenges faced by host cities, are likely to affect the vision on event portfolios and their specific characteristics. To conclude, a portfolio incorporates different events in a coherent manner. It targets and reaches diverse market segments and serves diverse city objectives.

Whole populations and event portfolios

Traditionally, almost all of the event management literature focuses on individual events (Getz, 2012). This is problematic for changing the outlook towards multiple events. The problem with looking mainly at single events is that it provides a narrow understanding of events and their contextual background. This established tradition fails to take into account the evolution and sustainability of events within their environment (Ziakas, 2014a). Since the development of events is influenced by the environmental conditions and the contexts in which they evolve, it is imperative to know how different events grow within a host community and, in turn, what the influences are on individual events. Getz (2012) calls for the need to pay attention on whole populations of events by applying organisational ecology as a conceptual and methodological frame in order to consider the meaning and measurement of the health of a given portfolio or population of events.

Getz (2012) defines a whole population of events as the full complement of organised, periodic events that are held within a given area. Whole populations of events have a close relationship with event portfolios. Nonetheless, it should be emphasised that event portfolios are different from whole populations in that they are managed policy tools of selected events. In other words, an event port-folio is neither a collection of events that comprise a host community's whole population of events, nor a coincidental assortment of miscellaneous events, but instead a strategic configuration that is more than the sum of its individual events (Ziakas & Costa, 2011a, 2011b).

An event portfolio is created through compiling selected events from the whole population of a host community's events (Ziakas, 2014a). Consequently, the development of event portfolios is contingent upon the existence of a robust or healthy population of events from which specific events can be selected for inclusion. Getz argues for whole-population studies in which the full interac-tions and interdependencies of events and their environment can be examined. Thus, city planners need to consider from the outset, and then constantly, the whole population of events within the host community as they manage event portfolios. According to Getz (2012), no portfolio can be managed effectively in the long-term without taking into account interactions with other events and institutions in the community.

A usual population of events includes primarily the genres of festival, ritual, game, spectacle, theatre, music and business, which entail a range of cultural, sports, arts, and mixed or hybrid performances. Events can also be classified according to their scale and the instrumental roles they serve in the host com-munity, such as tourism, celebration, recreation, commerce, and education. The common classification types include mega-events such as the Olympics and the Football World Cup, major large-scale events such as the Eurovision Music Con-test and Special Olympics and small-scale local or regional events. A separate notable category covers the hallmark or iconic events that are embedded as per-manent institutions within their community and whose international recogni-tion enhances the host destination brand through their tangible and symbolic value. Examples of such events include the Wimbledon Tennis Tournament, the Boston Marathon, the New Orleans Mardi Grass, or the Rio Carnival. Hallmark events thus contribute positively to destination image and brand and as such are core products in a destination's portfolio (Todd, Leask, & Ensor, 2017).

Andersson, Getz and Mykletun (2013a) applied the organisational ecology theory to the context of festival populations in three Norwegian counties unveil-ing the pattern of festival size pyramid in which the base consists of a large number of small, recurring festivals, and the apex includes only a few, large festivals. This study demonstrates that small-scale periodic events constitute the foundation of a healthy population or portfolio upon which a city can create or bid for a limited number of hallmark large-scale events. As cities, due to their larger size and resources, have the capacity to host events of all scales, the festival size pyramid is perhaps more apt to urban than rural areas (Andersson et al., 2013a). Thus, the spatial characteristics of a host community are a key determinant of portfolio volume and composition. As Andersson et al. (2013a) posit:

> Urban areas are much more likely to generate both large and small festivals, and a higher proportion of them. This is primarily a function of resources available and higher demand. Cities also have greater potential for 'resource partitioning', that is for finding a niche in terms of target audiences, including tourists, and for achieving a more balanced range of market-driven revenues and government funding sources (pp. 99-100).

However, the question of what constitutes a healthy or balanced population of events within different urban or rural communities, is not easy to determine given the topic complexity and the dearth of research and knowledge in this area. The viability of an event population must be considered within the context of external forces acting upon them from an organisational population ecology perspective (Getz & Andersson, 2016).

A whole population of events tends to accelerate during their legitimation, but thereafter, maximum density is reached as competition for resources imposes limits on the population (Andersson, Getz, & Mykletun, 2013b). As such, the balance (*homeostasis*) of a population is a relative term influenced by external factors that exist in each destination and should not be pursued as a means to an end. As Getz (2013) maintains, homeostasis (i.e., a stable equilibrium) within an event population is not necessarily the norm, nor even desirable. All event populations should be dynamic: tolerating diversity and uncertainty, fostering innovation, and ceasing unviable events.

Therefore, taking a laissez-fair (or no intervention) approach might be more appropriate, with the policy of letting the births and deaths occur as they might. But this approach will certainly meet resistance, especially as many events are valued as institutions or traditions, or have the support of powerful interests, and they will tend to seek subsidies and active support. In fact, there are powerful lobby groups for various event sub-sectors, including sports and the arts.

The organisational ecology perspective brings forth a series of pressing questions such as how other events and environmental forces impact upon single events and vice versa, how a healthy portfolio or population of events can be sustained, given resource limits and ongoing competition, or if some events in the portfolio or population should be allowed to fail (Andersson et al., 2013b). Still, what is clear concerns the spatial characteristics of host communities that substantially influence the contextual dynamics shaping the growth of events and the implementation of event portfolio development strategies. Consequently, looking at whole populations of events within their environment, as they organically grow or are strategically managed, can shed light on the conditions and the best means to develop event portfolios (Ziakas, 2019).

Attention to the growth dynamics of whole event populations brings to the fore the matter of self-sufficiency or self-sustained portfolios. According to Getz (2013), although portfolio managers can set to delimit self-sufficiency by achieving steady growth in overall portfolio value, this might be difficult to define when multiple goals are pursued in a triple-bottom-line perspective. Thus, self-sufficiency is a difficult concept to apply to event portfolios, given that portfolio managers (like local government or tourist agencies) do not usually receive direct revenue from events. Return on Investment (ROI) is often defined in terms of tax revenue, job creation or bed-nights – all of which yield no financial return to the portfolio managers. In this context, growth and self-sufficiency goals might be substituted by a steady-state approach in which minor fluctuations are tolerable within a fixed number of events.

Portfolio of events and destination capitals

From an operational perspective, a key concern appears when it comes to the coordination of portfolio development, where available resources should be allocated, goals be prioritised and joint strategies be implemented to equally distribute benefits and meet the requirements and perceptions of all interested stakeholders (Ziakas, 2014a). This calls for the development of a process-oriented portfolio approach. Such an approach incorporates design, management and leveraging of an event portfolio, and aims to develop balancing mechanisms among all the principles of sustainable development, including socio-cultural, economic and environmental outcomes (Ziakas, 2014a). The local context where portfolios operate should be scrutinised in order to understand the complexities of event-related processes in a city and its unique set of developmental needs which a portfolio of events might be able to satisfy. From this perspective, Sharpley's (2009) framework of destination capitals might serve as a good starting point.

Sharpley (2009) argues that every destination has a unique combination of environmental, political, social and cultural characteristics; as a result, every destination has its distinctive development needs. Therefore, local development should be based on the exploitation of the particular set of destination capitals that exist within an area. Destination capitals may include human, political, economic, environmental, technological and socio-cultural dimensions. Identifying the development needs and opportunities as well as external forces that might influence the process (e.g., political, economic, legal or environmental), city event planners can establish their major event portfolio strategies which would reflect these local capitals. In this instance, a portfolio of events will meet all the requirements for the sustainable development of a host destination. It would reflect the local context and the development objectives and would act as an appropriate leveraging tool.

Summary

The purpose of this chapter was to introduce portfolios of events as strategic tools employed by many cities to capitalise on the economic, socio-cultural, political and reputational benefits from staging successful events. The important role of event portfolios was explored through the prism of place-making, competitive identities and destination capitals. In order to become an eventful city and maximise the benefits from events, a city should utilise a portfolio approach, where events are strategically selected and managed in unison to deliver an array of positive long-term outcomes. One of the essential tasks for event portfolio managers is to explore and evaluate the overall population of events in a city in order to identify key events to be included into a portfolio. The next step is to correlate these events with a set of destination capitals to further develop these assets through different leveraging strategies. The next chapter will thoroughly review the concept of leveraging and its application to an event portfolio level.

References

Andersson, T., Getz, D., & Mykletun, R. (2013a). The 'festival size pyramid' in three Norwegian festival populations. *Journal of Convention & Event Tourism*, **14**, 81-103. doi:10.1080/15470148.2013.782258

Andersson, T., Getz, D., & Mykletun, R. (2013b). Sustainable festival populations: An application of organizational ecology. *Tourism Analysis*, **18**(6), 621-634. doi:10.3727/108354213X13824558188505

Anholt, S. (2007). *Competitive Identity: The new brand management for nations, cities and regions*. New York: Palgrave Macmillan.

Anholt, S. (2010). A political perspective on place branding. In F. M. Go & R. Govers (Eds.), *International Place Branding Yearbook 2010: Place branding in the new age of innovation* (pp. 12-20). Basingstoke: Palgrave Macmillan.

Chalip, L. (2005). Marketing, media and place promotion. In J. Higham (Ed.), *Sport Tourism Destinations: Issues, opportunitiea and analysis* (pp. 162-176). Oxford: Elsevier Butterworth-Heinemann.

Chalip, L. (2006). Towards social leverage of sport events. *Journal of Sport & Tourism*, **11**, 109-127. doi:10.1080/14775080601155126

Chalip, L. & Costa, C. A. (2005). Sport event tourism and the destination brand: Towards a general theory. *Sport in Society*, **8**(2), 218-237. doi:10.1080/17430430500108579

Dansero, E., & Puttilli, M. (2010). Mega-events tourism legacies: the case of the Torino 2006 Winter Olympic Games – A territorialisation approach. *Leisure Studies*, **29**(3), 321-341. doi:10.1080/02614361003716966

Derrett, R. (2003). Making sense of how festivals demonstrate a community's sense of place. *Event Management*, **8**(1), 49-58. doi:10.3727/152599503108751694

Dredge, D., & Whitford, M. (2010). Policy for sustainable and responsible festivals and events: institutionalisation of a new paradigm – a response. *Journal of Policy Research in Tourism, Leisure and Events*, **2**, 1-13.

doi:10.1080/19407960903542235

Foley, M., McGillivray, D., & McPherson, G. (2012). *Event Policy: From theory to strategy*. New York: Routledge.

Getz, D. (2005). *Event Management and Event Tourism* (2nd ed.). New York, NY: Cognizant Communication Corporation.

Getz, D. (2008). Event tourism: Definition, evolution, and research. *Tourism Management, 29*(3), 403-428. doi:10.1016/j.tourman.2007.07.017

Getz, D. (2012). *Event Studies: Theory, research and policy for planned events* (2d ed.). London: Routledge.

Getz, D. (2013). *Event Tourism: Concepts, international case studies, and research.* New York, NY: Cognizant Communication Corporation.

Getz, D., & Andersson, T. (2016). Analyzing whole populations of festivals and events: An application of organizational ecology. *Journal of Policy Research in Tourism, Leisure and Events, 8*, 249-273. doi:10.1080/19407963.2016.1158522

Markowitz, H. (1952). Portfolio selection. *The Journal of Finance, 7*(1), 77-91. doi:10.2307/2975974

Markowitz, H. (1991). *Portfolio Selection: Efficient diversification of investments* (2 ed.). Cambridge: Blackwell.

McClinchey, K. A. (2015). 'Something greater than the sum of its parts': Narratives of sense of place at a community multicultural festival. In A. Jepson & A. Clarke (Eds.), *Exploring Community Festivals and Events* (pp. 137-156). New York: Routledge.

Misener, L., & Mason, D. S. (2008). Urban regimes and the sporting events agenda: A cross-national comparison of civic development strategies. *Journal of Sport Management, 22*, 603-627. doi:10.1123/jsm.22.5.603

Misener, L., & Mason, D. S. (2009). Fostering community development through sporting events strategies: An examination of urban regime perceptions. *Journal of Sport Management, 23*, 770-794. doi:10.1123/jsm.23.6.770

Moilanen, T. & Rainisto, S. K. (2009). *How to Brand Nations, Cities and Destinations: A planning book for place branding.* New York, NY: Palgrave Macmillan

Olsen, C. S. (2012). Re-thinking festivals: a comparative study of the integration/ marginalization of arts festivals in the urban regimes of Manchester, Copenhagen and Vienna. *International Journal of Cultural Policy*, 1-20. doi:10.10 80/10286632.2012.661420

Pernecky, T., & Lück, M. (2013). Editors' introduction: Events in the age of sustainability. In T. Pernecky & M. Lück (Eds.), *Events, Society and Sustainability: Critical and contemporary approaches* (pp. 1-12). Abingdon: Routledge.

Pine, B. J., & Gilmore, J. H. (1999). *The Experience Economy*. Boston, MA: Harvard Business Review Press.

Quinn, B. (2010). Arts festivals, urban tourism and cultural policy. *Journal of Policy Research in Tourism, Leisure and Events, 2*, 264-279. doi:10.1080/19407963 .2010.512207

Richards, G. (2015a). Events in the network society: The role of pulsar and iterative events. *Event Management, 19*(4), 553-566. doi:10.3727/1525995 15x14465748512849

Richards, G. (2015b). Developing the eventful city: Time, space and urban identity. In S. Mushatat & M. Al Muhairi (Eds.), *Planning for Event Cities* (pp. 37-46). Ajman, United Arab Emirates: Muncipality and Planning Dept.

Richards, G., & Palmer, R. (2010). *Eventful Cities: Cultural management and urban revitalisation*. Amsterdam: Butterworth-Heinemann.

Richards, G., & Rotariu, I. (2015). Developing the eventful city in Sibiu, Romania. *International Journal of Tourism Cities,* **1**(2), 89-102. doi:10.1108/IJTC-08-2014-0007

Ryan, C. (1995). Introduction. In L. Barnes, T. Winikoff, C. Murphy, & A. M. Nicholson (Eds.), *Places not Spaces: Placemaking in Australia*. Sydney: Envirobook.

Sharpley, R. (2009). *Tourism Development and the Environment: Beyond sustainability?* London, England: Earthscan.

Silvanto, S., & Hellman, T. (2005). Helsinki—the festival city. In L. Lankinen (Ed.), *Arts and Culture in Helsinki* (pp. 4-9). Helsinki, Finland: City of Helsinki.

Smith, A. (2016). *Events in the City: Using public spaces as event venues*. New York: Routledge.

Stern, C. & Stalk, G. (eds.) (1998). *Perspectives on Strategy from The Boston Consulting Group*. New York: Wiley.

Stone, C. (1989). *Regime politics*. Lawrence: University of Kansas Press.

Todd, L., Leask, A., & Ensor, J. (2017). Understanding primary stakeholders' multiple roles in hallmark event tourism management. *Tourism Management,* **59**, 494-509. doi:10.1016/j.tourman.2016.09.010

Whitford, M. (2009). A framework for the development of event public policy: Facilitating regional development. *Tourism Management,* **30**, 674-682. doi:10.1016/j.tourman.2008.10.018

Ziakas, V. (2013). A multidimensional investigation of a regional event portfolio: Advancing theory and praxis. *Event Management,* **17**, 27-48. doi:10.3727/15259 9513x13623342048095

Ziakas, V. (2014a). *Event Portfolio Planning and Management: A holistic approach*. Abingdon: Routledge.

Ziakas, V. (2014b). Planning and leveraging event portfolios: Towards a holistic theory. *Journal of Hospitality Marketing & Management,* **23**(3), 327-356. doi:10.10 80/19368623.2013.796868

Ziakas, V. (2019). Issues, patterns and strategies in the development of event portfolios: configuring models, design and policy. *Journal of Policy Research in Tourism, Leisure and Events,* **11**(1), 121-158. doi:10.1080/19407963.2018.1471481

Ziakas, V., & Costa, C. (2011a). Event portfolio and multi-purpose development: Establishing the conceptual grounds. *Sport Management Review,* **14**, 409-423. doi:10.1016/j.smr.2010.09.003

Ziakas, V., & Costa, C. A. (2011b). The use of an event portfolio in regional community and tourism development: Creating synergy between sport and cultural events. *Journal of Sport & Tourism,* **16**(2), 149-175. doi:10.1080/1477508 5.2011.568091

3 Event Portfolio Leveraging

In order to exploit the strategic value of an event portfolio, a set of leveraging activities should be designed and implemented by event portfolio managers (Ziakas, 2014a). Such activities could be focused on the relationships among different events and their stakeholders. They can synergise events with one another and with the host destination's overall product and service mix (Ziakas, 2010, 2014a; Ziakas & Costa, 2011). This chapter thoroughly considers the concepts of leveraging and cross-leveraging and their application.

Introducing the concept of leveraging

The concept of leveraging shifts the focus from the mere analysis of event impacts and their ad-hoc effects towards the development of an analytical framework to understand how events can be leveraged in a long term perspective and what strategies can be implemented to achieve and increase positive outcomes from events (Chalip, 2004, 2006; O'Brien, 2007; O'Brien & Chalip, 2008). Chalip (2006) argues that, although impact studies provide useful information about the positive or negative impacts of events on economic and social development, tourism promotion or environmental sustainability, they do not explain why these outcomes occur. Thus, impact studies are insufficient for strategic event planning and management (Bramwell, 1997).

The term *leveraging* is derived from business literature and refers to the long-term strategies through which corporations seek to achieve the highest return to their investments (VanWynsberghe, Derom, & Maurer, 2012). Leveraging involves the identification of the existing assets of a corporation and the further creation and enhancement of the value of these assets to benefit the business (Boulton, Libert, & Samek, 2000). The analogy between the business leveraging approach and events can be briefly described as follows: leverage initiatives are "those activities which need to be undertaken around the event itself, and those which seek to maximise the long-term benefits from events" (Chalip, 2004, p. 228). The concept of event leveraging can be viewed, first, as a knowledge of the potential that events can generate for the host destination and its residents and, second, as an intention to realise this potential on different levels of community operations (Quinn, 2013). This approach emphasises the necessity of pre-event planning as well as during- and after-event analysis and evaluation.

Smith (2014, p. 21) argues that in order to achieve expected positive results from leveraging initiatives, a leveraging approach needs to be "...an integral part of the decision-making process in the early stages of event planning...". In other words, it is essential for city event managers to design, implement and evaluate tactics that employ all the opportunities that events offer to the community. Traditionally, events have been used in an 'ad-hoc' manner and the shift towards the leverage concept leads to a wider integration of events into the public policy domain (Richards & Palmer, 2010; Smith, 2014).

Impacts vs leveraged outcomes

To understand the core idea of the event leverage concept, it is essential to emphasise the difference between event impacts and leveraged outcomes. The impacts of events can be defined as the automatic effects of event projects (Smith, 2014). Preuss (2007a) argues that event impacts are often caused by a short-term impulse and affect the event environment (e.g., city economy, social wellbeing, local business development), directly through the event. For example, mega-events are capable of generating new jobs, business opportunities, enhancing the destination image and increasing tourist flows. Because of the substantial investment in event-related infrastructure, such effects can be materialised only due to the results of a particular event staged in a city (Smith, 2014). Negative impacts such as increased prices for services, inappropriate development, noise, crime and a tarnished destination brand can also occur (Jago, Dwyer, Lipman, Lill, & Vorster, 2010). All these impacts differ from leveraged outcomes that have been deliberately planned and undertaken around an event to maximise the long-term benefits from staging this event. An event itself is not the intervention. It represents a temporally limited set of assets. The main task for the event managers is to identify these assets and utilise them in order to achieve positive results (O'Brien, 2006).

Event-led and event-themed leveraging

Smith (2014) distinguishes between event-led and event-themed leveraging. When event-led leverage projects are closely linked to events and try to expand positive impacts that are normally expected from staging of events, event-themed leverage activities, in their turn, can be defined as general initiatives, which are planned to capitalise on and maximise the opportunities derived from hosting an event. In the latter case, an event is used as a hook to achieve more benefits which are not related directly to its hosting. The main advantage of event-themed initiatives is that they can help to extend the reach of events and benefit "a wider group of beneficiaries in a wider set of policy fields" (Smith, 2014, p. 27). Although these suggestions have been related, in the first instance, to the staging of large-scale international sporting events, it is possible to assume that the leveraging tactics could be also implemented while planning small community events with such leverage objectives as, for example, fund raising, charity or community members support.

The current literature demonstrates the potential of small-scale events in generating an array of leveraging opportunities for the host communities (e.g., Gibson, Willming, & Holdnak, 2003; O'Brien, 2007; Ritchie, 2004; Ritchie, Mosedale, & King, 2002). For example, tourism seasonality can be overcome by running a rugby season in off-tourism periods (Higham & Hinch, 2002). Ritchie (2005) and Wilson (2006) argue that small-scale sport events are capable of generating substantial benefits for the local economy through using available infrastructure and providing secondary expenditure opportunities. Overall, leveraging implicates strategic thinking and decision-making where both outcomes and the ways to achieve them are planned in advance (Smith, 2014).

Event portfolio as a leverageable resource

To sustain and enhance benefits through event leveraging, the concept of a strategically developed event portfolio should be employed (Parent & Smith-Swan, 2013). Chalip (2004) has developed a general framework (Figure 3.1) where an event portfolio is envisaged as a leverageable resource for the economic development of a host city. Chalip (2004) distinguishes between the immediate and long term leveraging activities of a portfolio. The former are designed to increase visitor spending, lengthen visitors' stays, retain events expenditures and enhance local and regional business relationships by building new markets and supply chains. In the long-term perspective, events are used as means to construct and enhance destination image. This process encapsulates destination showcasing via event advertising and reporting as well as using events in advertising and promotion for the host destination (Pereira, Mascarenhas, Flores, & Pires, 2015). Westerbeek and Linley (2012) argue that the development of a strong event portfolio may significantly improve long-lasting impressions about a host destination.

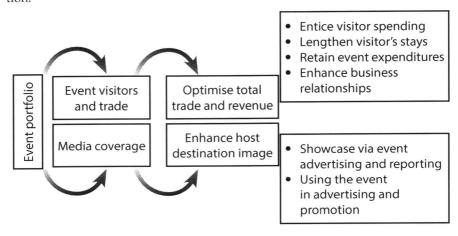

Figure 3.1: Portfolio leveraging. Adapted from: Chalip (2004, p. 229).

Portfolio leveraging for tourism

Although Chalip's leveraging model (2004) emphasises the important role of event portfolios in economic and business spheres, it does not cover another critical dimension of a city development, namely event tourism. To fill this gap, Ziakas (2014a) has adopted the Chalip's framework to event tourism and has suggested several additions to the general leveraging framework. If a city goal is to maximise benefits from event visitors, the following strategies should be incorporated:

♦ *Amplify visitation.* Events should appeal to a wide range of audiences and be responsive to tourists' needs and interests, providing unique experiences which are integrated with the destination's product mix.

♦ *Diversify tourism product.* The creation and inclusion of disparate events in a portfolio can enrich the local tourism product mix.

♦ *Schedule selected events off-season.* This means is able to help in regulating the seasonal character of the tourism product and redirecting tourism flows.

♦ *Rejuvenate destination.* The premise of this strategy is that the creation or attraction of events can improve the image of a destination and attract the interest of tourists.

◆   *Consolidate destination assets.* In coordinating event implementations, the
    destination's strengths and attributes should be consolidated in a joint
    scheme in order to create the value of the tourism proposal to the target
    audience.

◆   *Bolster destination's authenticity.* The key idea of this strategy is to create
    event experiences that are valued by or perceived as unique and authentic
    for tourists (Ziakas, 2014a).

Portfolio leveraging and social development

Along with economic and tourist leveraging perspectives, portfolios of events
can also be used as a means to foster the community social development and
engagement. The idea of an event's social value is generally grounded in the
anthropological theory that highlights the concepts of *liminality* and *communitas* (Turner, 1969, 1974). Liminality refers to the collective sense of the sacred
and ritualistic uncertainty which participants experience within the 'space-time'
environment of an event. The presence of the sacred aspect defines the event as
liminal, when normal social boundaries are intermitted and new social construc-
tions are explored (Ziakas & Costa, 2012). The unified sense of community that
appears temporarily due to such collective experience is called 'communitas'
(Turner, 1974).

Chalip (2006) proposes two key objectives to generate and cultivate liminality while staging events, namely, fostering social interaction and prompting a
feeling of celebration. A framework for the social leverage of events (O'Brien
& Chalip, 2008) has been suggested, based on the assumption that liminality,
which is created during an event, in turn generates opportunities for social leverage. The first opportunity is the communitas engendered by the events and the
second is the attention of media and sponsors.

Social leverage may result in generating a range of positive social effects, for
example, uniting people, increasing civic pride, promoting wellbeing, encouraging volunteering, and strengthening community networks. The implementation of complementary event activities which increase personal identification
and social interaction can increase the value of the main event (García, 2001).
An introduction of cultural or arts programming elements to a sport event, for
example, can broaden the range of entertainment provided to attendees and
strengthen the event's appeal to those market segments that otherwise might
not be reached.

Ziakas and Costa (2012) add the concept of 'event dramaturgy' to the social
leverage discourse. Event dramaturgy can be described as a process of constructing and extracting meanings through event symbolisms that enable members of
the community to instantiate the sense of community connection and identification (Ziakas & Costa, 2010). From the perspective of community development,

event dramaturgy is understood as an array of symbolic projections, which reflect the values of local people and address community issues. Understanding events as symbolic social spaces that reflect the local community's history, culture and heritage, and the associated design of event meanings can help in the cultivation of liminality within an event and in the further integration of events into the community development agenda (Ziakas & Costa, 2010, 2012).

Issues with event portfolio leveraging

A set of problems related to event and portfolio leveraging can be identified in the current literature. For example, Smith (2014) enquires about who should be responsible for the development and implementation of leveraging strategies? Event leveraging initiatives are usually separate from the delivery and management of event projects; thus it is difficult to relocate responsibilities for their planning. Ziakas (2010, 2014a) argues that success of leveraging depends on inter-relationships between community stakeholders and event managers. Community organisations that have expertise and experience in relevant policy fields are capable of delivering leveraging projects in their particular fields. For example, the Greenest City initiative was developed by the City of Vancouver in conjunction with the 2010 Winter Olympic Games (VanWynsberghe et al., 2012). However, the realisation of leveraging projects relies on events, so the involvement of event organisers is crucial. This process has its advantages and disadvantages. On the one hand, event organisational committees are often temporary organisations, focused on specific management questions. They are not suited for long-term leveraging initiatives. On the other hand, the removal of leveraging from the management of an event may lead to difficulties in delivering leveraging in an optimal manner (Smith, 2014).

Another significant challenge of leveraging is funding. Delivering effective initiatives demand access to solid funding and investment. In most mega-events projects, the majority of available funds is spent on building infrastructure and staging. Thus, the resources allocated to specific leveraging initiatives are limited and are vulnerable to the criticism that they exist only to justify the bid (Smith, 2014).

Potential problems associated with leveraging initiatives can also emerge during the evaluation phase of the implemented strategy. Researchers find it hard to separate the impacts of the event from the effects of supplementary initiatives (Smith, 2014). Moreover, there has not been much research undertaken on the effectiveness and efficiency of leveraging initiatives. As a result, it is often difficult to determine if benefits from leverage occur at the expense of other stakeholder groups. This problem is primarily related to the need for critical evaluation of event leverage so that it facilitates the equal distribution of benefits amongst stakeholders (Ziakas, 2015).

In view of these challenges, an event portfolio can be seen as a strategic opportunity to establish leveraging as a central organising principle and integral part of decision-making. Events should be chosen and delivered on the basis of their potential to provide and leverage desirable outcomes. In the case of a well-planned event strategy, special funds may be reserved for approved leveraging projects. In addition, the appointment of a coordinating entity can facilitate the process of assembling events, and establish connection among different stakeholders in order to coordinate the leveraging, financing and evaluation of results (Ziakas, 2014a).

Cross-leveraging opportunities in an event portfolio

The value of an event portfolio derives from both the interconnectedness and inter-relationships of events, and their separate contribution to the overall capacity to build a strong image of an event destination (Chalip, 2005; Ziakas, 2013; Ziakas & Costa, 2011). This calls for examining events in relation to one another within a portfolio in order to identify the key means that provide the synergy among them. Chalip and Costa (2005) maintained that the strategic incorporation of sport events into destination branding requires that each event be cross-leveraged with others in the destination's event portfolio.

Ziakas (2014b) distinguishes three basic types of event portfolio cross-leveraging:

(a) cross-leveraging the different recurring events of the portfolio, b) cross-leveraging the whole portfolio with one-off mega- or large-scale events, and c) cross-leveraging the portfolio of recurring events and/or one-off events with the host community's product and service mix (pp. 330-331).

The goal of cross-leveraging is to enable the development of synergy among the events in the portfolio to achieve and sustain the benefits and planned legacies of hosted events (Ziakas, 2014b). To achieve that, portfolio managers need to know how events complement each other and, in turn, how they can be complemented by the attractions, amenities, products, and services of a host community. This is a complex and demanding task that can be hindered by the innate fragmentation of the event sector and the conventional practice of focusing on the management of single events. For this reason, a paradigm shift is required in the way we currently view, study, and evaluate events. The portfolio perspective is conducive to this potential for developing a comprehensive interdisciplinary framework. This can provide the common ground for looking at particular areas, such as marketing, policy, leverage, community and economic development, as well as tourism-related aspects. The range of applications can be as diverse as the purposes that event portfolios are employed to serve in a host community, and a synergistic approach can help policy-makers to effectively integrate portfolios as versatile tools in local development (Ziakas, 2019).

To sum up, cross-leveraging is about understanding interrelationships, fostering synergies, and enhancing complementarities (Ziakas, 2014a). This holistic outlook can enable the formulation and implementation of joint strategies and can ultimately help managers find the best means to leverage event portfolios.

The choice of appropriate cross-leveraging tactics depends on the community resources, institutional structure of the host community, and political and business environment, as well as stakeholder interests and intentions. However, to date, there is an essential lack of emphasis by empirical studies related to the leveraging or cross-leveraging potential of host cities' event portfolios. One of the issues arising relates to the inclusion of one-off large-scale events into the city events programme or portfolio. The next section outlines the relevant discussion about this matter in the literature.

Event portfolios and one-off large-scale events

To build and expand the knowledge base related to the leveraging and cross-leveraging of event portfolios for multiple community purposes, it is critically important to take into consideration the arising research discourse on the ongoing legacy of mega-events and strategies of including such events into the local portfolio (Ziakas, 2014a). On one hand, event portfolios can hardly be compatible with such events because of their specific requirements, massive investment and preparation (Ziakas, 2014a). As Getz (2013) argues, adding a mega-event to a city's portfolio will instantly overload the system and divert attention and resources. On the other hand, the development of an event portfolio can build capacity (infrastructure, know-how, and social capital) for hosting mega-events. Therefore, hosting such kinds of events would allow the community to capitalise on the event portfolio and the positive impacts it generates (Ziakas, 2014a). Moreover, large-scale one-off events can fulfil different roles, for example, they can contribute substantially to growth and innovation, environmental sustainability and other public policy objectives (Clark, 2008).

The relationship between one-off events and event portfolios is still an undisclosed area in event studies. For event organisers, an event portfolio could represent a strategic community asset to draw resources and capitalise on the whole capacity of a host destination to stage events (Ziakas, 2014a). For a host community, the staging of a well-planned mega-event can also bring significant benefits and opportunities, particularly in a situation wherein a city has already achieved its event-related 'critical mass' (Getz, 2013). Some current research suggests that one-time events can play a strategic and sustainable role in event portfolios, however an integration of the overall destination experience with such events is required (e.g., Taks, Chalip, Green, Kesenne, & Martyn, 2009). It is evident that appropriate strategies should be identified and employed with regard to incorporation of one-off events into a destination's portfolio (Ziakas, 2014a).

In the academic discourse, the benefits and impacts associated with hosting mega-events are reflected in the concept of proactively planned sustainable long-term legacies (Leopkey & Parent, 2012). Legacy with regard to sporting large scale events can be defined as "all planned and unplanned, positive and negative, tangible and intangible structures created for and by a sport event that remain longer than the event itself" (Preuss, 2007a, p. 211). Positive legacies can include new infrastructure, urban revival, increased tourism and business opportunities, sport infrastructure (e.g., Cornelissen, Bob, & Swart, 2011; Gratton & Preuss, 2008; Kaplanidou & Karadakis, 2010; Parent & Smith-Swan, 2013). Potentially the negative legacy of mega events for a host destination can be increased prices for services and housing, high construction costs, tarnished brand and reduced destination pride due to problems at the event, excessive energy and water usage, 'white elephants' (i.e. unused facilities), and evictions (e.g., Jago et al., 2010; Parent & Smith-Swan, 2013; Preuss, 2007b).

As a multi-dimensional phenomenon, legacy plays an important role in all phases related to the event management: bidding, preparing for the event, staging the event and having a plan for the post-event phase (Hiller, 1998, 2006). Even the bidding process itself, without securing the right to host an event, can bring many positive benefits for a city (Clark, 2008).

The resulting legacy of mega-events represents a valuable leverageable resource (Boukas, Ziakas, & Boustras, 2013; Ziakas & Boukas, 2012). Based on Chalip's (2004) general event leveraging model, and Weed's (2008) Olympic tourism leveraging model, Boukas et al. (2013) have developed a framework for leveraging post-Olympic Games tourism. According to this framework, there are two opportunities for leverage, namely, the legacy of the Games and its effects on the cultural heritage of the host city. This requires the implementation of synergetic cross-leveraging strategies with the goal to optimise sport-related and cultural-related benefits. The authors suggest two key tactics to attain these strategic objectives. The first is to utilise the Olympic venues for organising events and other activities; the second uses the Olympic legacy and heritage themes in the media to reinforce the host city's image. The researchers also propose four derivative means to leverage post-games Olympic tourism: the design of Olympic-related attractions, the packaging of sport and cultural attractions, the attraction of conferences and exhibitions, and the development of an event portfolio.

The significance of the suggested framework lies in the fact that it shifts the attention from leveraging a mega-event itself and extends the objectives of leverage beyond sport to cultural heritage tourism (Ziakas, 2014a). Thus, an interdisciplinary approach can be employed to facilitate the development and implementation of cross-leveraging initiatives. Ziakas (2014a) concludes that, in this context, events from a local portfolio need to be cross-leveraged with a mega-event's legacy, engendering a range of positive outcomes in the post-event period.

Although the above mentioned framework paves the way to a more sustainable and integrated decision-making with regard to the development of appropriate events strategies, and legacy management, it covers only tourism, and to some extent (post-event venues utilisation) sport dimensions. Even the design of an event portfolio, according to the framework, reflects the tourist-oriented strategy approach. It seems reasonable to widen the research focus of post-event legacy leveraging and include such dimensions as social and business development, urban regeneration, and environmental issues. For instance, the FIFA Soccer World Cup in Germany 2006 produced substantial environmental improvements through a special Green Games Programme, and Manchester's Commonwealth Games 2002 revitalised several deprived districts of the city (Clark, 2008). As Jago et al. (2010) argue, a mega-event should be a part of a long-term development and marketing plan, acting as a catalyst for bringing forward development opportunities.

Summary

The purpose of this chapter was to scrutinise the complex dimensions of the leveraging and cross-leveraging of singular events and whole portfolios of events. It has been emphasised that the incorporation of different events into a portfolio requires an integrative way of viewing the different community purposes that events serve in unison. A series of interrelated events can be synergised and cross-leveraged to derive positive outcomes through a holistic planning approach that places events together and balances their different purposes. A portfolio constitutes a strategic patterning of events and their interrelations. Events can be symbiotically interrelated and benefits maximised in a number of ways: through cultivating markets, transferring knowledge, utilising common theming, and mobilising shared resources (Ziakas & Costa, 2011).

Understanding leveraging and cross-leveraging opportunities, as well as mechanisms within the pre-, during-, and post-event periods could shed light on the potential of utilising a series of events to capitalise on the host community's capacity. Although leveraging strategies seem to provide long-term positive outcomes, several issues with this approach have been identified and discussed. The problems of decision making, funding and evaluation have been raised and discussed. In addition, the potential of a strategic relationship between one-off large-scale events and event portfolios has been examined. Although major or mega events often bring organisational and political challenges, their inclusion in a portfolio can bring a lot of positive short-term impacts and long-term outcomes. The perspective of portfolio leverage provides a robust ground for the exploration of the relationship among different events and their stakeholders. The next chapter will look at the concepts of portfolio networking and stakeholder management.

References

Boukas, N., Ziakas, V., & Boustras, G. (2013). Olympic legacy and cultural tourism: Exploring the facets of Athens' Olympic heritage. *International Journal of Heritage Studies,* **19**(2), 203-228. doi:10.1080/13527258.2011.651735

Boulton, R. E. S., Libert, B. D., & Samek, S. M. (2000). A business model for the new economy. *Journal of Business Strategy,* **21**(4), 29-35. doi:10.1108/eb040102

Bramwell, B. (1997). Strategic planning before and after a mega-event. *Tourism Management,* 18(3), 167-176. doi:10.1016/s0261-5177(96)00118-5

Chalip, L. (2004). Beyond impact: A general model for sport event leverage. In B. W. Ritchie & A. Daryl (Eds.), *Sport Tourism: Interrelationships, impacts and issues* (pp. 226-252). Clevedon: Channel View.

Chalip, L. (2005). Marketing, media and place promotion. In J. Higham (Ed.), *Sport Tourism Destinations: Issues, opportunitiea and analysis* (pp. 162-176). Oxford: Elsevier Butterworth-Heinemann.

Chalip, L. (2006). Towards social leverage of sport events. *Journal of Sport & Tourism,* **11**(2), 109-127. doi:10.1080/14775080601155126

Chalip, L., & Costa, C. A. (2005). Sport event tourism and the destination brand: Towards a general theory. *Sport in Society,* **8**(2), 218-237. doi:10.1080/17430430500108579

Clark, G. (2008). *Local Development Benefits from Staging Global Events*: Organisation for Economic Co-operation and Development (OECD). https://www.oecd.org/cfe/leed/localdevelopmentbenefitsfromstagingglobalevents.htm

Cornelissen, S., Bob, U., & Swart, K. (2011). Towards redefining the concept of legacy in relation to sport mega-events: Insights from the 2010 FIFA World Cup. *Development Southern Africa,* **28**(3), 307-318. doi:10.1080/03768 35x.2011.595990

García, B. (2001). Enhancing sport marketing through cultural and arts programs: Lessons from the Sydney 2000 Olympic Arts Festivals. *Sport Management Review,* **4**(2), 193-219. doi:10.1016/s1441-3523(01)70075-7

Getz, D. (2013). *Event Tourism: Concepts, international case studies, and research.* New York, NY: Cognizant Communication Corporation.

Gibson, H. J., Willming, C., & Holdnak, A. (2003). Small-scale event sport tourism: Fans as tourists. *Tourism Management,* **24**(2), 181-190. doi:10.1016/S0261-5177(02)00058-4

Gratton, C., & Preuss, H. (2008). Maximizing olympic impacts by building up legacies. *The International Journal of the History of Sport,* **25**(14), 1922-1938. doi:10.1080/09523360802439023

Higham, J., & Hinch, T. (2002). Tourism, sport and seasons: The challenges and potential of overcoming seasonality in the sport and tourism sectors. *Tourism Management,* **23**(2), 175-185. doi:10.1016/S0261-5177(01)00046-2

Hiller, H. H. (1998). Assessing the impact of mega-events: A linkage model. *Current Issues in Tourism,* **1**(1), 47-57. doi:10.1080/13683509808667832

Hiller, H. H. (2006). Post-event outcomes and the post-modern turn: The Olympics and urban transformations. *European Sport Management Quarterly,* **6**(4), 317-332. doi:10.1080/16184740601154458

Jago, L., Dwyer, L., Lipman, G., Lill, D. v., & Vorster, S. (2010). Optimising the potential of mega-events: An overview. *International Journal of Event and Festival Management*, **1**(3), 220-237. doi:10.1108/17852951011078023

Kaplanidou, K., & Karadakis, K. (2010). Understanding the legacies of a host Olympic city: The case of the 2010 Vancouver Olympic Games. *Sport marketing quarterly*, **19**(2), 110-117.

Leopkey, B., & Parent, M. M. (2012). Olympic Games legacy: From general benefits to sustainable long-term legacy. *The International Journal of the History of Sport*, **29**(6), 924-943. doi:10.1080/09523367.2011.623006

O'Brien, D. (2006). Event business leveraging the Sydney 2000 Olympic Games. *Annals of Tourism Research*, **33**(1), 240-261. doi:10.1016/j.annals.2005.10.011

O'Brien, D. (2007). Points of leverage: Maximizing host community benefit from a regional surfing festival. *European Sport Management Quarterly*, **7**(2), 141-165. doi:10.1080/16184740701353315

O'Brien, D., & Chalip, L. (2008). Sport events and strategic leveraging: Pushing towards the triple bottom line. In W. A & M. D (Eds.), *Tourism management: Analysis, behaviour and strategy* (pp. 318-338). Oxfordshire, England: CABI.

Parent, M. M., & Smith-Swan, S. (2013). *Managing Major Sports Events: Theory and practice*. New York, NY: Routledge..

Pereira, E. C. S., Mascarenhas, M. V. M., Flores, A. J. G., & Pires, G. M. V. S. (2015). Nautical small-scale sports events portfolio: A strategic leveraging approach. *European Sport Management Quarterly*, **15**(1), 27-47. doi:10.1080/1618 4742.2015.1007883

Preuss, H. (2007a). The conceptualisation and measurement of mega sport event legacies. *Journal of Sport & Tourism*, **12**(3), 207-228. doi:10.1080/14775080701736957

Preuss, H. (2007b). FIFA World Cup 2006 and its legacy on tourism. In R. Conrady & M. Buck (Eds.), *Trends and Issues in Global Tourism 2007* (pp. 83-102). Berlin, Germany: Springer Berlin Heidelberg.

Quinn, B. (2013). *Key Concepts in Special Events Management*. London: SAGE.

Richards, G., & Palmer, R. (2010). *Eventful cities: Cultural management and urban revitalisation*. Amsterdam, the Netherlands: Butterworth-Heinemann.

Ritchie, B. W. (2004). Exploring small-scale sport event tourism: The case of Rugby Union and the Super 12 competition. In B. W. Ritchie & A. Daryl (Eds.), *Sport Tourism: Interrelationships, impacts and issues* (pp. 135-154). Clevedon: Channel View.

Ritchie, B. W. (2005). Small-scale sport event tourism: The changing dynamics of the New Zealand Masters Games. In M. Novelli (Ed.), *Niche Tourism: Contemporary issues, trends and cases* (pp. 157-170). Oxford: Elsevier Butterworth-Heinemann.

Ritchie, B. W., Mosedale, L., & King, J. (2002). Profiling sport tourists: The case of Super 12 Rugby Union in the Australian capital territory, Australia. *Current Issues in Tourism*, **5**(1), 33-44. doi:10.1080/13683500208667906

Smith, A. (2014). Leveraging sport mega-events: new model or convenient justification? *Journal of Policy Research in Tourism, Leisure and Events*, **6**(1), 15-30. doi:10.1080/19407963.2013.823976

Taks, M., Chalip, L., Green, B. C., Kesenne, S. & Martyn, S. (2009). Factors affecting repeat visitation and flow-on tourism as sources of event strategy sustainability. *Journal of Sport & Tourism,* **14**(2-3), 121-142. doi:10.1080/14775080902965066

Turner, V. (1969). *The Ritual Process: Structure and anti-structure.* Chicago, MA: Aldine Publishing.

Turner, V. (1974). *Dramas, Fields, and Metaphors.* New York, NY: Cornell University Press.

VanWynsberghe, R., Derom, I., & Maurer, E. (2012). Social leveraging of the 2010 Olympic Games: 'sustainability' in a City of Vancouver initiative. *Journal of Policy Research in Tourism, Leisure and Events,* **4**(2), 185-205.

Weed, M. (2008). *Olympic Tourism.* Oxford: Butterworth-Heinemann.

Westerbeek, H., & Linley, M. (2012). Building city brands through sport events: Theoretical and empirical perspectives. *Journal of Brand Strategy,* **1**(2), 193-205.

Wilson, R. (2006). The economic impact of local sport events: Significant, limited or otherwise? A case study of four swimming events. *Managing Leisure,* **11**(1), 57-70. doi:10.1080/13606710500445718

Ziakas, V. (2010). Understanding an event portfolio: the Uncovering of interrelationships, synergies, and leveraging opportunities. *Journal of Policy Research in Tourism, Leisure and Events,* **2**(2), 144-164. doi:10.1080/19407963.2010.482274

Ziakas, V. (2013). A multidimensional investigation of a regional event portfolio: Advancing theory and praxis. *Event Management,* **17**(1), 27-48. doi:10.3727/152599513x13623342048095

Ziakas, V. (2014a). *Event Portfolio Planning and mManagement: A holistic approach.* Abingdon: Routledge.

Ziakas, V. (2014b). Planning and leveraging event portfolios: Towards a holistic theory. *Journal of Hospitality Marketing & Management,* **23**(3), 327-356. doi:10.1080/19368623.2013.796868

Ziakas, V. (2015). For the benefit of all? Developing a critical perspective in mega-event leverage. Leisure Studies, 34(6), 689-702. doi:10.1080/02614367.2014.986507

Ziakas, V. (2019). Issues, patterns and strategies in the development of event portfolios: configuring models, design and policy. *Journal of Policy Research in Tourism, Leisure and Events,* **11**(1), 121-158. doi:10.1080/19407963.2018.1471481

Ziakas, V., & Boukas, N. (2012). A neglected legacy: Examining the challenges and potential for sport tourism development in post-Olympic Athens. *International Journal of Event and Festival Management,* **3**(3), 292-316. doi:10.1108/17582951211262710

Ziakas, V., & Costa, C. A. (2010). 'Between theatre and sport' in a rural event: Evolving unity and community development from the iside-out. *Journal of Sport & Tourism,* **15**(1), 7-26. doi:10.1080/14775081003770892

Ziakas, V., & Costa, C. A. (2011). Event portfolio and multi-purpose development: Establishing the conceptual grounds. *Sport Management Review,* **14**(4), 409-423. doi:10.1016/j.smr.2010.09.003

Ziakas, V., & Costa, C. A. (2012). 'The show must go on': event dramaturgy as consolidation of community. *Journal of Policy Research in Tourism, Leisure and Events,* **4**(1), 28-47. doi:10.1080/19407963.2011.573392

4 Event Portfolios and Stakeholder Networks

Stakeholder theory and management are of great importance within the events sector (van Niekerk & Getz, 2019). The focus of this chapter is on stakeholder cooperation and management within an event portfolio. First, the nature of inter-organisational relationships in the event sector will be examined. Second, the effects of strategic collaboration between different actors in a portfolio network will be analysed. Last, the characteristics of institutional structures and specifics of portfolio governance will be introduced and discussed.

Inter-organisational relationships in the event sector

Implementation of an effective event policy and strategy requires collaboration, coordination and partnership among different stakeholders, including organising and supporting boards, public sector bodies, community groups and volunteers (Ziakas, 2014; Ziakas & Costa, 2011). Hence, the understanding and management of an array of stakeholders' interests and motives has been seen as a critical aspect of event portfolio development (Getz, 2013; Ziakas, 2014).

Any event has the capacity to bring different actors together and foster community networks through participation, involvement in planning of event-related operations and the decision-making process (Misener & Mason, 2006; Ziakas & Costa, 2011). Larson (2009a) envisages events as "creating an imaginary space where different actors project their imagination on how the event can fulfil their interests" (p. 393). Literature on events acknowledges the importance of building relationships among different interest groups during the organisational phase of every event project. Misener and Mason (2006) highlight the significance of an analysis of the nature of event-related organisational networks and relationships in different political and cultural contexts. Mapping and analysing stakeholder networks identifies the key players, their expectations and intentions. Understanding the connections in a stakeholder web may result in the development of sustainable strategies that not only meet the needs of different power groups but also utilise the full potential of these groups in event planning. At least two theoretical approaches can be used to analyse and evaluate event stakeholder relationships, namely, stakeholder theory and network theory.

Event stakeholders

Freeman (2010) defines stakeholders as "any group or individual who can affect or is affected by the achievement of the organisation's objectives" (p. 46). Freeman's model of stakeholder management includes such stages as evaluation of stakeholders, management of stakeholders in order to accomplish organisational objectives, and measurement of stakeholder satisfaction with the organisational outcomes (Freeman et al., 2010). The influence of stakeholder theory on event management is well-documented and widely discussed (e.g., Andersson & Getz, 2008; Buch, Milne, & Dickson, 2011; Getz, Andersson, & Larson, 2007; Merrilees, Getz, & O'Brien, 2005; Sciarelli & Tani, 2013). Different event stakeholders have different levels of power and influence and can be mapped, managed and evaluated according to a diversity of parameters. For example, Getz et al. (2007) emphasise such major stakeholder roles as: 'facilitator', individuals and organisations that provide an event with essential resources; 'regulator' whose approval and cooperation are required (usually government agencies); 'allies and collaborators', who provide intangible help and can act as marketing partners (professional associations and tourism agencies); 'co-producers' – independent organisations that participate in the organisational process; 'the audience and the impacted', the groups and individuals affected by an event.

O'Toole (2011) applied an alternative, project management approach and distinguished primary, secondary, internal and external event stakeholders. Primary stakeholders – attendees and sponsors – are very focused and interested in the success or otherwise of the event. Secondary stakeholders, for example, local police, are interested only if an event passes a threshold of importance. Internal stakeholders are directly involved in event planning and realisation of an event project. This is an organising committee. External stakeholders have strong interest in an event, but are not directly involved in its planning and production. This group includes local residents, local business and suppliers.

In an event portfolio context, the analysis of stakeholder groups can also lead to the determination of the significance of particular stakeholders. This, in turn, can stimulate the establishment of new directions and development of specific stakeholder strategies. Mitchell, Agle and Wood (1997) suggest the concept of salience in corporate stakeholder analysis. Salience is a tri-dimensional construct, which includes such attributes of a stakeholder as their power to influence the organisation, legitimacy of relationship with the organisation and urgency of the stakeholder's claim on the organisation. Managers should take into account only those stakeholders that possess all three influential attributes.

Apart from identification of the key stakeholders who can influence the development of events and the whole portfolio of events in a destination, it is critically important to understand the motives of stakeholders and how those motives affect the inter-organisational relationships (Ziakas, 2014). Hede (2008) proposes a framework where the Triple Bottom Line (TBL) concept is incorporated into the stakeholder theory for the purpose of identifying key stakeholders' interests towards a particular event. The research shows that among fourteen identified event stakeholder groups only three (government, residents and community groups) appear to have interests in all three domains of the TBL, namely the economic, social and environment spheres. The TBL stakeholder framework proposed by Hede (2008) provides a basis for specifying and ranking the objectives of an event with regard to the main stakeholders' interests and priorities. This framework can be utilised by event and destination managers to develop strategies that simultaneously meet the needs of a number of stakeholders, rather than implement different strategies for each stakeholder.

Overall, stakeholder theory emphasises the relationships between an event or portfolio of events and its stakeholders, placing a particular event project in the centre of the investigation. However, the organisation of an event also depends on how different groups of stakeholders communicate and interact with each other within the actors' network. Network theory adds a new dimension to the stakeholder theory, taking into consideration complex and dynamic processes between participants of the network, which may change the structure or innovate an event network (Richards & Palmer, 2010).

Inter-organisational networks and collaboration

Stakeholder networks can operate as institutionalised units with formal structure and hierarchy, or as non-institutionalised units with invisible structure and non-specific objectives (Ziakas & Costa, 2010). Goal-directedness in a network is characterised by the establishment of an administrative entity that plans and coordinates activities of the network. Processes in such networks are constructed around specific shared goals (Kilduff & Tsai, 2003). When individual actors are not guided by any central network agent and actors form ties and partnerships based on their own interests, then this particular network operates using seren-dipitous trajectories (Kilduff & Tsai, 2003).

The planning and leveraging of event portfolios involve multiple stakehold-ers who have different or competing needs, interests and expectations (Reid, 2011). It is a complex task that requires flexible and inclusive management. A major challenge is to assemble a web of fragmented event stakeholders and to foster collaboration towards devising common strategies for a series of different events. As the number of events grows and more stakeholders are involved, the amount of risk factors and issues affecting an event portfolio can increase dra-matically. To sketch inter-organisational relationships and collaboration, event portfolios can be viewed as enduring symbolic spaces of interaction between different stakeholders (Figure 4.1).

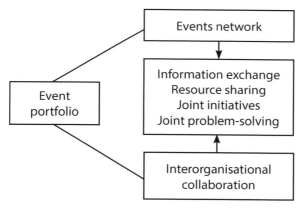

Figure 4.1: Event portfolio network. Adapted from Ziakas (2014, p.158).

From this perspective, an events network covers a variety of organisations from different business and administrative sectors, which are engaged in rela-tionships with the purpose of achieving their goals. As Ziakas and Costa (2011) argue, events networks are usually formed randomly and typically have an informal nature. Stokes (2007) has identified three main factors that influence the nature of inter-organisational relationships within event tourism networks: the impact of power and political issues; the importance of trust; and the importance of a shared commitment. Other aspects which also affect the network actors' relationships include the degree of relationship and network formality, network permanency and clustering, the fluidity of membership, and the actor's position in the network hierarchy. A lack of integrated network strategy often leads to isolation of some organisations and to the limitation or absence of cooperation ties between them (Weed, 2003).

Event stakeholder interactions and exchanges form a collaborative network working together in event implementations across the portfolio. This collaboration is shaped by information exchange, resource sharing, joint initiatives and joint problem-solving. Information exchange refers to any type of communication or data sharing regarding events in a city. Resource sharing delineates the use of facilities, equipment, funding and staff. Joint initiatives include marketing, fund raising and event operations. Joint problem-solving refers to common actions to solve emerging problems with regard to planning and delivering a portfolio of events (Ziakas, 2014).

Effective collaboration can be strengthened by enhancing norms of reciprocity and trust. On the grounds that event organisations are embedded into the social structures and cooperate effectively with other non-event organisations, a host community can enable the deployment and common utilisation of resources, facilities, skills, knowledge and human labour in managing its event portfolio. In other words, different organisations should exchange information and resources in the hosting of events.

The establishment of trust and moral obligation is a critical component in the development of inter-organisational relationships (Perrow, 1993; Uzzi, 1997; Zaheer, McEvily, & Perrone, 1998). They foster reciprocity among organisations and ensure mutually beneficial and long-standing relationships, thereby strengthening their collaborative relationships (Oliver, 1990; Podolny & Page, 1998; Provan, Veazie, Staten, & Teufel-Shone, 2005). The strengthening of collaboration patterns by increased levels of trust and reciprocity (Perrow, 1993; Provan, Nakama, Veazie, Teufel-Shone, & Huddleston, 2003) functions as a means to generate social capital (Podolny, & Page, 1998). Likewise, the event portfolio can become a space for the generation of social capital by developing and enhancing relationships of trust, mutual recognition and obligation as well as assistance among organisations. To this end, inter-organisational linkages should promote collaboration and reciprocity that supports joint decision-making and problem-solving in event implementation and cross-leveraging strategies.

Such strong stakeholder ties can enable coordination and build community capacity in portfolio management and leveraging, thereby achieving intended outcomes. However, the inter-relationships among different actors within an events network can also be characterised by power games, coalition building and change dynamic (Andersson, & Getz, 2008; Larson, 2002, 2009a). The formation of an event portfolio strategy in a city leads to the introduction of the notion of a 'political market square', where various stakeholders operate with a varying degree of power and influence, negotiate, form alliances and affect the decision-making process in the event industry (Getz, 2012; Larson, 2009b). A critical aspect affecting the realisation of the event portfolio approach concerns the conditions of an institutional structure that establish the organisational environment, where events are planned, delivered and leveraged (Ziakas, 2014).

Institutional structures and portfolio governance

From a planning and governance standpoint, the conditions of an institutional structure that establish the organisational environment, where events are planned, delivered and leveraged, play a critical role in forming a comprehensive policy that can enable the employment of joint efforts and cross-leveraging strategies among different events (Ziakas, 2014).

An institutional structure encompasses the institutionalised systems of local governance and administration that facilitate the incorporation of events into policy agendas and enable collaboration between event stakeholders and policy-making bodies. The formal structures of governance and administration can drive the formulation and implementation of joint event strategies in terms of legitimising their role as policy tools and employing the necessary resources and assets in event policies. While the formal structures are instrumental agents for the planning and management of event portfolios, informal modes of institutional organisation (e.g., culture, customs, etc.) can influence their nature, scope and outcomes. Therefore, the interaction effects of formal and informal institutional structures and logics should be taken into account to develop a comprehensive understanding of their role and evaluate which systems or structures are the most appropriate (and under what conditions). The components of effective institutional structures include:

- ◆ Employing participatory planning that encourages the involvement and participation of event stakeholders in the portfolio planning process and empowers them in decision-making;

- ◆ Establishing an environment of dialogue and mutual understanding that fosters common values and goals;

- ◆ Enhancing collaboration through sharing of information and resources;

- ◆ Placing conflict resolution mechanisms; and

- ◆ Creating a system to ensure accountability and equal distribution of events' impacts and benefits (Ziakas, 2014, p. 127).

Planning for event portfolios depends on the development of a comprehensive policy that defines their underlying purpose, design logics and strategic priorities. It also sets the ground for the formulation and implementation of leveraging and cross-leveraging strategies. The concepts of policy universe and policy community (Rhodes, 2002) can be applied at this stage. The policy universe is the large population of actors and independent interest groups interacting and competing with each other for influence over policy. The interaction and interdependencies between event stakeholders and the policy community that handles sectoral issues encompass the event policy network. The policy network can be understood as the linking process, the outcome of those exchanges within a policy community. Within this context, the event policy network should view an event portfolio as a strategic opportunity that can promote joint tactical planning and enhance mutual relationships in order to accomplish multiple policy purposes (Ziakas, 2014). The integrated strategic planning for leveraging an event portfolio can set common policy purposes for economic, tourism, social and sport development (Ziakas, 2019).

An event policy network must have strong, enduring relationships between event stakeholders and the policy universe. Economic action is embedded in the structure of social relations between actors, including kinship links, and thus the organisations operate embedded within a broad social nexus (Granovetter, 1985). In the business context, embeddedness is seen as the degree to which firms are embedded in local economies through relationships with competitors, customers, suppliers, regional business organisations and public sector fora (Markusen, 1994). As such, event-network embeddedness refers to either the overlap between social and economic linkages that influence event implementations and leverage strategies or the nesting of event-related linkages within other social relationships.

In this context, event organisations should be embedded into the socio-cultural, political and economic structures of a host community. This means that the institutionalisation of these entities, either in local government structures or in voluntary non-profit bodies, should give these organisations the 'voice', the power and autonomy to act on problems, distribute funds, and design, as well as implement, event policy programmes. This could incorporate an event portfolio in the community structures. As Getz and Andersson (2008) postulate in the context of festivals, the longevity and sustainability of events stem from institutional embeddedness, committed stakeholders and resource dependence on local government.

Planning in general is only one part of an overall decision-action process. It encompasses various activities such as bargaining and negotiation, compromise, coercion, interests, values, choice, and, of course, politics (Hall, 1998). In this context, governance constitutes a controlling mechanism that oversees the nature and structure of relationships between a multiplicity of stakeholders conducive to achieving shared goals through a more deliberative, inclusive, democratic, transparent and legitimate way of decision-making (Dredge & Whitford, 2011).

In terms of governance, the major question is: what agency will be responsible for the planning, management and leveraging of event portfolios and for the coordination of the associated activities and processes? Since the planning and implementation of event portfolios is grounded in a holistic outlook, the different events should be viewed in concert as instruments for community, economic, sport and tourism development. In this regard, an event portfolio provides the basis in which a common approach may be developed among different policy communities and event stakeholders to cross-leverage the events of a host community's portfolio. To realise this potential, host communities need to establish appropriate support mechanisms for the coordination of all aspects of event portfolio management (Ziakas, 2010).

The appointment or creation of a coordinating entity can be a foundational step toward developing an event portfolio policy to facilitate the processes of assembling events as well as establishing necessary alliances among different event stakeholders. Accordingly, inter-organisational cooperation between event stakeholders and the policy-makers can be achieved by setting a common policy and particular objectives for the event portfolio, thereby determining the choice of particular cross-leveraging strategies to be employed (Ziakas, 2010). A coordinating entity can also control funding of the portfolio and how funds should be allocated across the array of events, or at least provide guidance for financing the portfolio operation.

Undoubtedly, funding for portfolios is vital for their development, growth and extended life span. Public funding is the primary source of financing with selected events included in a portfolio to be subsidised from the government. This requires the establishment of criteria for selecting what events should be funded. Common criteria include the feasibility and return on investment, the event fit with the host destination and its contribution to enhancing its image and brand as well as its contribution to the overall portfolio value. Funding can also be used as a mechanism to develop and manage mutually beneficial relationships between the host community and the event portfolio. In this regard, long-term contracts provide security to both the event and the host community by signalling that a long-term relationship is to develop and thereby enhancing continuous interaction among stakeholders (Kelly & Fairley, 2018). Furthermore, given the entrepreneurial orientation of event governance, business-minded financing sources are increasingly used, stemming from the profitability of event operations such as sponsorship. These practices, of course, depend on the nature and ability of each event to attract and generate surplus revenues. Not all events have this capacity, but still their role within a portfolio can be significant and thus should be supported.

An important issue that needs to be factored into portfolio governance is the ownership of events. These can be owned by the city itself, private companies or voluntary organisations. It is common for portfolios to consist of a mix of events owned by public, profit and voluntary agencies. In this case, the portfolio complexity and its governance requirements increase as a wide range of stakeholders with different agendas have to be coordinated. The establishment of community partnerships or strategic alliances between agencies involved could facilitate portfolio governance and regulate intersecting responsibilities. In contrast, a city which owns the events of its portfolio can more efficiently oversee and manage the whole portfolio network. However, this might decrease inclusiveness, representation or engagement in the portfolio of different stakeholder groups. From a tourism standpoint, Destination Management Organisations (DMOs) have a key part in portfolio networks creating or bidding to host events. Nonetheless the role of DMOs needs to be balanced along with private and non-profit voluntary event owners who can bring in diversity and multiplicity in the portfolio.

Along these lines, event portfolio governance can be seen as a new form of public–private policy making shaped by the public sphere (i.e., the space of dialogue and participation) wherein stakeholders deliberate on and take action to achieve common goals (Dredge & Whitford, 2011). Despite the risk that the blurring of public–private interests may lead portfolios to be largely controlled by corporate and state interests (while short event timelines may prevent debate and engagement), the development of a discursive public sphere characterised by creative engagement and mediation of actors through a balancing third point of view is an essential support mechanism for portfolio governance as it enables dialogue and negotiated trade-offs between stakeholders to take place. Dredge and Whitford (2011) argued that an understanding of governance requires the appreciation of the institutional context, the issue drivers and influences that get pushed onto the political agenda and into the public sphere and the full range of stakeholders involved in event policy. On this basis, an appreciation of the public sphere can be developed along with how this shapes the space of dialogue, communication and information-sharing, which can enable stakeholder inclusiveness and participation in event portfolio planning and governance. From this perspective, a discursive public sphere is critical for transparent and accountable governance. This would also assist the application of an asset-based community development approach as a means of forming a more action-oriented, community-based approach to leveraging the social assets of events (Misener & Schulenkorf, 2016).

In addition, attention to how the public sphere of event portfolios is constituted, by whom and for what purposes and interests, could provide insights into issues of inequality and the shortcomings of event development policies (Moscardo, 2008). Actually, it is found that event policies often contain redundant rhetoric, are ad-hoc and reactive, are developed by an insular policy community and do not contain enough proactive, theoretically informed initiatives (Whitford, 2009). A comprehensive event portfolio policy should redress these shortcomings and establish appropriate governance mechanisms for enabling coordination.

Portfolio governance, hence, should aim to cultivate a space for leveraging the generated social capital by building a discursive public sphere (Dredge & Whitford, 2011) in which stakeholders negotiate their interests and take collective action to achieve common goals. Such a comprehensive portfolio policy and governance coordination should be grounded in a holistic event development paradigm that effectively addresses the economic, physical, social and political environments of events in order to either enhance the positive and/or prevent the negative impacts of events on the host community (Whitford, 2009).

Summary

The chapter thoroughly delved into the conditions of developing a sustainable and manageable event portfolio network. The nature of relationships among a range of stakeholders with different interests was considered. The implementation of an event portfolio strategy needs to garner local collaboration, synchronise policy agendas, solidify stakeholder networks, and increase identification among residents. Overall, a well-managed event portfolio has the potential to provide a common ground that would unite different stakeholders and enable the usage of an integrated set of event-related resources in the long-term. The next chapter will analyse and critically evaluate different aspects of event portfolio design and implementation.

References

Andersson, T. D., & Getz, D. (2008). Stakeholder management strategies of festivals. *Journal of Convention & Event Tourism,* **9**(3), 199-220. doi:10.1080/15470140802323801

Buch, T., Milne, S., & Dickson, G. (2011). Multiple stakeholder perspectives on cultural events: Auckland's Pasifika Festival. *Journal of Hospitality Marketing & Management,* **20**(3-4),311-328. doi:10.1080/19368623.2011.562416

Dredge, D., & Whitford, M. (2011). Event tourism governance and the public sphere. *Journal of Sustainable Tourism,* **19**(4/5), 479-499. doi:10.1080/09669 582.2011.573074

Freeman, R. E. (2010). *Strategic Management: A stakeholder approach.* Cambridge: Cambridge University Press.

Freeman, R. E., Harrison, S. J., Wicks, C. A., Parmar, L. B., & De Colle, S. (2010). *Stakeholder Theory: The state of the art.* Cambridge: Cambridge University Press.

Getz, D. (2012). Event studies: Discourses and future directions. *Event Management,* **16**(2), 171-187. doi:10.3727/152599512x13343565268456

Getz, D. (2013). *Event Tourism: Concepts, international case studies, and research.* New York: Cognizant Communication Corporation.

Getz, D., Andersson, T., & Larson, M. (2007). Festival stakeholder roles: Concepts and case studies. *Event Management,* **10**(2), 103-122. doi:10.3727/152599507780676689

Getz, D., & Andersson, T. D. (2008). Sustainable festivals: On becoming an institution. *Event Management,* **12**, 1-17. doi:10.3727/152599509787992625

Granovetter, M. (1985). Economic action and social structure: The problem of embeddedness. *American Journal of Sociology,* **91**(3), 481-510.

Hall, C. (1998). The politics of decision making and top-down planning: Darling Harbour, Sydney. In D. Tyler, M. Robertson, & Y. Guerrier (Eds.), *Tourism Management in Cities: Policy, process and practice* (pp. 9-24). Chichester: Wiley.

Hede, A.-M. (2008). Managing special events in the new era of the triple bottom line. *Event Management, 11*(1), 13-22. doi:10.3727/152599508783943282

Kelly, D. M., & Fairley, S. (2018). The utility of relationships in the creation and maintenance of an event portfolio. *Marketing Intelligence & Planning, 36*, 260-275. doi:10.1108/MIP-11-2017-0270.

Kilduff, M., & Tsai, W. (2003). *Social Networks and Organizations*. Thousand Oaks: SAGE.

Larson, M. (2002). A political approach to relationship marketing: case study of the Storsjoyran festival. *The International Journal of Tourism Research, 4*(2), 119. doi:10.1002/jtr.366

Larson, M. (2009a). Joint event production in the jungle, the park, and the garden: Metaphors of event networks. *Tourism Management, 30*(3), 393-399. doi:10.1016/j.tourman.2008.08.003

Larson, M. (2009b). Festival innovation: complex and dynamic network interaction. *Scandinavian Journal of Hospitality and Tourism, 9*(2-3), 288-307. doi:10.1080/15022250903175506

Markusen, A. (1994). Studying regions by studying firms. *Professional Geographer, 46*(4), 477-490.

Merrilees, B., Getz, D., & O'Brien, D. (2005). Marketing stakeholder analysis: Branding the Brisbane Goodwill Games. *European Journal of Marketing, 39*(9/10), 1060-1077. doi:10.1108/03090560510610725

Misener, L., & Mason, D. (2006). Creating community networks: Can sporting events offer meaningful sources of social capital? *Managing Leisure, 11*(1), 39-56. doi:10.1080/13606710500445676

Misener, L., & Schulenkorf, N. (2016). Rethinking the social value of sport events through an Asset-Based Community Development (ABCD) perspective. *Journal of Sport Management, 30*(3), 329-340. doi:10.1123/jsm.2015-0203

Mitchell, R. K., Agle, B. R., & Wood, D. J. (1997). Toward a theory of stakeholder identification and salience: Defining the principle of who and what really counts. *The Academy of Management Review, 22*(4), 853-886.

Moscardo, G. (2008). Analyzing the role of festivals and events in regional development. *Event Management, 11*, 23-32. doi:10.3727/152599508783943255

O'Toole, W. (2011). *Events Feasibility and Development: From strategy to operations*. Amsterdam: Butterworth-Heinemann.

Oliver, C. (1990). Determinants of interorganizational relationships: Integration and future directions. *Academy of Management Review, 15*(2), 241-265.

Perrow, C. (1993). Small firm networks. In R. Swedberg (Ed.), *Explorations in economic sociology* (pp. 227-402). New York, NY: Russell Sage Foundation.

Podolny, J., & Page, K. (1998). Network forms of organization. *Annual Review of Sociology, 24*, 57-76.

Provan, K., Veazie, M., Staten, L., & Teufel-Shone, N. (2005). The use of network analysis to strengthen community partnerships. *Public Administration Review, 65*(5), 603-613. https://www.jstor.org/stable/3542526

Provan, K. G., Nakama, L., Veazie, M., Teufel-Shone, N., & Huddleston, C. (2003). Building community capacity around chronic disease services through a collaborative inter-organizational network. *Health Education and Behavior*, **30**(6), 646-662.

Reid, S. (2011). Event stakeholder management: Developing sustainable rural event practices. *International Journal of Event and Festival Management*, **2**(1), 20-36. doi:10.1108/17582951111116597.

Rhodes, R. (2002). Putting people back into networks. *Australian Journal of Political Science*, **37**(3), 399-416. doi: 10.1080/1036114021000026337.

Richards, G., & Palmer, R. (2010). *Eventful Cities: Cultural management and urban revitalisation*. Amsterdam: Butterworth-Heinemann.

Sciarelli, M., & Tani, M. (2013). Network approach and stakeholder management. *Business Systems Review*, **2**(2), 175-190. doi:10.7350/BSR.V09.2013

Stokes, R. (2007). Relationships and networks for shaping events tourism: An Australian study. *Event Management*, **10**(2), 145-158. doi:10.3727/152599507780676652

Uzzi, B. (1997). Social structure and competition in interfirm networks: The paradox of embeddedness. *Administrative Science Quarterly*, **42**(1), 35-67.

van Niekerk, M., & Getz, D. (2019). *Event Stakeholders: Theory and Methods for Event Management and Tourism*. Oxford: Goodfellow Publishers.

Weed, M. (2003). Why the two won't tango! Explaining the lack of integrated policies for sport and tourism in the UK. *Journal of Sport Management*, **17**(3), 258. doi:10.1123/jsm.17.3.258.

Whitford, M. (2009). A framework for the development of event public policy: Facilitating regional development. *Tourism Management*, **30**, 674-682. doi:10.1016/j.tourman.2008.10.018

Zaheer, A., McEvily, W., & Perrone, V. (1998). Does trust matter? Exploring the effects of interorganizational and interpersonal trust on performance. *Organization Science*, **9**(2), 141-159.

Ziakas, V. (2010). Understanding an event portfolio: the Uncovering of interrelationships, synergies, and leveraging opportunities. *Journal of Policy Research in Tourism, Leisure and Events*, **2**, 144-164. doi:10.1080/19407963.2010.482274

Ziakas, V. (2014). *Event Portfolio Planning and Management: A holistic approach*. Abingdon: Routledge.

Ziakas, V. (2019). Issues, patterns and strategies in the development of event portfolios: configuring models, design and policy. *Journal of Policy Research in Tourism, Leisure and Events*, **11**(1), 121-158. doi:10.1080/19407963.2018.1471481

Ziakas, V., & Costa, C. A. (2010). Explicating inter-organizational linkages of a host community's events network. *International Journal of Event and Festival Management*, **1**(2), 132-147. doi:10.1108/17852951011056919

Ziakas, V., & Costa, C. A. (2011). Event portfolio and multi-purpose development: Establishing the conceptual grounds. *Sport Management Review*, **14**(4), 409-423. doi:10.1016/j.smr.2010.09.003

5 Critical Aspects of Portfolio Design

In this chapter, critical aspects of event portfolio planning and design will be examined. First, the principles of portfolio design will be introduced. The disparity between organic and formalised portfolios will be explained. The chapter then will analyse a diversity of portfolio development approaches with recent examples from different destinations. The concepts of meta-event and multiple portfolios will be introduced. After that the chapter will examine four event portfolio strategies, including symmetrisation, specialisation, multi-constellation, and macro-expansion. Several event portfolio design frameworks will be introduced and discussed. Finally, a holistic model of event portfolio design will be presented and the conditions of critical mass will be explained.

Principles of portfolio design

In line with the current tendency to shift focus from single events to portfolios of events, the aspects of portfolio design become increasingly important from both academic and industry perspectives. Richards, Marques and Mein (2014) point out that at the level of event portfolio:

> the need arises to design beyond the confines of the event itself, into infrastructure and orgware (organisational structures and process). Events themselves then become structures, which in turn shape social, economic and cultural practises (pp. 208-209).

The planning and design of a portfolio of events contributes to a city experience-scape (O'Dell, 2005) or even results in the development of distinctive event-scapes (Richards et al., 2014), which are places where the consumption of experiences of pleasure, entertainment and sociability occurs. Ziakas (2014) argues that the design of an event portfolio is a primary task for city event planners. This process entails strategic decision-making, portfolio concept development, packaging of events, scheduling the event-related activities, overall portfolio coordination and development of a synergetic value of the portfolio parts. Prior to decision-making regarding which events to consolidate in an event portfolio, it is crucial to audit the entire population of events in a destination (Getz, 2005; Ziakas, 2014). Local and regional, small and medium events in the course of time have the potential to transform into more substantial tourist and investment attractions (Andersson, Getz, & Mykletun, 2013). Hence, the continuous analysis and evaluation of existing local events is a fundamental requirement for the development of a balanced and successful portfolio of events (Getz, 2012). The design of an event portfolio is a dynamic process that:

> *entails the strategic decision-making on the events to be included…, involves a meticulous account of the exogenous factors that impact on the event portfolio, which event characteristics should be fostered within the portfolio and which leveraging strategies to be employed* (Ziakas, 2014, p. 163).

The fundamental principles for effective event portfolio design are the following:

1   **A common ground** for building community capacity to capitalise on an event portfolio serves to develop an internal logic that facilitates the assembling of events as well as inter-organisational collaboration among different event stakeholders (Ziakas & Costa, 2011a).

2   **Strategic planning** is required to prevent the innate risks of events' relatedness such as exhausting local resources, hosting monotonously repetitive event elements or exceeding demand for events (Ziakas & Costa, 2011b).

3   **The Triple Bottom Line** (Hede, 2008; O'Brien & Chalip, 2008) should be at the core of an event portfolio strategy in order to balance the economic and social outcomes of events and facilitate the fair distribution of benefits and the balanced dissemination of economic, social and environmental impacts (Campbell, 1996).

The above principles demand the embeddedness of event portfolios into the environment and structures of their host community. Besides, the nature and qualities of portfolios are based on the particular needs and characteristics of host communities, which can enable the effective deployment of local resources in portfolio strategies. Portfolio embeddedness is multifaceted, integrating contextual, operational and socio-cultural dimensions (Ziakas, 2013). The contextual dimension comprises the local policy setting, economic and market conditions as well as stakeholder networks, resource capacity and community characteristics that affect portfolio planning and management. The operational dimension determines and regulates portfolio composing strategies, including the selection of events, their frequency, size, and market orientation. Lastly, the socio-cultural dimension encompasses different local viewpoints on events and their symbolic meanings within the local community (Ziakas, 2013).

Organic and formalised portfolios

It is possible to identify two different types of event portfolios, namely, organic and formalised. An organic portfolio does not have an institutional status or a formal portfolio strategy, but still its nature and character exhibit basic portfolio characteristics. A formalised portfolio constitutes planned structures systematically patterned and regulated by an explicit portfolio strategy (Ziakas, 2019).

While the number of host communities and destinations that develop formalised portfolios continues steadily to grow as a result of their direct investment in events, it is also apparent that cities develop organic portfolios. As such, the organic portfolios are fundamental, since they comprise the base upon which formalised portfolios can be developed or alternative forms (re)arranged.

The planning approach can enable top-down centralisation or conversely bottom-up decentralisation in power and decision-making. It appears that the majority of event portfolios up to now, either organic or formalised, employ top-down planning intended to facilitate coordination, stakeholder management and their institutionalisation.

Portfolio focus and development approaches

Event portfolios are shown to have considerably different composition and policy focus. For example, Gainesville in Florida, being a relatively small university town with a passion for sports, and having an inventory of sports facilities, hotel capacity, and a volunteer pool, developed a small-scale sport event tourism portfolio (Gibson, Kaplanidou, & Kang, 2012). This example shows that the creation of small-scale event portfolios are appropriate policy options when they comply with a community's resources and infrastructure.

Another example is the case of the medium-sized city of London, Ontario in Canada, which by creating an organic grouping of sport events with an emphasis on ice sports, attempted to market itself as a hosting sport event destination brand (Clark & Misener, 2015). Gothenburg in Sweden has developed a diverse portfolio of events that encompasses a mix of local, regional, hallmark and mega-events staged all year round in order to maximise tourism demand for events.

On the other hand, Innsbruck in Austria capitalises on a major sport event portfolio without adopting a clearly defined portfolio approach and focusing on sport and its infrastructure/experience to host major sport events (e.g., the Winter Olympic Games), while Helsinki in Finland appears to host a rather haphazard combination of events, without employing a strategic approach towards building an event portfolio (Ziakas, 2019).

Overall, the heterogeneity of event development methods that are followed by host communities and destinations is a reflection of local needs and characteristics, which influence the ways that strategies are formulated for developing their event calendars in an effort to achieve an array of purposes.

The lack of a clear and comprehensive strategy is a common characteristic of event development approaches followed by cities. For example, in the case of Termoli, a small coastal destination in Southern Italy, which attempted to reposition its tourism product, from the classic sun, sea, sand (3S) model, through an organic portfolio of sport events, it was found that the lack of an overarching strategy significantly reduces the power of sport events in building a sustainable competitive destination (Presenza & Sheehan, 2013).

Similarly, in the aforementioned example of London, Ontario there was found a lack of an overarching strategy to connect the different portfolio components such as sport with the arts and cultural events (Clark & Misener, 2015). Another example is Portimão, a resort in Portugal's major tourism region of Algarve, which employed a nautical small-scale sports event portfolio approach to enhance its destination image and construct a nautical destination brand, but this effort was constrained by an unclear definition of goals and a lack of coordination among different events (Pereira, Mascarenhas, Flores, & Pires, 2015). This case illustrates that even when a confined portfolio approach (nautical brand) to events is employed, an overall strategic vision may be lacking to thoroughly foster synergies and enhance complementarities, hence resulting in missed opportunities for cross-leverage. Moreover, as demonstrated in the case of Cook Islands, the strategic development of its event portfolio is dependent upon the collaborative capacity of the supporting events network (Dickson, Milne, & Werner, 2018).

Different event portfolio foci can impact variably on the perceptions of variety in life and on the likelihood-to-move to another city. As shown in the literature, quality-oriented event portfolios (i.e., portfolios focusing on few, but primarily international top-events) are more promising for attracting new residents in large cities than quantity-oriented portfolios (i.e., portfolios focusing on diverse, but primarily local and non-top events) by offering them higher levels of perceived variety in life (Dragin-Jensen, Schnittka, & Arkil, 2016). However, the kind of events offered in the portfolio (i.e., sport vs. cultural events) is not found to play an important role.

Multiple portfolios

Multiple event portfolios may also exist within one city, focusing on certain types of events or owed by different agencies. In this case, it is important for the city to identify and coordinate overlapping or competing portfolios to minimise conflicts and consumer demand cannibalisation. The establishment of a community coalition or a local coordinating agency could undertake this task overseeing individual and multiple portfolios and enabling cross-leverage.

The value of a city's individual portfolio may be enriched through cooperation with adjacent portfolios in the region and thereby creating an additional synergy for cross-leverage of multiple portfolios. In particular, Mariani and Giorgio (2017) analysed the Pink Night festival, which takes place in the Northern Italian Adriatic coast, and is shared by more than 60 municipalities across a wide geographic area, demonstrating that these competing destinations deliberately cooperate to plan, manage and develop this thematic festival. They defined this type of festival as a meta-event:

> A collection of coordinated, synchronised and intertwined events, occurring in a wide geographic area and encompassing two or more nearby competing destinations, which collaborate to better market themselves and/or to reposition themselves in the marketplace. It is part of the event portfolio of two or more DMOs and allows them to collaborate to conjointly garner the benefits of event tourism. It addresses both the tourists and the hosting communities of the destinations involved (Mariani & Giorgio, 2017, p. 101).

A meta-event is a novel conception that surpasses existent event taxonomies in terms of magnitude (mega-event or hallmark) and spatiality (regional or local event). This is because it encompasses a tourism product comprising complex layers of organisational and spatial collaboration between competing destinations. The meta-event notion opens up the possibility to conjointly leverage one or multiple event portfolios by two or more competing host communities.

In this vein, a meta-event reveals the programmatic synergies and complementarities that are engendered, since the intertwined events are planned to be compatible with each other and to meet different customer needs and objectives (Ziakas, 2019). From this perspective, multiple competing destinations can leverage their own event portfolios conjointly, thus surpassing the spatial confines of a host community's portfolio set by administrative boundaries, and expanding the impacts of collaborative portfolios to wider areas. This might lead to the development of strategic alliances between different host communities to design conjoint event portfolios and achieve diversification, not through one portfolio, but through events included across collaborative portfolios that distribute their benefits widely (Ziakas, 2019).

Event portfolio strategies

The different approaches taken by cities to develop event portfolios exemplify the creation of particular strategies that bring forward a range of structural portfolio traits and pertinent courses of action. Ziakas (2019) models these organisational trajectories based upon the logics of emerging portfolio design patterns and planning practices. Four strategies are identified, grounded in the traits of portfolio overall events' composition, their scale, multiplicity in terms of a portfolio's capacity to serve multiple purposes, portfolio size and reach. The four portfolio strategies include: symmetrisation, specialisation, multi-constellation, and macro-expansion.

♦ **Symmetrisation** focuses on the proportionate clustering of events, where a pyramid model is used to create a balanced portfolio of events by classifying them in terms of their type and scale. The aim of symmetry is at the core of this strategy. Subsequently, the portfolio composition is symmetrical consisting of a majority of small-scale and fewer medium-scale events with some occasional large-scale events. The strategy aims to harmonise the portfolio's reach to different target markets while balancing the use of resources, by keeping an analogous size for the portfolio (medium to high) dependent on available resources, and subsequently, tending to have also medium-to-high multiplicity. This strategy has its roots in the event tourism domain with Edinburgh and Gold Coast being the closest examples.

♦ **Specialisation** employs a domain concentration to enable specialisation by focusing primarily on certain types of events and associated purposes that they can serve. For example, there can be portfolios specialising in sport, cultural events or major events and economic, tourism or sport development. Subsequently, this is an asymmetrical strategy, which opts to invest in selected types and scale events and thereby reach niche markets. As a result, the size of the portfolio is more likely to be small and have low multiplicity. The portfolios of Gainesville (Gibson et al., 2012), Portimão (Pereira et al., 2015), and London (Ontario) (Clark & Misener, 2015) are examples of this strategy.

♦ **Multi-constellation** concerns a multiform synthesis, where the portfolio exhibits high variety in its composition by encompassing a broadly varied and asymmetrical array of event types. The aim of this strategy is to move beyond mere diversification and achieve the amalgamation of a large number of different and predominantly small-scale events, combined with a selected number of medium-sized events, to meet a range of objectives. Subsequently, the size of the portfolio is large and its multiplicity high in order to reach wide markets. An example of this strategy reported in the literature is the case of the rural community Fort Stockton in Texas that assembled a large number of varied sport and cultural events to develop an organic portfolio as a tool in its overall development (Ziakas, 2007).

♦   **Macro-expansion** concerns the intent for spatial expansion and magnitude dispersion, where the portfolio broadens its reach and size spreading its impacts and strategic outcomes to wider metropolitan or national areas. This strategy may be formulated from scratch and implemented at a national level. For example, Scotland (Visit Scotland, 2015) and Wales (Welsh Government, 2010) have developed their own national event portfolios. A variation of this strategy can be the creation and management of multiple portfolios in the same geographical area. Multiple portfolios can also enable collaboration among neighbouring communities through the staging of meta-events allowing them to leverage their own event portfolios conjointly and thereby expand their impacts to wider areas. This strategy can be either symmetrical or asymmetrical comprising events of all scales aimed at achieving a wide range of purposes. Subsequently, the portfolio's size is large and its multiplicity high while the reach is continuously expansive. In the case of multiple portfolios, the blending of constitutive independent portfolios can be multifarious, increasing substantially their composite complexity as interacting systems.

Table 5.1 encapsulates the event portfolio strategies and their predominant traits. Their understanding suggests a road map for the competitive positioning and sustainable growth of event portfolios. The selection of a suitable strategy and design model can enable the effective leveraging of event portfolios and their incorporation into the overall product mix of the host community or destination.

Table 5.1: Event portfolio strategies. Source: Ziakas (2019, p. 152).

Event portfolio strategies	Portfolio composition	Events scale	Portfolio multiplicity	Portfolio size	Portfolio reach
Symmetrisation	Symmetrical, proportionate	Pyramidal clustering	Medium to high	Medium to high	Balanced
Specialisation	Asymmetrical, similar	Any focused	Low	Small	Niche
Multi-constellation	Asymmetrical, diverse	Small, medium	High	Large	Wide
Macro-expansion	Symmetrical or asymmetrical	All scales	High	Large	Expansive

Event portfolio design frameworks

The analysis of the literature demonstrates an increasing demand for the development of a comprehensive event portfolio design framework that explains key processes of portfolio composition. One of the first theoretical attempts to conceptualise portfolio design belongs to Getz (1997, 2005, 2008). In the original pyramid model by Getz (1997, p.113), a range of values was specified, and a hierarchy based on both function and quantity was indicated (see Figure 5.1).

The possible values for individual events cover a wide range of quantifiable and qualitative measures of worth from different stakeholder perspectives and environmental sustainability. This corresponds with the notion that value is a multistakeholder construct, especially when events are intended to meet a range of public and private goals. If tourism is the sole consideration, then the primary goal is likely to be the establishment of a full calendar of events, of different types, to attract desired target segments. The possible measures of value for specific events can be expanded to cover the event portfolio, and fit into the balanced scorecard model.

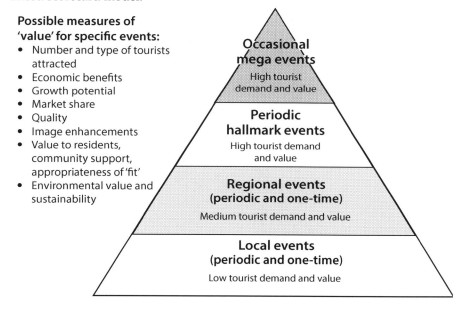

Possible measures of 'value' for specific events:

- Number and type of tourists attracted
- Economic benefits
- Growth potential
- Market share
- Quality
- Image enhancements
- Value to residents, community support, appropriateness of 'fit'
- Environmental value and sustainability

Occasional mega events
High tourist demand and value

Periodic hallmark events
High tourist demand and value

Regional events (periodic and one-time)
Medium tourist demand and value

Local events (periodic and one-time)
Low tourist demand and value

Figure 5.1: The pyramid model for an event-tourism portfolio. Source: Getz (1997, p. 133). Reproduced with permission by Cognizant Communications Corporation.

Getz has also revised the pyramid model for a community orientation, placing one-time major events (not 'mega') at the top, indicating their infrequency (see Figure 5.2). Permanent hallmark and iconic events will have high tourism and community value, with hallmark events in particular being viewed as valued traditions that satisfy a range of community-oriented goals. The base of this pyramid consists of the population of local and regional events that are primarily for and by residents. This differentiation of tourism and community-oriented event portfolios reflects a common approach in Australian cities, but of course, there is overlap.

Viol, Todd, Theodoraki, and Anastasiadou (2018) have adapted the revised pyramid model to commemorative events, placing occasional one-time major anniversaries at the pinnacle. Below this are iconic-historic commemorative events, then lower down are local and regional commemorative events. At the base are, any number of events in a permanent commemorative infrastructure, representing topics of local or regional importance.

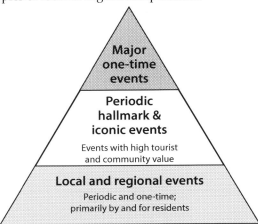

Figure 5.2: Revised portfolio model for a community orientation.

Getz (2013) suggests several scenarios for portfolio development. Thus, scenario A, where the portfolio is managed for immediate, maximum tourism and economic gain appeals to destinations that are just entering event tourism and tends to put their names on the international event map. Scenario B where a diverse portfolio is managed for long-term, TBL sustainability is a strategy that corresponds to the contemporary paradigm of sustainable urban development. Scenario C focuses on a portfolio managed for increasing long-term benefits. It concentrates on niche audience markets rather than on mass tourism or mass consumption of the event product. A strong focus provides competitive advantages in branding, promotion and managing of the portfolio.

Ziakas (2007) argues that the overall purpose of the portfolio should be identified, taking into consideration historical, political, cultural or even existential characteristics of a community. All the driving forces that can influence the objectives of an event portfolio should be analysed and discussed among organising bodies and host community stakeholders. An event portfolio approach envisages all different types of events as resources, which can be utilised in line with the event strategy.

Any portfolio design should be guided by a strategic vision. On a conceptual level, the destination vision is grounded in the *competitive advantages, comparative advantages* and *internal values of destinations*. An interplay of these components determines the formulation of goals and objectives for public events, which are directed towards delivering an authentic city experience.

♦ **Comparative advantages** usually pertain to a destination legacy, heritage, or related available resources. These include location, climate, visitor attractions, social and economic conditions (Getz, 2013).

♦ **Competitive advantages** refer to the activities and achievements that improve the profile of a city and emphasise its points of difference. This includes an effort to develop relevant strategies, establish regional development agencies, partnerships, effective marketing and industry competence (Getz, 2013). Anholt (2007) argues that building a competitive identity of a place requires a joint strategy of highlighting and promoting the things that a destination has or does, including its people, traditions, attractions, companies, products and services. Public events in this case play a role of reputational assets that attract international and national attention and influence the formation of positive stereotypes and place images.

♦ **Internal values** manifest themselves in the community's culture, history and beliefs. This is an inner mentality of the population projected through the creation of shared meanings. A city's residents will never know most of their neighbours; however, in their minds lives the image of the communion (Anderson, 1991). Internal values can be described in terms of cultural and ethnic diversity, community vibrancy, historical roots and heritage that are transmitted through events and, again, outline place uniqueness. Events become vital particles of a city's existence. They influence the formation of the city character and transform the way people perceive it.

Antchak and Pernecky (2017) discuss several parameters that determine the nature of a portfolio design reflecting the contextual background in destinations. These are *formality, intentionality, directionality* and *rhythmicity*. Formality refers to the level of standardisation of portfolios, operating procedures, protocols and rules. The opposing values of formality are 'standardised' and 'amorphous'. Intentionality determines to what extent portfolio approaches and initiatives are strategic and intended to achieve certain outcomes. The opposing values are 'purposive' and 'unintended'. Directionality describes the orientation of the approaches, either on the supply-side market-led initiatives or demand-side community engagement in portfolio design. Rhythmicity refers to the ability of city event managers to modify their approaching due to the context changes and revision of objectives, with values being 'intensive' and 'passive'.

Portfolio programming is a complicated area of event planning and management. Whitford (2009) argues that it is imperative for cities to identify those events that are most suitable for their profile enrichment and can complement other urban objectives and goals. One of the main tasks of portfolio managers is to consider how events complement one another and how these connections can lead to the integrative synergy of events in the portfolio (Ziakas, 2014).

Antchak (2016) brings forward a systematic approach for putting together and designing an event portfolio. According to this approach, portfolio design involves an interplay of *Composing* and *Synergising* strategies (Figure 5.3).

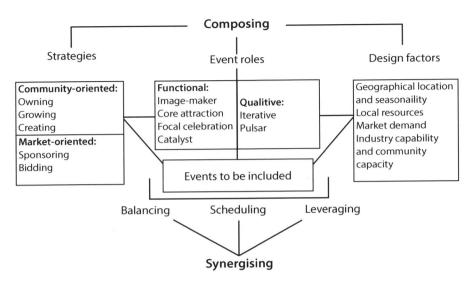

Figure 5.3: Event portfolio design. Adapted from Ziakas (2014) and Antchak (2016).

As a process, Composing includes a set of tactics to construct a competitive and diverse portfolio of major events. It entails strategic decisions with regard to the selection of events, event roles and factors that influence the process. Synergising focuses on the development of the overall portfolio value, its unity. Portfolio synergy provides event managers with an opportunity to balance events and their outcomes, to manage the portfolio calendar and proactively plan any leveraging strategies. In a synergetic portfolio, events complement one another and produce an integrative network of objectives, resources, stakeholders and expertise.

Composing

The composition of event portfolios contains the parameters of specialisation (i.e., event genres/types level of concentration or diversification) and sanctioned scale/periodicity of events. These make up the overall form of portfolios. Figure 5.4 displays on horizontal axis the specialisation level of homogeneous (focusing on an event genre) vs. heterogeneous (diversified event genres) portfolios. The vertical axis illustrates the small-scale/periodic vs. large-scale/one-off emphasis of events in the portfolio. In the middle of this axis, medium-sized events can be placed, also considering the degree to which events are highly or lowly periodic.

It is possible to delineate five strategies for assembling a portfolio of events in a destination. These strategies are divided into two groups. Community-oriented strategies include owning, growing and creating of events. Market-oriented strategies are represented by sponsoring and bidding for events.

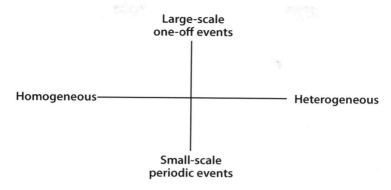

Figure 5.4: Composition of event portfolios. Source: Ziakas (2019, p. 148).

Community-oriented strategies: owning, growing and creating

The key advantage of *owning* events is that a city controls the event's properties and rights. Such events are "essentially community owned" (Getz, 2013, p. 134). They have stable institutional structures, usually with a board of directors and permanently hired event managers. The direct involvement of local government provides such events with public funding, low rent expenses and free promotion campaigns. Such locally-distinctive events should constitute the basis for the portfolio planning. Owned events generate the highest return on investment across many criteria with the minimum of investment. Local major events are fully co-branded with the host place. Their functions include being a visitor attraction, image promotion, delivering community benefits, including a sense of pride and being sustainable. The support of such events on an annual basis and their inclusion in portfolio guarantees the development of sustainable long-term assets and continuous positive outcomes, for example, permanent jobs. Owned events can become an attractive anchor for other smaller local events that can be bundled together with the main event to increase visitations and a sense of festivity and celebration.

Growing of existing events that are already at a city's disposal is another strategy of composing a portfolio of events. Ziakas (2014) argues that, in order to compose a successful portfolio, the audit of the whole population of events in a city is required. A so-called 'picking the wins' tactic, when promising events are identified and a decision to support and invest is taken, should be a general responsibility of all the involved stakeholders, including local DMOs and authorities. Sometimes growing occurs in natural conditions without any intervention from the city government, otherwise the event is directly supported by the city council in order to widen the city's events programme and attract more visitors and participants.

There are at least three key strategic reasons for creating new events in a portfolio. New events can be developed to fill existing gaps in the annual programme. They can be built in response to market demand and to meet city status requirements. Getz (2013) argues that creation of events is a more sustainable strategy in comparison to, for example, buying events from outside. A locally created event provides city event managers with a strategic advantage in terms of controlling the event-related processes and meeting particular goals when it comes to timing, targeting and a positive city image. In order to succeed, created events should be fully integrated into the community's fabric and city's perceptions. They should possess characteristics of distinctiveness, otherwise, the possibility of a 'copycat' challenge exists. As Richards, Marques and Mein (2014) argue, there is a tendency for cities to create events because their competitors have them or because the status of the city allegedly requires such events. This is a risky tactic as if an event is not an integral part of the city, it is unlikely to succeed.

Creating and growing events has been considered as a preferable but long-term and resource-consuming portfolio composing strategy. At the same time, home-grown or created events have a lot of advantages. The rights for home-grown events are usually controlled by the city. Such events are rooted in the community traditions and history, and they are more likely to meet the perception of residents and get their support. What is more important, the home-grown events are an excellent permanent platform for an array of leveraging initiatives and long-term legacy projects.

Market-oriented strategies: sponsoring and bidding

The strategy of *sponsoring* major events widens the portfolio horizon in a city, as it provides event organisers and promoters with an opportunity to get some financial support from the city to host their event. Sponsored events are not owned by the city; they should meet key criteria stated by the city authorities in order to get investment and become part of an annual portfolio of major events. Sponsoring strategy provides a periodic refresh of the portfolio offered in event destinations. It is also a good source of support for new creative event ideas and grass roots projects in the city.

Bidding is one of the most popular strategies of securing one-off events for portfolios. Getz (2013) argues that destinations bid for events to achieve clear-cut objectives that cannot be realised in other ways, otherwise, there is no strategic necessity to make huge investment in the bidding process. Many destinations nowadays increasingly use this strategy to secure predominantly sporting events. Such events have been expected to bring economic wins and enhance the city's profile. As Foley, McGillivray and McPherson (2012) argue, such an approach is common for relatively peripheral event destinations to secure the recognition of the city's brand. The smaller cities, however, do not have sufficient funds to bid on a regular basis and normally they participate in collective national bids to secure the rights to host mega and major events.

There are several pitfalls with the bidding element in portfolio design, including the relationships between the host city's brand and the brand requirements of the event owners and sponsors who accompany every important international event. City event managers very often become dependent on external event-related agencies and, as a result, their organisational creativity is limited. The restrictions that come together with large events may negatively affect local business, community satisfaction and image promotion.

Another issue with the bids is the element of 'unknown'. Bidding on, and then hosting, a large sporting event is an expensive and risky project with some potential of bad legacies. The short-term duration of an event might significantly affect the image and competitiveness of the host destination. Finally, sporting events represent the majority of biddable events on the international market. This is understandable due to the specific character of cultural celebrations and their traditional embeddedness in a community life. It is impossible to bid for the Rio Carnival or Octoberfest; however, as the example of the European Capitals of Culture project demonstrates, the cultural element in bids is getting more salient (e.g., Richards, Dodd, & Palmer, 2014). For a period of one year, a city-winner organises a series of cultural events and festivals with a strong European orientation. Such events invariably enrich the city's event programming. As Getz (2013) argues, bidding can help to fill the gaps in the portfolio by adding specific types of events that are oriented towards a particular audience segment. However, the more sustainable methods are to create new events or grow already existing events.

Event roles

A variety of composing strategies guarantees the inclusion of diverse events in a portfolio. Each of the events can play its own strategic role and contribute to the overall portfolio content and depth. The research findings allowed identification of functional and qualitative roles of major events.

Functional roles reflect the purposeful intention behind hosting one or another event in the cities (Clark & Misener, 2015). This may include tourism promotion when events play a role of a core tourist attraction and generate sufficient economic contribution (Getz, 2013). This is the case of large-scale one-time events and local festivals, which motivate visitation, as well as local and regional participation. Some events catalyse development, transformation and renovation of city-scapes, including construction of new venues, re-construction of city centres and waterfronts.

Ziakas (2014) suggests that a host destination can utilise the following roles of events in a portfolio:

♦ *Events as core attractions*. Events under this strategy are used to attract visitors whose primary reason for travelling to the host destination is the event.

◆ *Events as focal celebrations.* Events under this strategy are anchors of community identity, values and civic esteem that result in social capital development.

◆ *Events as complementary features.* Events under this strategy are used to complement and reinforce the benefits bestowed by major events of the two previous strategies.

Functional roles are not anchored. Each event can play several roles within a portfolio, delivering multiple experiences and meeting numerous objectives.

Qualitative roles of events can be of iterative or pulsar nature. Iterative events are usually annual community-embedded events that "generally have a maintenance function – bringing people together on a regular basis to cement strong social ties and generating bonding social capital" (Richards, 2015, p. 557). Iterative events bring local people together. They accomplish a maintenance function, strengthening the connections within a community, bonding social capital, preserving traditions and developing a sense of belonging. Iterative events are usually community-owned events, deeply rooted in the community structures. They are not necessarily small events, but events that reflect and regularly celebrate a unique local identity.

Pulsar events, on the contrary, "are potential moments of change that can lead to the development of new structures, links, and opportunities..." (Richards, 2015, p. 557). Pulsar events deliver dynamic changes in the host place. They challenge local event industry capacity and may require a significant investment of resources. Pulsar events meet the criteria of large-scale international festivals and sporting tournaments. This type of event is delivered by sponsoring new, or bidding on, important international major events that require investment and new infrastructure. A balanced combination of pulsar and iterative events in the portfolio provides a diverse spectrum of experience for both locals and visitors and develops eventfulness (Richards, 2015). Richards illustrates the interplay between iterative and pulsar events in Barcelona's portfolio, which connects the local spaces with the global flows achieving to produce a range of effects such as image change, tourism growth, and urban regeneration. The mix of iterative and pulsar events within a portfolio can give a change of pace and a diversity of experience bringing together different stakeholders and target audiences.

The dominance of one or the other composing strategies could lead to the shift of accent in the city event strategy. For example, if a city is focused on multiple bids for economic benefits, it concentrates on the delivery of pulsar events that bring changes but do not guarantee regular community interactions, which are important for social cohesion (Richards, 2015). On the other hand, if the city event strategy is oriented on the development and growth of local existing events, the pulsar changes of the city structures are less noticeable.

The use of diverse composing strategies results in varied proportions of iterative and pulsar events in the portfolio. As these roles relate to different event qualities and objectives, the task for portfolio managers is to monitor and manage the compositional structure of the portfolio in order to balance the influence of iterative and pulsar events in the host city.

In addition, portfolio managers need also to decide on the role of sport or cultural events in relation to other events, and the role of hallmark periodic events or one time major events. Similarly, the roles of sport and the arts as portfolio elements need to be determined. Along the same lines, managers should formulate strategies that can incorporate one-off sport mega-events into a host city's portfolio and enable their cross-leveraging with its recurring smaller-scale events.

Composing and design factors

As portfolio composing occurs within changing urban environments, event managers should take into consideration internal and external factors that might influence portfolio composition. It is possible to identify at least four critical design factors: (1) geographical location and seasonality, (2) local resources, (3) market demand, and (4) industry capability and community capacity.

Geographical location and seasonality

For event owners or promoters, accessibility of a host destination often plays a critical role in decision-making. Portfolio managers should carefully evaluate their geographical location and its accessibility and either try to turn it into a competitive advantage or diminish its negative impact. For example, the geographical remoteness of a destination or accessibility issues can have implications both for timetabling and for cost. As a result, it could affect the assortment of events and audience numbers. Portfolio design requires an extensive evaluation of this factor in order to mitigate the influence of distance and organisation and travel costs. Moreover, geographical location impacts on the availability and capacity of target markets. Geography, however, can also play a positive decisive role in event bidding campaigns, when a decision to host an event is made due to the suitability and benefits of the destination's location. Cities can try to capitalise on their unique natural environment and wildlife, which are comparative advantages. The task is to compose a portfolio in a way that it attracts different categories of event visitors, and particularly those who seek for an authentic experience of the place, notwithstanding its geographical location and accessibility.

Since large-scale public events require open spaces, *seasonality* is an influential factor for the host cities. The problem of off-peak seasons has been extensively analysed in event tourism literature (e.g., Connell, Page, & Meyer, 2015; Getz, 2012). For portfolio planning, decisions could be made to bid and host a variety of major business events that could provide additional visitor-nights for the local hospitality industry during the off-peak season and engage relevant city venues.

Although this is a different type of event, of a specialist nature which is normally not considered as part of city portfolios, cooperation between business event organisers and host cities seems to be promising for all the involved stakeholders.

A more sustainable and long-term strategy involves creation of new events to combat seasonality. In this case, however, a strong collaboration with the local community is required, as locals represent a key source market for events (Connell et al., 2015). Without the support of the local community, it is unlikely to realise any initiatives with regard to solving seasonality issues.

Local resources

Local resources constitute another important portfolio design factor that determines the feasibility and quality of the portfolio design. Ziakas (2014) describes local resources for portfolios as the unique capital of a host destination that can support the organisation of events. This includes available infrastructure, financial support, and network collaboration. There is a strong imperative for event portfolio managers to achieve a certain level of alignment between portfolio structure and available resources. The task is to select the 'right' events without exceeding the available infrastructure and amount of public money. Feasibility studies of the 'supply' side, including available venues, parks, transport system, accommodation and public investment, are required to determine the perspectives of an event and allocation of event-related resources.

Ziakas (2014) argues that an effective use of local resources within a portfolio leads to resource interchangeability, which refers to the utilisation of the same resources by different events in the portfolio. This requires collaboration and common understanding of the resource inter-dependencies and limits (Ziakas, 2013). For example, the same venues can be used as spaces for different types of events (e.g., arts, food markets, fan zones and music festivals). Strategic portfolio planning helps to avoid competition between event organisers and to plan the utilisation of the facilities in advance.

Market demand

Market demand can be described as the level of the potential market and audience for an event (Ziakas, 2014). It also relates to the attractiveness of an event offer and to the benefits visitors expect to get from visiting an event (Getz, 2013). There are internal and external types of demand that should be taken into consideration by the city event managers. The internal demand refers to the availability of an internal market and audience for a particular event, to be held in a city. The common strategy is to conduct market research and surveys to evaluate the perspectives of a particular event or a series of events. The analysis of the internal situation on the event market facilitates in identifying current gaps in the portfolio planning or specific shortfalls in terms of economic growth, tourism development and community engagement. The next step is to find or create an event that could deliver positive outcomes and reduce the influence of those gaps.

The external demand occurs when an external market player, like an international sporting federation or right holder expresses an interest on staging an event in a particular destination. This is a chance for a destination to capitalise on this external opportunity, host the event and thereby enhance its international profile and competitive identity as an events destination.

Key benefits of the demand evaluation were clearly formulated by Getz (2013):

> *The leisure and sport markets offer virtually unlimited potential for competitive advantage, if only more is known about the motivations and social worlds of people with special interests* (p. 387).

If the expectations of event attendees (both visitors and locals) are clearly understood, then event managers can adjust event programming and offer a unique and authentic portfolio of events.

On occasion, the demand manifests itself from the perspective of bottom-up planning when the community demand directly informs the portfolio composing. Such 'market intelligence' (Getz, 2013) also enables the identification of the gaps in event programming. The bottom-up and demand-side approaches open new avenues for portfolio design, planning and development. As Getz (2013) suggests, such approaches liberate entrepreneurship and innovation in the event industry.

Industry capability and community capacity

Industry capability to plan and host major events refers to managerial and organisational expertise and strategic networking. The growing experience of a city in the planning and management of large-scale events increases the level of managers' and the whole industry's capability to organise and host events of international and national significance. This also refers to a strategic use of volunteers' pools and sharing of knowledge among the local and regional event sectors.

Industry capability is linked with the overall community capacity. This is a well-developed concept in tourism and events studies. As Moscardo (2008) argues, hosting events can catalyse skill development, knowledge exchange, and problem solving. In this instance, the relationships among event stakeholders play a critical role.

The processes for community capacity-building in event portfolio planning and management need to be grasped. Wider community involvement and stakeholder participation is essential. Since event portfolios are shaped and delivered by a network of event stakeholders (Getz & Page, 2016), it is necessary to look at their interactions, exchanges, synergies and cooperation (Huxham & Vangen,

2005; Jarman, 2018; Larson, 2009) within the broader impacted local population context that entails residents' attitudes about the portfolio, community participation in, and inclusiveness of the portfolio. Thus, applying an event portfolio network perspective is useful to assess the development of partnerships and fostering of collaboration as well as coordinate stakeholder management strategies (Adongo & Kim, 2018). The resulting development of social capital constitutes the lifeblood of an event portfolio, which can potentially deliver long-lasting benefits to a host community or destination providing that derives from efforts to build community capacity and enable inclusive bottom-up participatory planning across the portfolio. This process can be facilitated by engaging all stakeholders with a common understanding of the issues so that a discursive public sphere is generated (Dredge & Whitford, 2011) enabling inclusive community participation, dialogue and cooperation in the production, management and leveraging of the portfolio.

The composing process cannot succeed if it is not supported by a stable and embedded system of stakeholder relationships. The ability to coordinate stakeholders through the implementation of different tactics, including protocols and group meetings, gives the city event managers an opportunity to purposefully negotiate with the interested event-related agents and direct joint efforts to the realisation of event projects.

Portfolio synergising

Synergy is understood as "integration across projects so that allocation of resources can be done in a more efficient way, either by sharing resources among projects or by improving project performance from the results of other related projects" (de Souza, Carneiro, & Bandeira-de-Mello, 2015, p. 127). Ziakas (2014, p. 135) highlights the necessity of the development of synergetic means to "attain, magnify and sustain benefits and planned legacies of events". The process of synergising facilitates the contiguity of events and related initiatives.

Capitalisation on the portfolio values entails identification of strategies and tactics that enhance synergy among events in the portfolio. There are three components of event portfolio synergising: balance, scheduling and leveraging.

Portfolio balance

Balance is a cornerstone of portfolio integral value. Due to the contextual peculiarities, balancing can be approached in different ways. Portfolio balance can refer to the correlation between selected events and associated outcomes. In this scenario, the decisions regarding the extent of event support or its inclusion into a portfolio depend upon the estimated performance indicators and specified conditions, which derive from a feasibility study. The balance in a portfolio can be achieved by the allocation of the specified roles an event could play in order to achieve specific outcomes. Some events, generally cultural celebrations, provide liveability, others, for example, sporting events, provide economic benefits and international exposure. Often, the same event is expected to provide several outcomes. This is an investment-oriented approach. A different approach is when portfolio managers focus on a balance between different genres of events or target audiences. The goal is to achieve a balanced representation of different entertainment levels that people want to see and participate in.

One of the critical components of a balanced portfolio design is event accessibility. A portfolio should contain free city events that deliver a sense of festivity to all the residents and visitors. However, some events are more commercially-oriented. In this case, the task of the city events team is to monitor the level of fees and negotiate ticket price scale with the rights holders or promoters.

Balancing in event portfolios can be considered as compatibility between the demand of the host community and the supply side that is provided by the city event managers. In order to succeed, events in the portfolio should be more city-oriented in terms of their embeddedness and connectivity with the city's cultural, heritage and historic roots. Here the concept of balance goes beyond the event realm, and represents a strategic accumulation of unique place assets. A portfolio can be authorised to play a role of a destination network, where events are used to consolidate a wide range of local attractions in order to transmit an authentic value of the city and its people.

Portfolio scheduling

The character of event portfolios is shaped by programming decisions that fix the timing and fit of events amongst them. Strategic coordination of events requires appropriate scheduling, when events do not conflict with each other or with other occurrences in the host city (Ziakas, 2014). Such coordination allows event portfolio managers to bundle different events of different genres and target audiences and deliver this package as a joint unique experience. Bundling refers to a deliberate staging of multiple events together on the same or adjacent dates (Xu, Wong, & Tan, 2016). By bundling two or more events together, city event managers amalgamate their resources and management of events, providing event organisers with an ability to work and communicate with various audiences. For example, in 2014, in Auckland, several events of different genres (the NRL Auckland Nines tournament, a concert of Eminem and the Lantern Festival) were staged during the same weekend to increase the 'buzz' effect, attract a huge audience and deliver a nation-wide promotion campaign. Staging of multiple events concurrently provides an effective relocation of available city resources, including infrastructure, promotion budgets and pools of volunteers. A series of bundled events create an attractive festive atmosphere in a city and new or smaller events benefit from co-scheduling by sharing the audience base and publicity with larger well-known city events.

Portfolio leveraging

The potential of an event portfolio as a leveraging tool has been already discussed in Chapter 3. In terms of portfolio integrity and synergy, leveraging strategies could consolidate different event-led and event-themed initiatives (Smith, 2014) that extend the benefits from hosting large-scale events and contribute to the development of other areas of city life. Leveraging expands the portfolio usefulness and integrates events into a wider business and community environment. Leveraging the synergy of an event portfolio can increase a city's ability to plan for improvements in other industries and sectors. In this case, events play a role as contributors to the destination' prosperity, including new infrastructure construction, development of creative industries, employment, youth engagement and city brand promotion. Composing an event portfolio places leveraging on a more holistic and strategic basis. Indeed, it is more beneficial to develop and accumulate all the leveraging strategies within one entity rather than estimating and planning for discrete events. The portfolio approach allows looking beyond direct events impacts.

Critical mass in portfolio design

One of the critical stages in designing a successful portfolio of events is the achievement of a state of 'critical mass'. Critical mass refers to "minimum portfolio of events, venues, and related investment that is necessary to achieve a permanent, adaptable portfolio and self-sustaining growth in net benefits" (Getz, 2013, p. 150). Although no research has been conducted to explain the essence of the critical mass of events in event destination, Getz (2013, pp. 150-151) suggests a list of starting points for empirical testing, including:

◆   A basic level of event venues required for hosting different events;

◆   A basic number of permanent and one-off events in the city which guarantee the achievement of critical mass;

◆   Collaboration of key stakeholders, including partnership between government and private sector;

◆   Legitimation, which refers to "the process of making investment in events and venues desirable because of demonstrated benefits";

◆   Successful track-record in bidding and hosting major events.

One of the key factors for creating a critical mass is the number and variety of events included in a portfolio, their interrelationships and strategic roles. The main task for portfolio managers is to understand what types of events should be included and how they should correspond to the current political, economic or cultural agenda of a destination. The collaboration of stakeholders plays a vital role as it guarantees the support and sharing of expectations from all interested actors in the city event industry.

Summary

This chapter provides a set of theoretical constructs and tools to systematically design and develop event portfolios. From this standpoint, city event managers and policy-makers can assess the effectiveness of different configurations and strategies by examining their advantages and disadvantages as well as their competitive positioning. In this regard, the spatiality of portfolios should also be considered as the development and management of portfolios can have different dynamics in urban, regional, national, or island contexts (Ziakas & Boukas, 2016). In effect, a comprehensive event portfolio policy should establish an appropriate planning and operational approach resulting in a particular model of portfolio management and development.

The chapter introduced a model of portfolio design, centred around the processes of composing and synergising. Composing deals with the compositional structure of a portfolio. From a strategic perspective, city event managers should clearly understand what events to include (different genres), what assembling strategies to use (owning, creating, growing, bidding and sponsoring), what roles each of the selected events are to play within a portfolio (functional and qualitative) and what factors can affect portfolio success (geographical location and seasonality, local resources, internal and external demand, industry capability and community capacity).

The synergy within a portfolio of events, via balancing, scheduling and leveraging, provides the 'gleaning' of all the separate entities, including the events themselves, leveraging opportunities, scheduling and genre representation. The synergetic value of an event portfolio makes it an indispensable policy tool for city policy-makers who aim to construct and reinforce the uniqueness and attractiveness of their city for different audiences.

The state of critical mass might be seen as a good starting point for measuring achieved outcomes, reformulating city objectives with regard to events and setting new priorities and indicators of success. The evaluation of the whole portfolio of events calls for the development of new domains and methods that should connect portfolio design with the principles of sustainable development. The next chapter explores multiple methods of event portfolio evaluation.

References

Adongo, R., & Kim, S. (2018). The ties that bind: Stakeholder collaboration and networking in local festivals. *International Journal of Contemporary Hospitality Management*, **30**(6), 2458-2480. doi: 10.1108/IJCHM-02-2017-0112

Anderson, B. (1991). *Imagined Communities: Reflections on the origin and spread of nationalism*. London, England: Verso.

Andersson, T. D., Getz, D., & Mykletun, R. (2013). The 'festival size pyramid' in three Norwegian festival populations. *Journal of Convention & Event Tourism*, **14**(2), 81-103. doi:10.1080/15470148.2013.782258

Anholt, S. (2007). *Competitive Identity: The new brand management for nations, cities and regions.* New York, NY: Palgrave Macmillan.

Antchak, V. (2016). *Event Portfolio Design: Exploring strategic approaches to major events in New Zealand.* Auckland University of Technology, New Zealand., Unpublished Doctoral Dissertation.

Antchak, V., & Pernecky, T. (2017). Major events programming in a city: Comparing three approaches to portfolio design. *Event Management, 21,* 545-561. doi:10.3727/152599517X15053272359013

Campbell, S. (1996). Green cities, growth cities, just cities? Urban planning and the contradictions of sustainable development. *Journal of the American Planning Association, 62*(3), 296-312. doi:10.1080/01944369608975696

Clark, R., & Misener, L. (2015). Understanding urban development through a sport events portfolio: A case study of London, Ontario. *Journal of Sport Management, 29,* 11-26. doi:10.1123/jsm.2013-0259

Connell, J., Page, S. J., & Meyer, D. (2015). Visitor attractions and events: Responding to seasonality. *Tourism Management, 46,* 283-298. doi:10.1016/j.tourman.2014.06.013

de Souza, P. B., Carneiro, J., & Bandeira-de-Mello, R. (2015). Inquiry into the conceptual dimensions of project portfolio management. *Brasilian Business Review,* 118-148. http://www.redalyc.org/articulo.oa?id=123041059006

Dickson, G., Milne, S., & Werner, K. (2018). Collaborative capacity to develop an events portfolio within a small island development state: The Cook Islands. *Policy Research in Tourism, Leisure and Events, 10,* 69-89. doi:10.1080/19407963.2017.1409751

Dragin-Jensen, C., Schnittka, O., & Arkil, C. (2016). More options do not always create perceived variety in life: Attracting new residents with quality- vs. quantity-oriented event portfolios. *Cities, 56,* 55–62. doi:10.1016/j.cities.2016.03.004

Dredge, D., & Whitford, M. (2011). Event tourism governance and the public sphere. *Journal of Sustainable Tourism, 19*(4/5), 479-499. doi:10.1080/09669582.2011.573074

Foley, M., McGillivray, D., & McPherson, G. (2012). *Event Policy: From theory to strategy.* New York, NY: Routledge.

Getz, D. (1997). *Event Management & Event Tourism.* New York: Cognizant Communication Corporation.

Getz, D. (2005). *Event management and event tourism* (2nd ed.). New York: Cognizant Communication Corporation.

Getz, D. (2008). Event tourism: Definition, evolution, and research. *Tourism Management, 29*(3), 403-428. doi:10.1016/j.tourman.2007.07.017

Getz, D. (2012). *Event Studies: Theory, research and policy for planned events* (2d ed.). London: Routledge.

Getz, D. (2013). *Event tourism: Concepts, international case studies, and research.* New York: Cognizant Communication Corporation.

Getz, D., & Page, S. J. (2016). Progress and prospects for event tourism research. *Tourism Management, 52,* 593-631. doi:10.1016/j.tourman.2015.03.007

Gibson, H. J., Kaplanidou, K., & Kang, S. J. (2012). Small-scale event sport tourism: A case study in sustainable tourism. *Sport Management Review, 15,* 160-170. doi:10.1016/j.smr.2011.08.013

Hede, A.-M. (2008). Managing special events in the new era of the triple bottom line. *Event Management, 11,* 13-22. doi:10.3727/152599508783943282

Huxham, C., & Vangen, S. (2005). *Managing to Collaborate: The theory and practice of collaborative advantage.* London: Routledge.

Jarman, D. (2018). Social network analysis and the hunt for homophily: Diversity and equality within festival communities. *Journal of Policy Research in Tourism, Leisure and Events, 10*(2), 117-133. doi:10.1080/19407963.2018.14149 87.

Larson, M. (2009). Joint event production in the jungle, the park, and the garden: Metaphors of event networks. *Tourism Management, 30,* 393-399. doi:http://dx.doi:10.1016/j.tourman.2008.08.003

Mariani, M., & Giorgio, L. (2017). The 'Pink Night' festival revisited: Meta-events and the role of destination partnerships in staging event tourism. *Annals of Tourism Research, 62,* 89-109. doi:10.1016/j.annals.2016.11.003

Moscardo, G. (2008). Analyzing the role of festivals and events in regional development. *Event Management, 11*(1), 23-32. doi:10.3727/152599508783943255

O'Brien, D., & Chalip, L. (2008). Sport events and strategic leveraging: Pushing towards the triple bottom line. In Woodside, A. G. & Martin, D. (eds.) *Tourism Management: Analysis, behaviour and strategy,* 318-338. CABI. doi:10.1079/9781845933234.0318

O'Dell, T. (2005). Experiencescapes: Blurring borders and testing conncections. In T. O'Dell & P. Billing (Eds.), *Experiencescapes: Tourism, culture and economy* (pp. 11-33). Copenhagen: Copenhagen Business School Press.

Pereira, E. C. S., Mascarenhas, M. V. M., Flores, A. J. G., & Pires, G. M. V. S. (2015). Nautical small-scale sports events portfolio: A strategic leveraging approach. *European Sport Management Quarterly, 15,* 27-47. doi:10.1080/161847 42.2015.1007883

Presenza, A., & Sheehan, L. (2013). Planning tourism through sporting events. *International Journal of Event and Festival Management, 4,* 125-139. doi:10.1108/17582951311325890

Richards, G. (2015). Events in the network society: The role of pulsar and iterative events. *Event Management, 19*(4), 553-566. doi:10.3727/1525995 15x14465748512849

Richards, G., Dodd, D., & Palmer, R. (2014). *European Cultural Capital Report* (Vol. 5). Arnhem: ATLAS.

Richards, G., Marques, L., & Mein, K. (2014). Event design: Conclusions and future research directions. In G. Richards, L. Marques, & K. Mein (Eds.), *Event Design: Social perspectives and practices* (pp. 198-212). Abingdon: Routledge.

Smith, A. (2014). Leveraging sport mega-events: new model or convenient justification? *Journal of Policy Research in Tourism, Leisure and Events,* **6**, 15-30. doi:10.1080/19407963.2013.823976

Viol, M., Todd, L., Theodoraki, E., & Anastasiadou, C. (2018). The role of iconic-historic commemorative events in event tourism: Insights from the 20th and 25th anniversaries of the fall of the Berlin Wall. *Tourism Management,* **69**, 246-262. doi:10.1016/j.tourman.2018.06.018

Visit Scotland. (2015). Scotland the perfect stage: Scotland's events strategy 2015-2025. Retrieved from http://www.eventscotland.org/assets/show/4658

Welsh Government. (2010). Event Wales: A major events strategy for Wales 2010–2020. http://gov.wales/topics/culture-tourism-sport/major-events/event-wales -a-major-events-strategy-for-wales-2010-2020/?lang=en

Whitford, M. (2009). A framework for the development of event public policy: Facilitating regional development. *Tourism Management,* **30**(5), 674-682. doi:10.1016/j.tourman.2008.10.018

Xu, Y. H., Wong, I. A., & Tan, X. S. (2016). Exploring event bundling: The strategy and its impacts. *Tourism Management,* **52**, 455-467. doi:10.1016/j.tourman.2015.07.014

Ziakas, V. (2007). *An event portfolio in rural development: An ethnographic investigation of a community's use of sport and cultural events.* (Dissertation/Doctoral Thesis), ProQuest Dissertations and Theses Full Text database. (304831441).

Ziakas, V. (2013). A multidimensional investigation of a regional event portfolio: Advancing theory and praxis. *Event Management,* **17**(1), 27-48. doi:10.3727/152 599513x13623342048095

Ziakas, V. (2014). *Event Portfolio Planning and Management: A holistic approach.* Abingdon: Routledge.

Ziakas, V. (2019). Issues, patterns and strategies in the development of event portfolios: configuring models, design and policy. *Journal of Policy Research in Tourism, Leisure and Events,* **11**(1), 121-158. doi:10.1080/19407963.2018.1471481

Ziakas, V., & Boukas, N. (2016). The emergence of 'small-scale' sport events in 'small island' developing states: Towards creating sustainable outcomes for island communities. *Event Management,* **20**(4), 537-563. doi:10.3727/1525995 16X14745497664479

Ziakas, V., & Costa, C. (2011a). Event portfolio and multi-purpose development: Establishing the conceptual grounds. *Sport Management Review,* **14**, 409-423. doi:10.1016/j.smr.2010.09.003

Ziakas, V., & Costa, C. A. (2011b). The use of an event portfolio in regional community and tourism development: Creating synergy between sport and cultural events. *Journal of Sport & Tourism,* **16**(2), 149-175. doi:10.1080/1477508 5.2011.568091

6 Portfolio Evaluation and Impact Assessment

Chapter outline

☐ The evaluation of event portfolios is complex, requiring new theories, methods and measures;

☐ A multi-stakeholder approach to valuing event portfolios, considering both intrinsic values and extrinsic measures of worth;

☐ Four types of impact assessment and their application to portfolio evaluation;

☐ Key terms and concepts: value or worth; evaluation; impact assessment; asset; outputs; outcomes;

☐ The nature and use of logic and theory of change models;

☐ The relevance of organisational ecology theory;

☐ How financial portfolios evaluation informs event portfolio evaluation;

☐ Portfolio strategy models and their relevance to evaluation;

☐ How to assess values against costs and risks within portfolios.

The purpose of this chapter is to introduce and explore the main event portfolio evaluation and impact assessment methods. The principles of financial portfolio management are discussed, considering their applicability to event portfolio evaluation, which should be done with caution, as events are not merely financial assets. The chapter highlights that the evaluation of event portfolios is complex, requiring new theories, methods and measures. To develop a comprehensive evaluation system, it is emphasised that there is a need for a multi-stakeholder approach to valuing event portfolios, considering both intrinsic values and extrinsic measures of worth. The chapter discusses four types of impact assessment and their application to portfolio evaluation. Key terms and concepts are explained, including value, evaluation, impact assessment, asset, outputs, and outcomes. The relevance of organisational ecology theory to portfolio evaluation is stressed. The nature and use of logic and theory of change models are examined followed by a discussion of portfolio strategy models and their relevance to evaluation. Finally, it is illustrated how to assess values against costs and risks within portfolios.

Portfolio evaluation complexities

The challenges associated with event impact assessment (IA) and evaluation are magnified greatly when the scope expands from single events to portfolios. Complexity increases in terms of politics, theory and methods, while uncertainty and risk increase when long-term sustainability and the cumulative impacts of multiple events are considered.

Political complexity reflects the many and diverse stakeholders, the need to reconcile multiple and sometimes divergent goals, and issues surrounding the conduct of evaluation, the validity of impacts, and the use of conclusions. If a portfolio is managed in isolation by one agency, such as tourism or economic development, it possibly can escape some of the complications imposed by many competing voices, but in a city or destination with overlapping portfolios there must be a process established to achieve collaboration.

Theoretical complexity is acute, as we do not have theories to explain, let alone predict, how the interactions and synergies among numerous events and their environment will generate desired or unanticipated outcomes over a long period of time. Uncertainty and risks abound, and the establishment of a sustainable system, reflecting triple-bottom-line (TBL) goals, will be extremely challenging. We do not know how impacts will accumulate, so there is a need for more attention to theories of change, both to guide strategy and, through evaluation, contribute to the building of relevant theory. A great deal of uncertainty will generally apply regarding the resilience of events within the portfolio, and the portfolio itself, while its sustainability, in a TBL sense, cannot be managed with certainty.

Third, we do not have all the methods and measures at hand for undertaking impact assessment and evaluation of portfolios. This is a new field of inquiry and praxis, and a lot of trial and error might be needed before we can forecast impacts, measure progress, or determine the worth of event portfolios.

Evaluation and assessment terminology

The term *evaluation* has two connotations that are important. The first is to establish the merit or worth of an event or portfolio, with merit referring to whether or not goals have been attained, and worth (or value) meaning a determination (usually requiring multi-stakeholder input) of the desirability or legitimacy of the event or portfolio.

Worth is such a loaded term that it cannot usually be discussed without acknowledging the *intrinsic – extrinsic* dichotomy and underlying ideology or value perspectives. Many people assign intrinsic worth to events of certain types, meaning they do not feel the need to quantify costs, benefits, or return on investment because the events are inherently good within the context of culture, lifestyle or health. Others use events as instruments of public policy and corporate strategy, and they require quantification of return on investment – from tourist bed-nights generated by event tourism to brand recognition and sales generated by experiential marketing. Judgement, therefore, is a key to this form of evaluation, and the nature of available evidence is critical. Furthermore, there is no inherent reason for believing that any managed event portfolio holds intrinsic value – its collective worth has to be established through evaluation.

The second way we use the term evaluation refers to the applied research needed to detect and solve problems and otherwise to inform decision making. This is often called *programme evaluation*, and it includes determination of goal attainment. In this context it is more common to evaluate merit (did we achieve our goals?) than to place a value on an event. Most producers and supporters of events naturally believe their efforts are worthwhile, even though other stakeholders might not.

Programme or technical evaluation is often categorised as *formative, process* and *summative.*

♦ Needs assessments, stakeholder consultations, feasibility studies, impact assessments and evaluation of experiences all help shape the future and are therefore *formative* in nature.

♦ *Process* evaluation occurs during the course of an event with the intention of identifying and solving problems. In the context of a long-lasting programme or portfolio this form of evaluation includes monitoring (data collection plus identification of divergence from standards or specifications) and corrective measures such as fine-tuning of implementation. In cases of severe problems the whole strategy might have to be revisited.

♦ *Summative* evaluation includes both impact assessment and evaluation of merit and worth, and this information helps shapes the future. There is little value in doing an IA if it does not inform evaluation and strategic planning.

An *asset* is something owned (or controlled or invested in) that has value. It can be tangible, as in a venue owned by a city, or intangible, as in the potential value of event portfolios. InvestorWords.com describes *assets* in the context of an *investment portfolio*, pointing out the inherent dependence upon goals and the various parameters influencing investment decisions:

A compilation of assets working in concert designed to achieve a specific investment objective based on parameters such as risk tolerance, time horizon, asset preference, and liquidity needs. Portfolios are usually constructed with a mix of assets that have the potential to achieve the desired returns, while minimising risk and volatility through proper diversification and balance.

Venue development is capital intensive, but those kinds of assets have a long life and are real property that can be sold. Producing events is not necessarily expensive, especially when existing spaces and facilities are utilised. An event portfolio strategy therefore has at its core the matter of how dependent events are on built facilities or other capital-intensive infrastructure like transit, roads, sewers and electricity. In a small town, for example, it makes sense to utilise open spaces like parks and streets and existing, community-oriented facilities. Cities, on the other hand, tend to invest in expensive venues in order to compete in the national or global event marketplace.

In financial portfolios the assets are either cash or investments that can be converted to cash, whereas governments might consider the strength of the economy to be an asset with current and future value to be realised through taxation. A corporation can consider an event to have immediate sales value or longer-term brand value.

Seven types of *capital* can be invested to create events and portfolios, according to Mykletun (2009). He especially identified the importance of social capital, derived from networking among stakeholders. Cultural capital is evident in volunteering, human capital includes entrepreneurship, and in some cases natural capital (i.e. nature) is important. Physical capital covers infrastructure, including hospitality services. And of course, there is financial capital – often a limiting factor when organisers plan a new event. Finally, Mykletun discussed administrative capital, the kind that supportive policy makers and government agencies can provide. All of these forms of capital, or any blend, can be critical for event viability, but within a portfolio they are synergistically the basis of resilience.

Risk and uncertainty are inherent in investments and portfolio managers have to pay attention to how it can either be minimised by not taking big risks, or by preparing to mitigate negative consequences when adverse impacts occur. It is worth noting here that mitigation is a central feature of impact assessment. In this context a risk can be defined as the negative consequences of something going wrong, or a change in the environment that impacts upon events, and risks are magnified by uncertainty. Andersson, Getz, Gration, and Raciti (2017) identified *systematic* and *specific* risk factors for event portfolio management. Systematic risks are common to all event portfolios, such as an economic downturn affecting travel, while specific risks apply to individual events and portfolios. Both types of risk have to be considered in portfolio management.

Impact assessment

Impact assessment (IA) has traditionally focused on forecasting the impacts of a project, thereby informing decisions. IAIA (www.iaia.org) defines it this way:

> *Impact Assessment (IA) simply defined is the process of identifying the future consequences of a current or proposed action. The "impact" is the difference between what would happen with the action and what would happen without it.*

That traditional view of IA, as a forecasting exercise, is too limited. There are four applications that have to be considered, as explored in detail by Getz (2019).

♦ *Forecasting portfolio impacts:* We cannot reasonably expect to be able to accurately predict the consequences of large or complex event portfolios, and especially of overlapping portfolios, but it is possible to employ logic and theory of change models to guide strategies and how they are adapted.

♦ *Strategic IA*: Whenever a new or modified policy, strategy or plan is considered a strategic IA should be conducted. As theory for event portfolio management advances there will be an improved ability to forecast impacts and establish more effective management systems.

♦ *Post-event IA*: Assessing after an event is the most frequently occurring form of IA, and it has been mostly the economic impacts, in a tourism context, that have been considered. More comprehensive methods and measures are required to reflect TBL or balanced-scorecard approaches. For portfolios there is no end point, so the process of post-event IA has to be modified to incorporate outputs that will specifically inform portfolio planning.

♦ *Retrospective*: System-change assessment and evaluation is seldom attempted. The purpose is to retrospectively determine what happened as a consequence of taking certain actions or implementing policies and strategies. Applied to event portfolios the question would be: "how did our event portfolio change the economy – or the environment – or certain elements of our society and culture?" Clearly this kind of retrospective IA and evaluation is complicated by everything else that happens along the way, so isolating the particular impacts of events and the synergistic effects of portfolios is the great challenge.

Outputs and outcomes: These two terms are often used synonymously, but for IA and evaluation we need a clear differentiation. *Outputs,* in systems theory, are defined as the intended and measurable things produced by a transforming process (like an event), with the efficiency of resource acquisition/use and the effectiveness of management systems in achieving goals being primary considerations. For events these outputs are generally short-term and linked directly to the organisation's mandate, with the most frequent (and some would say most important) being: profit or revenues; attendance; and customer or guest satisfaction. In the context of a tourism-oriented event portfolio these outputs would be tourism attractiveness (i.e., the number and types of dedicated event tourists), their within-scope spending (to enable an estimate of direct economic contribution), and their satisfaction with the event and destination experience.

Many other potential goals can be pursued, including social, cultural and environmental, each with their own *key performance indicators* (KPI). The companion book *Event Evaluation* provides numerous suggested goals and KPIs for a fully comprehensive evaluation. For an event portfolio we could simply aggregate the goals and KPIs, but there will inevitably be additional considerations – as discussed in the ensuing sections. In particular, the definition and measurement of "direct economic contribution" is of special relevance within a tourism context (for details see *Event Impact Assessment*, also in this series).

Outcomes are defined as longer-term or permanent changes in a system, and therefore can be used synonymously with *impacts*. As an example, a tourist-oriented event or event portfolio aims to attract tourists, maximise their spending and provide a direct economic contribution. But a portfolio of events might seek to re-position a city in terms of its brand, strengthen its economy by pursuing a culture-led development strategy, and re-structure its hard and soft infrastructure to become globally competitive. While individual events sometimes set long-term, system-changing outcome goals, this is certainly the function of event portfolios.

Cumulative impact assessment: Since in portfolio management we are talking about synergies and long-term perspectives it is essential to consider cumulative impact assessment. The IA stresses the fact that repetitive actions (e.g., periodic events) and incremental changes over time can interact to generate undesired or unanticipated consequences, thereby necessitating attention to three types of interaction: additive, interactive and synergistic.

Additive impacts are an assembly of separate impacts; IA often uses a matrix to identify all possible impacts that might arise from a project and its components; within event portfolio there potentially will be a very complex web of possible outcomes using a triple-bottom-line approach.

Interactive impacts: sometimes impacts interact and together create a new impact, raising the possibility of cascading and synergistic effects; a cascade effect could be the interactions of multiple events causing a wave of publicity, image enhancement, and either/or: economic prosperity and/or damaging over-tourism

Synergistic impacts: The sum of interacting events is greater than the parts; this is desired for some outcomes (e.g., increased social capital and economic prosperity) but not for others (e.g., environmental or social stress).

Portfolio evaluation informed by financial management

Financial portfolio management is well developed, with professional advisory services being big business. Anyone with a financial plan involving investment knows about risk levels and 'balanced portfolios'. From this perspective (and it is not the only legitimate one) we can argue that all events within a portfolio are 'assets' with value contributing to the whole. Long-term growth is usually the ideal goal in financial portfolios, but for an event portfolio the desired 'value' is not necessarily monetary. This approach to event portfolio management is not well developed.

Governments, not-for-profit organisations, corporations and individuals all invest in events (individually or collectively) with the expectation of realising targets that encompass diverse goals: personal growth, enhanced quality of life, private profit, fostering brand value, stimulating economic growth, cultural development, social change and much more. Specific, measurable outputs are generally articulated for the short term, but when events are expected to contribute to longer-term changes in the economy, society or environment, then value creation becomes very complex and 'asset value' takes on new meanings.

Events are often valued intrinsically as creators of personal welfare or public good, but that is not a factor when a financial or economic perspective is taken. In a managed portfolio of events, each event is an asset that has to contribute to overall return on investment (ROI), and this can be done by fulfilling one or more particular roles such as attracting specific target segments, generating profit or surplus revenue, enhancing a city or destination image, cultivating new audiences/consumers, etc. These and other possible measures of value are discussed later.

Issues related to financial portfolio management

Some of the major issues or challenges facing financial portfolio management also apply to event portfolios, as discussed below.

The allocation of dividends or other value: Is there one manager of the event portfolio, or do many stakeholders expect a return? Are risks and potential benefits shared equally among stakeholders or shareholders and is this the subject of a legally binding contract (versus goodwill)?

Liquidity and holding periods: Liquidity refers to how easy it is to convert an asset into cash, and the holding period of an investment is the length of time predetermined for obtaining a desired ROI. Events are generally not bought and sold in an open marketplace, and they are difficult to convert into cash; venues can be bought and sold, but not necessarily for a quick return. Many events in a portfolio will be expected to become permanent institutions, while others can be abandoned by supporters (e.g., funding is withdrawn), terminated by owners (sometimes even before they are held!) run down over a period of time (e.g., through de-marketing), or substituted by a new event.

Return on Investment: Is the ROI expected in the short or long term, and is it expected to increase over time? A private company will want a quick ROI, whereas not-for-profits and government can (but do not always) take a long-term perspective on the value of events. When estimating ROI, investors in events need to take into account several factors. First, what is the current value of the event as an asset? For example, if 1 million in currency is put into an event, can that be fully recovered right away, as if it was cash? The answer is no, because any given event can lose money and it likely cannot be sold – it is not a liquid asset. Second, can the future value of the event (at any point in time) be estimated? (i.e., taking into account inflation, interest earned, operating and borrowing costs, opportunity costs and expected rate of return). Event and event portfolio investments cannot possibly make these estimations without assuming a great deal, and therefore taking risks. Costs can be estimated, but future value in monetary terms is extremely difficult, and if qualitative measures of value are introduced the entire issue of ROI becomes unsolvable and 'faith-based' projections enter the picture. In other words, event portfolio managers are not going to be able to make reasoned or valid claims of ROI in financial terms, but must rely upon a more subjective and multi-stakeholder evaluation of future value.

All capital has a cost: Does capital have to be borrowed, or are investments made from tax revenue? Part of the cost of borrowing is debt charges, while utilising taxes always raises the question of opportunity costs. The allocation of tax revenue by governments is always political and often controversial, a fact that is repeatedly demonstrated when cities think about bidding on mega events.

Risk taking is inherent in financial investments. Taking risks, including speculation such as that accompanying the hope that a mega event will help a city reposition or re-invigorate its economy, is a strategic option. Those bidding on events or producing them must realise there are risks, and they have to operate within a defined comfort zone that sets parameters on how much they can afford to invest and to lose. A related and most important issue is that of underwriting failure or losses, as in setting out exactly who is liable for losses or damages.

Understanding the investment environment, or marketplace is essential. First, are capital investments and bidding on events being made at the global level (e.g., 'world cities' bidding on mega events and competing with the biggest and best venues) or at a lesser level? Determining what league in which a city or destination is competing is a responsibility of senior decision makers, not portfolio or event managers. Second, how volatile is the marketplace, and are changes predictable? There is no doubt that risks increase when there is a lack of intelligence regarding competition, consumer trends, inflation, or other factors that influence potential ROI and event success. Third, relationship building is critical in establishing the kind of reputation for hosting events that inspires confidence in those making locational decisions, and this requires constant interaction with numerous stakeholders.

Direct or indirect investment: Owning and producing events is a direct form, with concomitant costs and risks, while supporting events in other ways (e.g., grants, subsidies, in-kind services) can pay dividends but with reduced risk. Many cities and destinations prefer to not own or produce events, while others see advantage in taking direct control. A related issue is whether or not direct control of an event portfolio is preferred to sub-contracting, and this raises the matter of fiduciary responsibility or principle-agent challenges (i.e., do the managers always act for the benefit of the investors?). Cities and corporations with professional event staff would appear to have an advantage when it comes to making investment decisions, but it is unlikely that there are many professionals skilled in translating financial portfolio management principles into event portfolio management.

Cash flow: Small businesses, and many events, suffer from cash-flow problems. No matter their past performance, savings or future value, they need cash or borrowing power to stay viable. Consequently, decisions about investing in events and venues have to consider not only their asset value and potential ROI but the provision of often-substantial operating funds and emergency-relief capital.

Transparency: The value of investments in equities or bonds is easily confirmed through public sources, but determining the present and future value of an event is all but impossible; guesstimates will often be necessary. Event portfolio managers will therefore often engage in 'faith based' investments and sometimes this goes wrong.

Principles of financial portfolio management

The most-cited principle is that of *diversification,* with the aim of *minimising risk.* For our purposes diversification could be by the type of investment (i.e., capital versus intangible support), in the types and sizes of event, permanent versus one-time events, single-purpose or flexible venues, spreading events seasonally and geographically, diverse target market segments, or other factors that might influence event success such as who to partner with. Many investors pool their resources and spread their risk by choosing mutual funds or market-indexed equity funds, and a diverse event portfolio spreads risks similarly. However, it has to be asked where the training and experience in event portfolio management comes from, as there is little published evidence.

Balance within a portfolio might be achieved by a mix of higher risk growth-oriented investments and lower risk 'value' assets such as proven revenue-generating events. This could take the form of a mix of old and new events (the old ones presumably having a known risk versus value ratio), or a mix of all types of venues and events. Balance also applies to limiting the impact of market volatility, but for events there could be many volatile factors to consider, such as tourism trends, consumer fads, competition and economic conditions affecting disposable income. Fund managers will look for this kind of balance by holding stocks, bonds and cash, but what is the equivalent for event portfolio managers? Furthermore, we do not have evidence of a balanced event portfolio that optimally spreads risks among stakeholders. These are on-going questions for researchers and theory building.

Synergy refers to interactions that generate gains or advantages greater than the sum of individual parts. A portfolio by nature is synergistic in that the value of a collection is greater than the value of individual assets. In business management, however, this term is usually reserved for discussion of the synergies possible through mergers and acquisitions (such as cost reductions, brand enhancement, cross-selling or fostering innovation), and is not something expected *within* a financial investment portfolio. But it is an important goal for event portfolio managers, and policy makers should be focused on maximising synergistic potential. One example is the sharing of events and venues by residents and tourists, resulting in more than can be accomplished if only tourists *or* residents are considered when making investments.

Taking a long-term perspective: Financial advisors are usually quick to admonish investors to stay in it for the long term, and not be distracted by short-term fluctuations in the marketplace. This is normally good advice, except when the long-term trend is negative! Will cities invest in venues and events if tourism trends turn downwards over many years? The future is uncertain, therefore a goal of minimising risks would lead to the strategy of having a portfolio that both delivers immediate and longer-term ROI.

Monitoring and revisions to investment portfolios are essential, as the environment is dynamic. New opportunities arise, risks can become magnified or reduced, asset value changes with competitive forces and consumer demand, and stakeholder goals will undoubtedly respond. Within a company monitoring and revisions can be an automatic process, sometimes undertaken exclusively by owners, whereas individual investors might do best to reply upon professional advisors. Event portfolio managers will of necessity be evaluating outputs and impacts, and constantly thinking about implications for policy and strategy. Changes to an event portfolio cannot be realised at a moment's notice, so responding to emergencies will be difficult. Perhaps the most difficult decision to make will be the termination of an event, as this might entail protests or financial losses.

Performance evaluation: In part this will be a process of monitoring change over time relative to a *benchmark*. Each event has a starting point, but in a city or destination there is no portfolio until some form of management is applied, so what is an appropriate benchmark? Key Performance Indicators and Key Impact Indicators have to be set, and agreed upon by stakeholders.

Markowitz and efficiency frontiers

Markowitz (1952) developed a method for assessing potential value versus risk in financial portfolios, and it has been utilised experimentally for events in research by Andersson et al. (2017). That research was conducted in the Sunshine Coast of Australia and considered four events from both tourist and resident perspectives, utilising situation-specific measures of asset value and risk.

Markowitz postulated that investors should construct an optimum portfolio that yields the maximum expected return with the minimum risk. This requires analysis of varying levels of expected return for individual events and the total-ity of the portfolio, and for events the possible measures of 'return' are not nec-essarily expressed in monetary terms. Judgement will be required, taking into account multiple value perspectives. Similarly, risk is multi-dimensional, rang-ing from the uncertainty associated with future economic conditions and com-petition to the possibility that costs will balloon. Later in this chapter a method for evaluating value versus risk is discussed.

Portfolio evaluation informed by organisational ecology

Even more daunting than evaluating managed event portfolios is the problem of assessing the impacts and worth of entire populations of events. There are no pertinent theories or methods to draw upon, but we can be informed by organi-sational ecology, especially with regard to the matter of a 'healthy' population of events and the evaluation of especially important factors including population dynamics, resource competition versus cooperation, and legitimation.

This body of research seeks to explain the rates of birth, growth, and mortality of a population of organisations in any given environment. In our context the *population* is all planned events, although for practical considerations it could be one type of event such as festival or sports.

Baum (1996) noted that all 'ecological' theories of organisations start with the premise that there are births and deaths (this is the basic analogy to natural ecol-ogy) and therefore the population is dynamic. Applied to events, there usually exists a free or semi-regulated market in which myriad events come and go in the public, private and not-for-profit sectors. Event portfolios seek to control this process to an extent, but the aim cannot be to ensure survival of every event – that would prove impossible in most environments – but to ensure the sustain-ability of the portfolio as a whole and to maximise its value-creation synergies.

A second premise of organisational ecology is that while there are definite types of organisation, such as festivals or sport events, there is diversity at the population level. Applied to event portfolios this raises the matter of whether or not a homogeneous portfolio is more desirable or effective in ensuring long-term sustainability. Third, and for a variety of reasons, organisations often have a problem adapting to changing environmental conditions. We do not know if portfolios of events have a higher or lower adaptability quotient, or how that would be measured, but a strategy to maximise adaptability might very well place a premium on diversification – just as financial portfolio managers stress it.

As an overarching concept, we can consider the 'health' of a population of living things. For animals, health can be defined narrowly as freedom from dis-ease and maintaining the ability to procreate. Of course, this does not imply there will be no sickness or death. For events and event portfolios that could be translated into this principle:

P1: The health of a population or portfolio of events must not be dependent upon the viability of single events nor the addition or subtraction of events within it.

The ability to achieve goals (which can be short term in nature and as selfish as making a quick profit, or long term and linked to system-wide changes) is of paramount importance to organisations. A secondary criterion of importance to organisations, and many events, is long-term resilience, simply because most events want to survive, and investments have to be amortised over many years. A second principle follows:

P2: A healthy population or portfolio of events must be resilient by virtue of an assured resource base, sound management and internal diversity.

A healthy population of events, therefore, is open to discourse about the goals of all the key stakeholders (i.e., government, the events, corporations, tourism agencies, arts community, residents, consumers, etc.) and how the goals can best be met. It is not primarily about ensuring the survival of individual events but fostering resilience (without being overly concerned about failures and 'deaths'). A healthy population of events will allow for growth or decline in numbers, within the context of available resources and changing priorities. Resource dependency is high among events, so resilience and goal attainment often depend upon consumer demand, as well as shifting government priorities and corporate strategies resulting in funding. A third principle follows:

P3: A healthy population or portfolio of events will be dynamic, constantly adapting to environmental pressures and to the shifting goals and priorities of its key stakeholders.

Here are some suggested evaluation criteria for event populations and portfolios, all of which require monitoring within a permanent management system:

♦ The number and types of start-ups (innovation should always be valued; certain policies/strategies might require incentives to generate the 'right' types);

♦ The number and types of failures/deaths (too many losses in one geographical area or of one type of event could be a sign of environmental stress, and could result in a failure to attain important goals);

♦ A measure of variety or diversity (too narrow a range of event types might lead to vulnerability; this corresponds with the notion of diversification in financial portfolio management);

♦ Growth/decline trends (one consideration would be that event numbers should increase with human population growth, at least in rapidly-growing urban areas);

♦ Stakeholder input, including resident and consumer satisfaction and support (consider both use and non-use values), the needs expressed by event organisations, and corporate/industry views on the impacts of events overall (e.g., on tourism);

♦ Financial performance of events and the organisations that produce/support them (look for warning signs such as accumulating debt, and signs of health such as surplus generated and re-investment).

It is often difficult to see value in major one-time events (the kind usually won through competitive bidding in particular) within an organisational ecology perspective. Their purpose and legacy would have to be specified as contributing to innovation, variety, resilience, financial success or the overall ability of periodic events to meet their goals. The resources devoted to bidding on and hosting one-time events could possibly detract from our suggested indicators of population and portfolio health. However, since bidding on one-time events implies some degree of event strategy and management, it is necessary to integrate their planning. Event portfolio managers have to justify every one-time event in terms of what it can do, by way of leveraging sustainable benefits, for the portfolio.

Evaluation models for event portfolios

Logic and theory of change models

Figure 6.1 shows a logic model for event evaluation and impact assessment. The diagram depicts a logical process for taking planned actions to achieve goals and evaluating the outputs (using KPIs). It also indicates how a portfolio of events, as part of a tourism strategy, sets outcome goals, employs key impact indicators (KIIs) and an action pathway that should ideally be based on theory, or at least experience. The validity of the logic must be clear, otherwise the exercise becomes an experiment that can contribute to theory building.

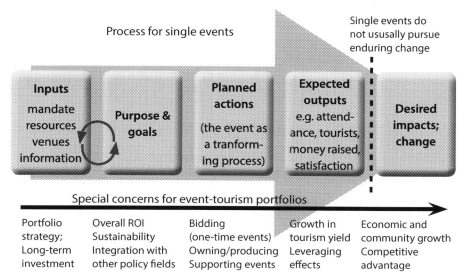

Figure 6.1: A logic model for event evaluation and impact assessment. Source: Getz (2018).

Both logic and theory of change (TOC) models are attributable to Weiss (1995), with TOC being the appropriate approach for social marketing and portfolios conceived as agents of change. As it is illustrated in Figure 6.2, the goal is social inclusion and integration, to be achieved through a path that requires the evaluation of short-term outputs and the assessment of long-term or permanent impacts/outcomes. Note that external forces might act to reinforce or impede progress towards these goals. Various assumptions of logic have to be made (especially in the absence of pertinent theory) and the entire logic chain must be tested for internal validity before implementation. As is the case with all event portfolio management, a precondition will be collaboration among stakeholders and commitment of resources. Evaluation of the adequacy of resources and support can be considered *formative*, while monitoring and evaluation of outputs can be considered to be *process* evaluation. *Summative* evaluation in this model would be in the form of periodic assessment of the suggested KIIs.

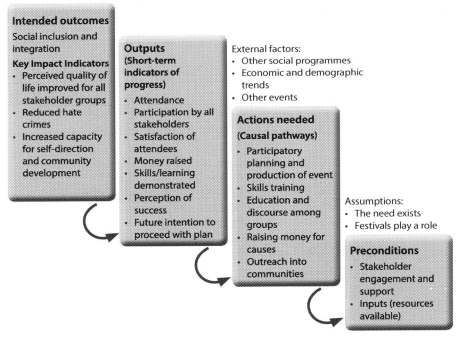

Figure 6.2: Theory of change model.

It is also important to consider that many long-term portfolio goals, other than those pertaining to its viability and resilience, are likely to be in the nature of social constructs requiring consensus among the stakeholders. Social and cultural goals in particular, such as inclusion and integration, require a working definition for the purpose of setting goals, actions and evaluation indicators. Economic goals can be more precisely formulated and the pertinent KIIs are readily available (e.g., to measure direct economic contribution).

Balanced Scorecards for portfolio evaluation

The original model of the Balanced Scorecard (Kaplan & Norton, 1992) features four dimensions labelled 'financial', 'customer', 'internal process', and 'learning and growth'. For each of these, objectives are to be formulated, plus key performance measures, action plans and evaluation, plus feedback. For the purposes of event evaluation, Getz (2018) adapted the model and labelled the quadrants 'customers and stakeholders', 'sustainability', 'organisational culture', and 'internal or transforming processes'. Applied to event portfolios Figure 6.3 represents yet another modification.

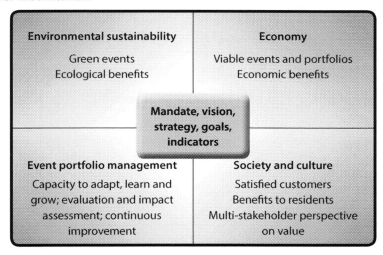

Figure 6.3: Adapting the Balanced Scorecard evaluation system to event portfolios.

There is no firm starting point when constructing or utilising the model. The 'economy' quadrant stresses both financial viability of events and the portfolio as a whole, plus the desired economic benefits attributed to event tourism. The 'society and culture' domain encompasses the satisfaction of customers and other stakeholders (especially residents) and no doubt reflects diverse value perspectives. Maintaining a triple-bottom-line approach, the 'environmental sustainability' quadrant emphasises both the greening of events and the positive role that events and the portfolio must play in achieving sustainable cities and destinations. In this regard, Getz (2017) outlined how events can become a positive force for urban sustainability across all policy fields. Fourth is 'event portfolio management'.

In the centre of the model are the basic requirements for any managed portfolio. The mandate, vision, strategy, goals and indicators give purpose and direction. Portfolio managers also seek to sustain the portfolio through learning, adapting to changing conditions, and implementing a permanent IA and evaluation system. It might be acceptable to pursue continuous improvement in management, but some portfolios might be managed for growth and self-sufficiency.

Satisfaction of multiple stakeholder goals and expectations is perhaps the trickiest part of portfolio management, as there can easily be diverse perspectives on goals and how to measure the portfolio's performance. Following the process of developing a Theory of Change will assist, as it is specifically designed to bring stakeholders together for the planning exercise and ensuing monitoring and evaluation.

Matrix models

Variation on the Boston Consulting Group Matrix

Getz (2013, p. 154) adapted the classic Boston Consulting Group Matrix which dealt with products within a life-cycle framework and measured relative market share against market growth. The Getz matrix is based on the standard practice of measuring 'asset value' against costs and risks, which is usually referred to as the risk to reward ratio (see Figure 6.4). This model advocates 'move or lower costs/risks' for events deemed to have high costs/risks and high asset value. A considerable amount of judgement is required, however, as risks are not always about increasing costs (being the usual consideration when investing) and values are not always quantifiable. Events within portfolios that are low in value and high in costs or risks should be moved or removed. Some can be grown, if they show potential for higher value, and hallmark events were indicated as possessing the greatest value for the lowest costs and risks. From a tourism perspective, high-value, one-time events maximise one or all of the following: tourist attractiveness, image enhancement, leveraging for business and trade growth, capacity building, strong local support and potential for repeat occurrence.

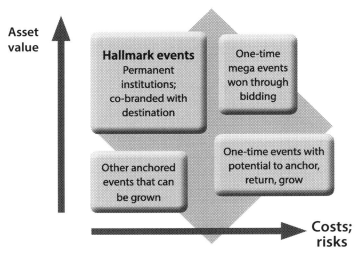

Figure 6.4: Value × risk/costs matrix model for event portfolios. Source: Getz (2013, p. 154). Reproduced with permission of Cognizant Communication Corporation.

While each portfolio will have a different mix, this model is normative in suggesting that the highest possible value with the lowest cost and risk accrues from hallmark events, which are defined as being traditional attractions for residents and tourists alike, permanent institutions in the community, and co-branded with the host city or destination. One-time mega events won through bidding typically require enormous investments both to bid and produce, and carry many risks, including political divisiveness that generates strong resistance movements, losing the bid, underestimating costs, and generating a legacy of debt and white-elephant facilities. 'Anchored events' are those attached to the city or destination by virtue of tradition, ownership or dependence on local venues and other resources, and some of these can be grown. Some one-time events can also be attracted or used as a basis for creating anchored events. This approach can be modified to consider types of events (i.e., sports, business, entertainment, cultural).

An initial consideration might be to divide events within portfolios, or entire portfolios, on the basis of intrinsic versus extrinsic value – although a mix is probably normal. Portfolios and events managed for economic benefits or private profit will require quantifiable ROI measures, while those managed for cultural or social benefits are often considered to hold intrinsic value that does not need justification. Can these two approaches be reconciled? It will require a concerted effort on the part of stakeholders, but when it comes to sharing goals, and the establishment of appropriate indicators of success or value, a city-wide strategy seems most likely to achieve the necessary agreement – perhaps through some compromises. It is local government that has both the broadest mandate and is closest to residents, thereby enabling close contact with all parties and strong leverage through its various policies and regulations – not the least of which are funding for events, provision of venues, health and safety provisions and place marketing.

Ossians' Matrix

Intended to focus on strategic options, Ossian's Matrix (Getz, 2013, p. 153, adapted from Ossian Stiernstrand) labelled the quadrants as 'short-duration events' (top left and bottom left), and 'long-duration events' (right side, top and bottom). Stiernstrand suggested the horizontal dividing line could be based on the percentage of tourists versus residents, specifically a 50/50 mix, and the vertical dividing line could be based on the frequency and length of events. With these criteria, the top-right quadrant would encompass long-duration events mostly for residents, and bottom-right would be annual, long-duration events of a large scale and mostly for tourists. Some combination of these could be hallmark and iconic events. On the top-left quadrant of Ossian's Matrix are short-duration events (one time, mostly for residents and small in scale) and bottom-right are one-time events, mostly for tourists and large in scale. Portfolio management from a tourism perspective would seek to move events into the bottom-right quadrant.

Value against risks and costs

Andersson, Getz and Jutbring (2019) conducted an experiment with professional event staff of the Swedish city of Gothenburg (Goteborg). They were seeking greater understanding of how event portfolios were managed in practice and trying out a method by which value could be assessed against risks and costs.

Gothenburg is a city of approximately half a million residents is as an example of successful event-tourism development and positioning as an event capital. Goteborg & Co. is the DMO and city agency with responsibility for events: bidding, supporting, marketing and producing. Its website, City of Events (http://goteborgco.se/en/our-activities/city-of-events/) proclaims that it pursues an event portfolio strategy within the context of urban sustainability.

The experiment requested ten participating event professionals to evaluate fourteen existing, periodic events as to value and risks. This had not been attempted previously. Both risk and value for each event were rated by each of the participants on a 1-5 scale. Respondents were forced to give two events grade 1, three events grade 2, four events grade 3, three events grade 4, and two events grade 5. This technique is similar to Q-sort (Block, 2008). In the more subjective part of the experiment respondents described in writing the characteristics of each event that led to their evaluation of its value and risk score.

Analysis identified three events with high perceived value and low risk, and four events with above-average value but also above-average risk. Several events were collectively assigned low value and high risk. There was no pattern to indicate that cultural events were perceived to be any different from sports. Although this type of exercise could potentially inform cities and destinations for strategic purposes, a more general value lies in the reasons given by the professionals for their ratings. High value was assigned to events that create substantial economic impacts, generate opportunities for bidding on other events, build social and cultural capital, and act as a platform for meetings and networking. Common risks include attendance decline or low visitor numbers, an exclusive target group, critical media coverage, a lack of public support, terrorism, and a threat that owners could move the event to another destination. Critical media coverage regarding negative impacts is also a possible threat to the festival. Other risks include a possible loss of public funding, lack of development of festival content over time, and lack of a strong brand.

Variations on this experimental method can certainly be developed. The main aims are to help portfolio managers in their strategic planning, and more generally to make explicit the criteria thought to be important when evaluating value and risks.

Process model for event portfolio evaluation

The process of event portfolio evaluation has no beginning and no end (see Figure 6.5). There are antecedents, including what could be called traditional formative evaluation such as needs assessment, feasibility studies, market research and strategy formulation, but because cities and destinations have a history of events and related policies the management and evaluation of portfolios will be an evolutionary process.

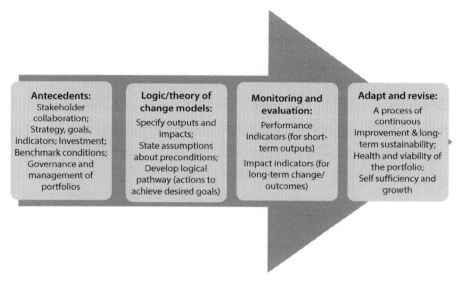

Figure 6.5: Process model for evaluation of event portfolios.

Research and documentation of benchmark conditions should inform the entire process, as many impact indicators require an assessment of actual change, and attribution of outcomes to actions taken.

What is critical is stakeholder collaboration, as many stakeholders have to be clear about their goals and how evaluation will be conducted and used. Any number of value perspectives can be relevant, and even within a narrowly defined event-tourism portfolio there will be venues, government agencies, for-profit companies, not-for-profit events and many interest or lobby groups to consider – not the least of which are the residents.

Collaboration on goals, or the benefits sought, will lead to the issues of risk and reward allocation: who is taking the various risks, and how will benefits be distributed? The ROI is going to be different for each stakeholder, with only some measuring it in monetary terms. Deliberate creation and management of synergies, to benefit all, will form a major part of the discussions, and this leads to the matters of diversification and balance within the portfolio. Without doubt the treatment of individual events within a portfolio will arise, as when they are considered to be assets, they might very well become redundant or otherwise disposable.

In some jurisdictions this collaboration might be a formal starting point for event portfolio strategies, but in many it will evolve and perhaps go through many iterations. The question of power will often arise, with those having regulatory power and those making monetary capital investments having major stakes in the process. Governance of the collaboration will be equally as important as the hands-on portfolio management.

It has been argued that logic and theory of change (TOC) models are required for event portfolio management. Logic models develop the pathways to goal attainment, with outputs specified for the short term, while TOC models are appropriate when events and event portfolios are conceived as agents of change, specifically intended to create longer-term or permanent system changes. Preconditions and assumptions must be taken into account in developing a collaborative TOC, and ideally these are worked out through the governance process. There will always be uncertainty, so in a way a logic and TOC models are experiments leading to theory development, but this is dependent upon IA and evaluation.

The monitoring and evaluation system is vital and has to be established within the governance and management models. The population of events within a city or destination, and those within a managed portfolio, will be dynamic, births and deaths must be monitored, with analysis of environmental conditions and internal process that lead to strengths, weaknesses, failures and start-ups. Key performance indicators are needed for the outputs desired along the way, and key impact indicators for the longer-term or permanent system changes being pursued.

With no end point, the portfolio evaluation process becomes focused on long-term sustainability, both in terms of adaptation (requiring revisions to goals, strategy or management) and how the events contribute to overall sustainable-city or destination goals), the overall health of the event portfolio (though individual events might come and go), and the satisfaction of all the stakeholders that the process is on track to deliver desired benefits. Unexpected and negative impacts might arise, so the system cannot be completely focused on goal attainment, it must encompass comprehensive impact assessment with formal and regular feedback from all stakeholders.

A final pair of questions: is it reasonable to expect a managed portfolio of events to become self-sufficient and to grow? Growth could be in the form of more events, or in magnification of desired outcomes (i.e., the ROI). If so, a different approach to investment and management will likely be necessitated, and therefore new evaluation criteria and methods. Kelly and Fairley (2018) published a case study of tourism-oriented, event portfolio management, with a focus on collaboration and stages in the process. This is unique research that suggests the need for comparative cases, and in particular longitudinal evaluation of portfolio management and evaluation systems.

Overall, portfolio evaluation is more complex than normal evaluation or impact assessment for single events, and the necessary theory, methods and measures have not been fully developed. A number of key issues will likely arise, starting with the need for collaboration and consensus among a multiplicity of stakeholder value perspectives, and the inevitable uncertainty that gives rise to many risks. When events are considered to be assets within portfolios they must be assigned value, and their contribution to overall portfolio success becomes a primary consideration. This potentially gives rise to conflicts related to the perceived intrinsic value of events versus determining their worth through quantitative, extrinsic measures such as economic impact. Portfolios, like populations need to be managed dynamically, and this could give rise to the desire by managers to change the composition and event to terminate support for single events.

Summary

The long-term perspective of portfolio management, stressing synergies and diverse benefits, as opposed to short-term outputs and return on investment, requires a form of cumulative impact assessment that has yet to be fully developed. These issues are reflected in the suggested process model (Figure 6.5) which has no firm beginning or end.

Theory of Change models are suggested as a tool for event portfolio evaluation, as they are intended for use when events and portfolios are designed as agents of change. Issues and propositions derived from financial portfolios, including investment strategies, have been suggested as a basis for informing event portfolio management and evaluation. Of these, the necessity for on-going monitoring and revisions must be stressed, as without a system there will be increased risk and reduced adaptability over the long term.

From organisational ecology theory several propositions have been put forward in this regard, including the admonition that portfolios cannot be dependent upon the viability of single events, and that a healthy portfolio must be resilient and dynamic. A number of evaluation criteria were suggested for monitoring the event population or portfolio assets.

There are several extant event portfolio models that can inform design, management and evaluation, each of which suggests the kinds of indicators needed for evaluation. These include a modified balanced scorecard, pyramid and matrix models. Because there will be wide variations in portfolio strategies and management styles, there can be no single model with universal applicability.

References

Andersson, T., Getz, D., & Jutbring, H. (2019) Balancing value and risk of tourist attraction: An explorative study of DMO professionals' assessments of an event portfolio, unpublished.

Andersson, T. D., Getz, D., Gration, D., & Raciti, M. M. (2017). Event portfolios: Asset value, risk and returns. *International Journal of Event and Festival Management*, **8**, 226-243. doi:10.1108/IJEFM-01-2017-0008

Baum, J. (1996). Organizational ecology. In S. Clegg, C. Hardy, & W. Nord (Eds.), *Handbook of Organizational Study* (pp. 77-115). London: Sage.

Getz, D. (2013). *Event Tourism: Concepts, international case studies, and research.* New York: Cognizant Communication Corporation.

Getz, D. (2017). Developing a framework for sustainable event cities. *Event Management*, **21** (5), 575-591. doi: 10.3727/152599517x15053272359031

Getz, D. (2018). *Event Evaluation.* Oxford: Goodfellow Publishers.

Kaplan, R., & Norton, D. (1992). The Balanced Scorecard - measures that drive performance. *Harvard Business Review*, **70**(7/8), 172-180.

Markowitz, H. (1952). Portfolio selection. *The Journal of Finance*, **7**, 77-91. doi:10.2307/2975974

Mykletun, R. J. (2009). Celebration of extreme playfulness: Ekstremsportveko at Voss. *Scandinavian Journal of Hospitality and Tourism*, **9**, 146-176. doi:10.1080/15022250903119512

Weiss, C. (1995). Nothing as practical as good theory: Exploring theory-based evaluation for comprehensive community initiatives for children and families. In J. Connell, A. Kubisch, L. Schorr, & C. Weiss (Eds.), *New Approaches to Evaluating Community Initiatives*. Washington: Aspen Institute.

Part II: Case Studies

7 Governmental Approach to Major Events in New Zealand

For the past 20 years, New Zealand, a country relatively remote in geographical terms, has been actively communicating with the international visitor market in order to construct a global brand for the country. As a tourist destination, New Zealand offers an impressive range of natural and cultural attractions, outdoor activities, urban tourism and a diverse event calendar. In 2017, the country welcomed 3.7m visitors, with the market forecast to grow by 7.5% in 2018.

The active role of the Government in the visitor economy makes New Zealand an attractive investment destination. Extensive marketing campaigns, significant expansion of transport connections, private investment in infrastructure and the hotel sector indicate that New Zealand will continue its sustainable tourism growth over the coming years.

Major events have been recognised as a powerful and successful instrument that can brand the country directly to the target audience. The ever-increasing numbers of international event visitors to New Zealand, as well as recent success in securing bids for such large-scale international events as 2011 Rugby World Cup, 2015 ICC Cricket World Cup, 2015 FIFA U-20 World cup and 2017 World Master Games, demonstrate the relevance of the employed strategy.

This chapter reviews a national event portfolio approach in New Zealand. The approach is characterised by a strong top-down orientation, where the Government plays the leading role in determining current economic and socio-cultural objectives for the major event industry, implementation of the national event strategy and evaluation of the investment in major events. The data for this chapter have been collected by document selection and analysis and by interviewing several industry experts.

First steps

In 1990s to early 2000s, the Government of New Zealand was providing support to major events, usually through a co-funding scheme, using cash grants as the main form of sustenance. This included bidding and hosting costs, investment in leveraging opportunities and assistance in conducting event feasibility studies. Decisions were made on a case-by-case basis. It was taken for granted that major events usually would be organised by private agencies and that Government participation was important only when an event advanced the government's objectives and brought benefits to the nation. This was a typical scenario of a policy related to events (Smith, 2012). The Government acted more as a regulative body or advisor, without actively contributing to the planning process.

The involvement of a large number of different institutional stakeholders in major events requires a strong coordination effort from the Government to avoid, for example, under-investment, duplication of services and operational issues. In response to this organisational and managerial demand, in 2001, an Interagency Events Coordinating Group (IAEG) was established. The IAEG was tasked to improve the coordination of government intervention in major events through the consideration of event proposals and information sharing among all interested agencies (Cabinet Office Wellington, 2004). As a group, the IAEG consisted of New Zealand Trade and Enterprise, Tourism New Zealand, Creative New Zealand, Sport and Recreation New Zealand, Te Puni Kokiri (Ministry of Maori Development), the Ministry of Tourism, the Ministry for Culture and Heritage, the Foundation for Research, Science and Technology, and the Ministry of Economic Development.

All these institutions directly or indirectly participated in the coordination of major events in New Zealand, which kept causing organisational issues even after the IAEG was created. For example, the IAEG had no allocated funding to specifically support major events and develop national bids. Different government agencies and ministries used their own budgets to fund only those events which fitted into their strategies without any alignment to the overall national vision and national priorities. Hence, the broader goals which could have been achieved through strategic planning and management of major events were not properly identified and supported.

There was also a lack of communication and coordination between the government agencies and the private sector. The IAEG had no accepted and shared criteria for assessing submitted event proposals. As a result, event organisers did not clearly understand how to cooperate with the Government, as all the decisions to support and fund events were taken on an ad-hoc basis.

It became obvious that a more strategic approach to planning and developing of major events in the country was necessary. In 2003, the IAEG was tasked to develop a national major events strategy.

New Zealand major event strategy

The strategy was launched in 2004. It presented an overview of a vision and key objectives for government intervention in the domain of major events. The Government intended to occupy a pivotal position in the national major event sector in order to achieve its goals for promoting sustainable economic and cultural development of New Zealand, as well as its brand profiling. The strategy addressed three key areas of international competitiveness, including:

◆ Retention of sustainable events that already occur;

◆ Growth of new and existing events; and

◆ Attraction of new major events to New Zealand (Cabinet Office Wellington, 2004, p. 13).

A "more focused engagement with industry stakeholders" (Cabinet Office Wellington, 2004, p. 14) was introduced as one of the key rationales behind the strategy. Ten priorities, which enable the Government to influence and better moderate the major event sphere, were identified:

◆ Enhanced co-ordination of events organiser activities;

◆ More sophisticated process for seeking and winning major events;

◆ Reduction in duplication of effort by event organisers and government agencies;

◆ Reduction in competition among New Zealand destinations to host the same event;

◆ Better use of available infrastructure, including natural assets;

◆ Focus on attraction of high quality, high yield events;

◆ Building events in low and shoulder seasons;

◆ Pooling of resources to gain efficiency;

◆ Improved standards; and

◆ Improved research (Cabinet Office Wellington, 2004, p.3).

Overall, the key objective of the strategy was to clearly state the role of the Government in attracting, retaining and growing major sporting and cultural events. The strategy responded to the existing coordination, informational and funding issues in the national major events sphere at that time. It also sent a clear message to the industry, in which the key responsibilities of the main public actors, and their objectives and expectations were outlined.

The New Zealand Major Events Fund (MEDF) was established in 2004 to support the strategy and allow the IAEG to fully exploit its capacity and expertise to coordinate the major events industry in New Zealand. The Fund was seen as "a key instrument of the strategy that enables government to address the problem of market failure through the provision of direct financial assistance" (Ministry of Economic Development of New Zealand, 2007, p. 11). The strategy emphasised a set of criteria for event funds allocation, including economic impacts, social and cultural benefits and international exposure. The allocation was planned by way of:

1   Seed funding to secure sponsorship or private sector investments;

2   Research grants for conducting feasibility studies;

3   Bidding and hosting costs;

4   Investment in leveraging activities.

(Ministry of Economic Development of New Zealand, 2007, p.13).

The Fund appropriated NZ$3.4 million per annum for 2005-2006 and 2006-2007. 41 major events were funded over the period September 2004 – June 2007, including the 2005 Volvo Ocean Race, 2006 ITU Triathlon World Cup, 2007 World Netball Championship, 2006-2007 Ellerslie Flower Shows (Ministry of Economic Development of New Zealand, 2007).

The responsibilities of the IAEG were widened, including the assessment of event proposals and allocation of major events funding through several funding rounds and evaluation of event bids. The secretarial functions of the IAEG were delegated to put the Major Events Group (MEG) within Ministry of Business, Innovation and Employment (former Ministry for Economic Development).

The establishment of strategy and the MEDF paved the way to the strategic use of events in New Zealand. Major events became a recognised and approved tool to deliver economic and social value to New Zealand's citizens and related national industries. The strategic vision on events was consistent with the 'Brand NZ' strategy, the aim of which was to promote New Zealand as an innovative, creative and technologically advanced country. Major events were seen as opportunities to leverage off-event activities and further national reputational and development goals. However, as it will be shown in the next section, the remained institutional structure predetermined a relatively passive role of the authorised government agencies in the realisation of the strategy's objectives.

Management and governance: New approach

The MEDF evaluation in 2007 indicated the IAEG's lack of a strategic vision regarding the support and delivery of major events. Although supported events had delivered reasonable investment returns, unused potential to gain greater benefits had been identified (Ministry of Economic Development of New Zealand, 2007).

As a voluntary group with informal membership, the IAEG reactively responded to the information and recommendations suggested by its secretariat in regard to specific major events and their funding. Therefore, the implementation of the overall strategy and related leveraging activities tended to be unsystematic and ineffective. One of the critical factors that determined that lack of strategic approach and the passive attitude was that for the majority of the IAEG members, events were not the 'core businesses'. It was unlikely to construct a synergetic environment of decision-making, where different agencies align their internal priorities with general IAEG's aims and objectives.

The case-by-case approach to the evaluation of an event's potential was guided by "one-third weightings to economic, socio-cultural, and international exposure criteria" (Ministry of Economic Development of New Zealand, 2007, p. 20). If an event seeks major events funding, it must demonstrate potential benefits across each of the three criteria. In order to broaden the investment opportunities, the IEAG was recommended to establish a portfolio approach to the evaluation of events and their further funding. A portfolio approach suggests that the overall balance of the mentioned criteria should be planned and measured at the portfolio level and not for separate events only.

In 2009, as a response to organisational and managerial concerns, the Government declared a change in its approach to major events in New Zealand. It was suggested to re-focus government actions from "being mainly an additional source of funding to becoming an integral partner with the events sector in helping to attract, retain, grow and deliver high quality events, and ensure major events deliver a lasting benefit to New Zealand" (Cabinet Office Wellington, 2009, p. 1). Table 7.1 presents the key features of the revised role of the Government in relation to major events.

Table 7.1: Key features of the shift in the national major event policy in New Zealand. Source: (Cabinet Office Wellington, 2009, p. 4).

Previous approach	Desired approach
Government is one source of funding for event support	Government works with others to actively develop the events sector for the long term benefit on New Zealand
Reactive focus on event funding in response to applications from event organisers	A balance of proactive strategic development of New Zealand's events 'landscape' with reactive support
Focus on funding as the primary tool to achieve governmental objectives	Applying a broader range of tools to generate the desired outcomes (e.g. development of volunteer programmes)
Transactional relationships with the sector around particular events	Ongoing partnership approach to adding value, including through information, co-ordination and strategic planning
Fragmented, ad-hoc approach to event leverage and legacy planning (mostly left to event owners)	Government leading leverage and legacy planning for events where there is significant national benefit

In order to achieve the desired goals, the Government focused on the delivery of a set of actions, including:

♦ **Strategic planning** for a proactive government role in major events. This is understood as undertaking of a leadership role across the major events sector, including identification of gaps in the national event calendar, exploration of event opportunities, coordination with local authorities and event organisers to ensure the delivery of a whole spectrum of benefits across New Zealand.

♦ **Leveraging and legacy planning.** Leveraging and legacy have been defined as broad and long-lasting benefits that "are set in motion than realised by events" (Major Events, 2016). The new approach envisaged leveraging and legacy activities as critically important sources to broader national, regional and local impacts from major events. A strategic framework has been suggested in order to develop appropriate leveraging/legacy opportunities during the initial feasibility and bidding stages.

♦ **Mapping New Zealand as a desirable host** for major events. Taking into account the increasing level of international competition, the Government intended to play a larger role in improving national competitiveness to attract and host large-scale events of international significance. This included identification of key markets for promoting New Zealand as an event destination, providing bidding assistance, building relationships with key international major event actors (sports federations, for example) and strategic conveying of 'success stories' to target markets and event organisers.

♦ **Disseminating learning and information** across the major events sector. The Government of New Zealand was to become a 'dissemination hub' of knowledge and experience on event support, organisation and management of bidding, development and support of volunteer and databases (Cabinet Office Wellington, 2009).

Due do the described changes and revised approach to Government involvement in major events, the Major Events Strategy was revised in 2010 (Ministry of Business Innovation and Employment of New Zealand, 2010). The revised strategy entailed the shift from a reactive funding model to a more strategic partnership with the major events industry. Accordingly, in 2011, the capacity of the MEDF was increased from NZ$3.4 million to NZ$10 million per year.

In order to exploit the potential of major events to make a significant contribution to the economic development of New Zealand, major changes have been made in the institutional structure of the agencies responsible for major events. In 2009, the decision-making regarding allocation from the MEDF was transferred from the IAEG to the Ministry of Business, Innovation and Employment. This step was justified by the desire to "better enable decisions to be made in light of broader, overarching, cross-government perspectives and better facilitate the mobilisation of resources to support government's involvement in major events" (Cabinet Office Wellington, 2009, p.3).

In 2012, the IAEG was dismissed. The key premise for this decision was inability of the IAEG to carry out a forward-looking role in identifying potential event opportunities that could be used to deliver long-term benefits from hosting major events. Instead, a Major Events Ministers Group was created (Ministers for Economic Development (Chair), Tourism, Foreign Affairs, Sport, and Culture & Heritage). The rationale was to increase ministerial oversight and achieve a situation where all the decisions regarding direct event investment and event leverage are taken collaboratively.

In addition, a Major Events Investment Panel was created to provide investment advice to the Ministers Group. The Investment Panel consists of two private sector representatives (including an independent Chair), and the CEOs of Tourism New Zealand, New Zealand Trade & Enterprise, Ministry for Culture and Heritage, Ministry of Business, Innovation and Employment, and Sport New Zealand. The Investment Panel considers major events applications and advise the Minsters Group on event investment, event leverage and legacy and event prospecting. This body allows both private and public sectors to have an input in investment decisions regarding delivering major events.

The authority of the Major Events Group within the Ministry of Business, Innovation and Employment, that initially functioned as a secretariat for the IAED, was widened and its activities re-focused on the broader major events attraction and delivering functions. Under the new name, New Zealand Major Events, it provides a secretariat support to the Event Ministers Group and Major Events Investment Panel. It positions itself as an advisor, a partner, an investor and a one-stop-shop for event organisers.

Another important outcome from the institutional changes was that for every funded event a special so-called 'sponsoring agency' was nominated to take responsibility for cross-government event leverage and legacy delivery. This was done to ensure that the Government could optimise the benefits sought from investment in major events and secure up-front leverage co-funding commitments during the investment process. Examples include New Zealand Trade & Enterprise hosting business VIP events alongside a major sporting event, or Tourism New Zealand organising special events and presentations for the key niche media that might visit the country for a particular event and could write positive reviews about New Zealand as a tourist and investment destination.

Portfolio performance evaluation and evolution

Recent analysis and evaluation reports suggest that major events prove to be a beneficial investment for the Government of New Zealand. The meta-evaluation of 55 major events that received an investment from the New Zealand Major

Events Development Fund in 2011-2015 indicates an approximate return on investment (ROI) of 113% and NZ$128.9 million of net economic benefit (Cabinet Office, 2016). To large extent, these results were achieved by the contribution to GDP from expenditure by overseas visitors who came to New Zealand to partici- pate or attend the events. In total, the supported events attracted 62,600 interna- tional visitors to New Zealand. Such results emphasise the strategic importance of hosting events which are capable of generating high numbers of international visitors.

The compositional structure of the national portfolio of major events in New Zealand demonstrates the predominance of one-off sporting events (76 per cent) which have received the major part of available funds. The data indicate the increase of the share of sporting events in the overall portfolio (Cabinet Office, 2016). This consistent pattern reflects the first priority stated in the updated major event strategy to make sensible investments in events with the most potential for economic return. The large-scale sporting events, are, in general, more aligned with the range of benefits that the Government aspires to achieve and capitalise on. However, a strong emphasis should be put also on achieving other positive outcomes.

In 2016, Ministry of Business, Innovation and Employment in collaboration with the Ministry for Culture and Heritage initiated a development of a Cultural Events and Content Strategy aiming at increasing the proportion of non-sport events in the national portfolio. Following the direction of a 'balanced portfolio approach' (Antchak & Pernecky, 2017; Getz, 2008) the MEDF has supported the growth of several 'home-grown' events, including the World of WearableArt, a touring fashion project, New Zealand IceFest, a biennial festival, and the Winter Games New Zealand, an elite international winter sport event.

Although the strategy highlights the necessity to spread supported events throughout the year in order to provide a relatively equal flow of visitors across peak (November-March), shoulder (April, October) and off-peak (May-Septem- ber), the majority of major events (57 per cent) have been held in the peak season (Cabinet Office, 2016). The explanation of such a distribution can be found in the weather variability in New Zealand. The majority of event organisers intend to organise their events during the summer months. This could guarantee signifi- cant numbers of local and international visitors. However, the 2013 evaluation of MEDF operation (Ministry of Business Innovation and Employment of New Zealand, 2013) illustrates disproportionally greater economic returns from off- peak and shoulder season events in relation to events hosted in the peak season. Thus, such events represent a clear leveraging potential for host destinations and their event-related industries. Hosting major events during the off-peak or shoulder seasons also helps to minimise the pressure on the infrastructure which might be extremely high during the peak season.

Geographically, the distribution of major events that received investment from the MEDF has been heavily concentrated in Auckland. The city hosted 17 out of the 37 events, included in 2016 evaluation (Cabinet Office, 2016). It is reasonable, taking into account the international status of Auckland as well as a well-developed infrastructure, including stadiums, hotels, and international airport and renovated harbour area. However, a more balanced distribution would be beneficial to grow both national and regional benefits and to develop event capability in smaller regions.

Summary

This chapter thoroughly described the key phases of the development of a portfolio approach to major events led by national authorities in New Zealand. As it was shown, the Government of New Zealand, as well as all key stakeholders had passed through several stages of institutional arrangements and relationship management. To summarise the results of this case study, a relationship marketing model, suggested by Parvatiyar and Sheth (2000) and for the first time applied in event portfolio studies by Kelly & Fairley (2018), will be used.

Relationship marketing is defined as the process of engaging in cooperative and collaborative activities to create or enhance mutual economic value (Parvatiyar and Sheth, 2000, p. 9). The process entails four stages, namely, *formation*; *management and governance*; *performance evaluation*; and *evolution*. Formation refers to the decisions regarding strategic goals, partnerships and mandates on event selection and funding allocation. Management and governance refers to relationship building and collaboration among stakeholders. Performance and evaluation deals with a variety of event portfolio evaluation strategies and evolution addresses further steps to maximise benefits and achieve strategic goals (Kelly & Fairley, 2018).

The two stages – formation and management and governance – in New Zealand have been developing in parallel and can be described as amorphous at the beginning and very structured at the current stage of operation. The IAEG group and its ad-hoc operational nature caused several organisational issues and proved to be, in general, unproductive. Although the supported events generated positive economic benefits, a flat institutional structure, coordinated by an advisory secretariat, and the absence of available joint IAEG funds led to unrealised leveraging opportunities, duplication of service delivery and limited success in establishing a proactive coordinated approach to major events. The development of the major event strategy in 2004 as well as the establishment of MEDF were aimed at improving the support of major events on the governmental level. However, IAEG as an advisory and facilitating group, did not possess enough authority and resources to lead this process.

The reactive operational style predetermined the following institutional changes. The IAEG was dismissed and a new cross-ministerial group was created. The operational functions were allocated to the MEDF within the Ministry of Business, Innovation and Employment. At the same time, the Government of New Zealand began playing a more active role in major events, considering event as one of the key pillars of the economy. Today, MEDF plays a role of a 'control centre' (Kelly & Fairley, 2018), providing recommendations on funding allocation, actively supporting bidding and developing leveraging and legacy strategies.

In terms of performance evaluation, several periodical evaluations were conducted in 2007, 2013 and 2016 to measure the achievement of specific objectives stated in the strategy. The applied matrices explored and compared the growth in the number of events and event visitors, ROI, average length of stay by international visitors, regional distribution of events and the overall portfolio contribution.

The evolution of the portfolio of major events in New Zealand is an ongoing process. Playing a role of a 'conduit to create and facilitate relationships among key stakeholders' (Kelly & Fairley, 2018, p. 272), MEDF paved the way to the development of regional and local event strategies. Major event strategies and approaches in Auckland, Wellington and Dunedin will be discussed in the next chapter. The leading role of the Government ensures consistency and strategic orientation on the long-term positive outcomes from hosting major sporting and cultural events all over the country.

References

Antchak, V., & Pernecky, T. (2017). Major events programming in a city: Comparing three approaches to portfolio design. *Event Management*, **21**(5), 545-561. doi:10.3727/152599517X15053272359013

Cabinet Office, Wellington. (2004). Government major event strategy. Wellington, New Zealand: Cabinet Economic Development Committee. Retrieved from http://www.med.govt.nz/majorevents/pdf-library/ nz-major-events/strategy-documents/major-events-strategy-2004

Cabinet Office, Wellington. (2009). Changes to the Government's approach to major events. Wellington, New Zealand: Cabinet Economic Growth and Infrastructure. Retrieved from http://www.med.govt. nz/majorevents/pdf-library/nz-major-events/strategy-documents/ changes-to-governemnt-approach-event-policy

Cabinet Office, Wellington. (2016). *Evaluation of the Major Events Development Fund*. Wellington, New Zealand. Retrieved from http://www.majorevents. govt.nz/pdf-library/nz-major-events/strategy-documents/evaluation-of-the-major-events-development-fund-cabinet-paper.pdf

Getz, D. (2008). Event tourism: Definition, evolution, and research. *Tourism Management*, **29**(3), 403–428. doi:10.1016/j.tourman.2007.07.017

Kelly, D. M., & Fairley, S. (2018). The utility of relationships in the creation and maintenance of an event portfolio. *Marketing Intelligence & Planning*, **36**(2), 260–275. Retrieved from doi:10.1108/MIP-11-2017-0270

Major Events. (2016). Leverage and Legacy Planning. Retrieved from http:// www.majorevents.govt.nz/resource-bank/leverage-and-legacy-planning/ definition

Ministry of Business Innovation and Employment of New Zealand. (2010). New Zealand major events strategy. Retrieved from http://www.med.govt.nz/majorevents/pdf-library/nz-major-events/strategy-documents/ME-strategy.pdf

Ministry of Business Innovation and Employment of New Zealand. (2013). Economic evaluation outcomes: Major events development fund. Wellington, New Zealand. Retrieved from http://www.med.govt.nz/majorevents/pdf-library/news/MEDF-evaluation-report.pdf

Ministry of Economic Development of New Zealand. (2007). Operation of the major events development fund: Evaluation report. Wellington, New Zealand. Retrieved from http://www.med.govt.nz/majorevents/pdf-library/nz-major-events/strategy-documents/evaluation-Major-Events-development-fund-2007.pdf

Parvatiyar, A. & Sheth, J. N. (2000) The domain and conceptual foundations of relationship marketing. In J. N. Sheth & A. Parvatiyar (Eds.), *Handbook of Relationship Marketing* (pp. 3-38). Thousand Oaks: Sage Publications.

Smith, A. (2012). *Events and Urban Regeneration: The strategic use of events to revitalise cities*. New York: Routledge.

8 Portfolio of Major Events in Auckland, Wellington and Dunedin

The overall purpose of this chapter is to analyse the inter-relations between institutional arrangements, event policy frameworks and applied portfolio approaches. The chapter aims to explore the influence of the public sector institutional and policy environments on the realisation of portfolio approaches in three cities in New Zealand, Auckland, Wellington and Dunedin. The cities have a core national status (Ministry of Business Innovation and Employment, 2012) in terms of economic, political and socio-cultural share, and represent a variety of different contexts.

Auckland is located in the North Island of New Zealand. It is the largest urban area in the country with a population of 1,415,500. It contains around 190 ethnic groups. Auckland is New Zealand's principle business centre and accounts for 35.3% of New Zealand's GDP as major national gateway for imports and exports (Statistics New Zealand, 2014). It is the most visited tourist destination in New Zealand, attracting around 70% of all visitors to the country (aucklandnz.com, n.d.). Auckland has been recognised in different international comparative studies such as Mercer Quality of Living Survey is 2015 and 2018, where it was ranked the third most liveable city in the world (Mercer, 2015, 2018).

Wellington is the capital of New Zealand and the main city in the Greater Wellington region. The region is the third largest in the country in terms of population, with 471,315 residents: 11.1% of the total national population (Statistics New Zealand, 2013). Wellington City's total population is 190,959 residents with 77% being of European ethnic origin. Geographically, the city is located at the south-western edge of the North Island. The city houses the national Parliament and the head offices of Government Ministries. It is an important centre for creative industries, including the film and theatre industry. Wellington is home to the country's major arts and cultural institutions such as the Royal New Zealand Ballet, New Zealand Symphony Orchestra and the National Museum of New Zealand, Te Papa Tongarewa. Wellington has been positioned as the 'coolest little capital in the world' and 'a smart capital' (wellingtonnz.com, n.d.). Lonely Planet Best in Travel 2011 ranked Wellington as fourth in its Top

10 Cities to Visit in 2011 (Lonely Planet, 2011). In 2014, Wellington was named the 12th city of the best quality of living in the world by Mercer (Mercer, 2014).

Dunedin is the second largest city in the South Island of New Zealand. It is located on the central western coast of the Otago region. The population of 120,249 residents ranks it fifth in size out of the 67 districts in the country. This represents 2.8% of New Zealand's total population, and 83% of residents belong to the European ethnic group. The city's primary industry is tertiary education, housing the University of Otago and Otago Polytechnic, and students represent 21% of the city's population. It is the oldest New Zealand city with a rich Scottish legacy. Dunedin is also a UNESCO creative city of literature and the 'heritage capital' of New Zealand.

The analysis of the data, collected for this chapter in 2015-2016, including interviews with the industry experts and relevant public documents, has revealed an interplay of the four elements which explain the relationship between local institutional contexts and applied portfolio approaches (see Figure 8.1).

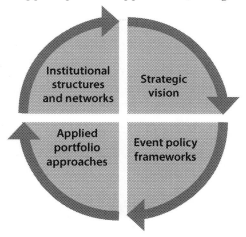

Figure 8.1: Local institutional context and portfolio approaches in Auckland, Wellington and Dunedin.

The first element, 'Strategic vision' examines the rationale for designing portfolios of major events in Auckland, Wellington and Dunedin. It describes the desire of city event planners to use major events as a tool to enhance and promote the expected desirable city profiles and their competitive points of differences. The second element, 'Institutional structures and networks', describes the current relationships in the public sector. The third element, 'Event policy frameworks', outlines the public policy aspects of major events programming in the cities. The fourth element, 'Applied portfolio approaches', describes the relatively different strategic initiatives in the cities, which incorporate diverse financial, planning and managerial aspects of event portfolio development.

Element 1: Strategic vision. City desirability through major events

The reason behind planning and delivering portfolios of major events is rooted in the vision that major events can significantly contribute to the development of city personality and distinctiveness or, in other words, unique place identity (see Table 8.1).

Table 8.1: City vision on the value of major events and destination attractiveness.

City	Vision on major events
Auckland	Events not only attract visitors beyond our borders, helping to grow the visitor economy, they also enhance and shape public perceptions of Auckland as an exciting and vibrant place to live and work as well as enhancing the quality of people's lives. Major event help us tell the story of our region and strengthen our identity. They raise awareness of Auckland as a potential destination through domestic and international media and digital coverage (ATEED, 2018, p. 4).
Wellington	Wellington events are highly valued by Wellingtonians. Residents and ratepayers have told us that events are what makes Wellington great. Events generate economic benefits, attract, inspire and retain talent and give a sense of community belonging and a sense of place. The arts and culture, sports, business and community sectors all organise events and rely on them for success both for themselves and for the broader community (Wellington City Council, 2012, p. 4).
Dunedin	Festivals and events play a role in creating great cities. They provide economic benefits, social connection, and a chance to share and highlight culture, identity and the things that matter to us. Through festivals and events, we show the best of ourselves and make Dunedin feel like home (Dunedin City Council, 2018, p. 9).

In Auckland, place identity has been expressed in the concepts of city liveability and ethnic diversity. Public documents describe liveability as being a globally connected city, an internationally competitive destination, a city that attracts talented people. Liveability reflects a diversity of experiences which visitors and locals can enjoy while exploring the city, including nature and urban attractions. Another aspect of liveability correlates with a sense of pride and enjoyment of being a city resident. Major events should "make people proud of who they are, where they live by making Auckland more interesting and exciting" (ATEED, 2011, p. 14).

Auckland's ethnic diversity is another key factor that contributes to the city's uniqueness. Some major events have been labelled as 'distinctively Auckland' because of their thematic orientation on celebrating cultural and ethnic variety. For example, the Pasifika Festival is an annual Pacific Islands-themed that presents a wide variety of authentic cultural experiences. Annually the event attracts over 200,000 visitors.

Another example is the three-day-and-night Lantern Festival, a big Asian festivity in the city during the Chinese New Year celebration. The festival is one of the biggest and most popular cultural celebrations in Auckland. The event celebrates the city's ethnic diversity and marks the end of Chinese New Year festivities. During the run of these events, city parks are transformed into stages where a diverse array of performances and celebrations highlight the city's multiculturalism and ethnic diversity.

Such events, to a major extent, are oriented on achieving positive social outcomes, or developing 'internal' characteristics of a desirable place. Other major events like large-scale sporting tournaments have been seen as a solid contribution to the 'external' city identity, including recognisable city image and visitor attractiveness. An example is the ITU World Triathlon Series. This is the International Triathlon Union's annual series of triathlon events, including stages in such destinations as London, Hamburg, Chicago and Cape Town. In 2015, Auckland hosted the second stage. The entire series usually is broadcast online, which guarantees a huge international exposure for a host city, showcasing attractive cityscapes. International visitors and supporters crowded the city streets, new facilities and fan zones were created, and some public spaces were thematised for the event.

While Auckland promotes itself as a multi-ethnic and liveable place, Wellington has been introduced as a vibrant centre of creativity and art:

> Embraced by a natural amphitheatre of ocean and hill, Wellington merges big city culture with small town charm. A lively energy pulses through what is celebrated as New Zealand's arts, film, coffee, culinary, craft beer, events and political capital (wellingtonnz.com, n/d).

Major events have been expected to demonstrate that the city is the best place to live in, to leverage the city's identity as a creative and cosmopolitan capital, and to enhance its image of an event city. The intention of the city's brand and event managers is to emphasise the competitive advantages of Wellington as a visitor and event destination. Visitors do recognise Wellington as a small compact city with a good nightlife, cafes, restaurants, walk-distance to all famous places. The compactness of the city centre provides event planners with a unique opportunity to embrace all the city attractions and showcase it as a unitary modern, creative event area.

Cuba Dupa, a street festival in Wellington, highlights and celebrates the creative spirit of Wellington. Cuba Street is an iconic creative district in the city. During the events, several streets in the city centre are closed for live music and dance performances. The New Zealand Festival is a biannual cultural event, hosted in Wellington. It brings the best live arts world experience to New Zealand, and is a leading multi-arts festival in Australasia. The festival includes over 300 large and small events and features more than 1000 national and international artists and writers. Another example of an iconic event is the World of WearableArt Show, an annual presentation of art, music, dance, drama and comedy. The show highlights the Wellington entertainment scene, fashion and creativity. Over 300 designers from New Zealand and overseas participate every year in this celebration.

In Dunedin, city brand managers invest a lot of effort in developing a distinctive city identity. A new Festival and Events Plan introduces Dunedin as "one of the world's great small cities" (Dunedin City Council, 2018, p. 9). Dunedin has been also viewed as a family-friendly and event-rich destination. It is a compact city of contrast, where wildlife attractions organically coexist with gothic architecture and modern arts. Many events in the city have been designed to highlight the diverse experiencescape and attract visitor attention. ID Dunedin Fashion Week, one of the leading national fashion events in New Zealand, for example, emphasises and celebrates the city's history of fashion and design, as well as its creativity and unique style. The events during the fashion week included retail exhibitions, workshops and demonstrations. The week culminated the ID International Emerging Designer Awards and the ID Dunedin Fashion Shows. The Dunedin Midwinter Carnival celebrates the winter experience in the city, and the key theme of the Carnival is the longest night in the year. Each year the Carnival attracts talented local artists and the wider regional community.

In brief, the city event planners in Auckland, Wellington and Dunedin understand the importance of the development of a unique place identity through major events, which can be utilised as a competitive advantage of the city. Different visions cultivated in the cities under study – liveable city, smart and cultural capital, event-rich city of contrast – have been planned to highlight the distinctiveness of the place and its desirability to visitors, locals and international business. The cities' overarching ambitions to become desirable places tend to be achieved using a strategic blend of city images and major events programmes, which attract national and international attention and highlight local points of difference.

The fundamental desire of the cities to posit their attractiveness and desirability through major events instigates the development and realisation of the event portfolio strategies. The assemblage of events in portfolios provides event planners with a strategic opportunity to extend a positive effect from staging events during the course of the year.

Element 2: Institutional structures and networks

This section introduces the second element of the suggested framework, 'Institutional structures and networks'. It covers and explores distinctive public sector arrangements and inter-organisational networks in the cities under study.

Institutional arrangements

As Antchak and Pernecky (2017) mention, the realisation of major event strategies in Auckland, Wellington and Dunedin has been affected by the establishment of new economic and destination development agencies: Auckland Tourism, Events and Economic Development (ATEED) in 2010, Wellington Regional Economic Development Agency (WREDA) in 2014 and Enterprise Dunedin in 2014. The creation of these council-controlled organisations (CCOs) aimed at integrating critical destination management activities, including economic development, industry and business growth, investment attraction, tourism and major events under the authority of a single institutional body.

As it is reflected in relevant official statements and public documents (Auckland Tourism Events and Economic Development, 2014; dunedin.govt.nz, n.d; WREDA, 2015), the overall rationale behind such changes in the institutional structures of the cities lies in the tendency to centralise strategic decision-making in all critical spheres of sustainable destination development. A more coordinated approach to economic growth, tourism and major events can decrease agency costs and duplication of efforts, and guarantee the realisation of region-wide, coordinated strategies in line with broader economic development objectives. While the CCO status obliges it to operate at 'arm's length' and be accountable to city councils, it provides some strategic benefits. For example, in Auckland, being 'one step away' from the city council allows ATEED to operate more commercially. In 2014-2015, ATEED invested NZ$14 million into major events. The investment returned NZ$85 million with 426,500 visitor nights (Auckland Tourism Events and Economic Development, 2015).

The formation of new economic development agencies has changed the way major events are planned and managed in the cities. In Auckland, a *separate management scheme* has been applied (Antchak & Pernecky, 2017). Major events have become a part of ATEED's portfolio of activities, while smaller local and regional events remain under the jurisdiction of Auckland Council (AC). ATEED is responsible for major event development, major event delivery and operational facilitation, major event investment and major event industry capability development (Auckland Tourism Events and Economic Development, 2013).

The arrangements in Wellington represented a *transformative stage* of major events management. Although one of the key tasks of a newly established WREDA was to manage portfolios of major events, the relocation of duties between Wellington City Council (WCC), which previously planned all the events (local and major), and WREDA was still in process. One of the key benefits of major events relocation to a relevant CCO is their integration with other critical areas of destination management. Economic development agencies play a role of a 'one-stop shop' for major events, which facilitates the implementation of events into a wider city development agenda.

In Dunedin, a *merged type* of public event management has been applied (Antchak & Pernecky, 2017). Dunedin City Council (DCC) delivers all public events, including major events. Although Enterprise Dunedin is responsible for destination marketing, the agency has not been involved in major events directly.

Overall, the creation of regional economic development agencies is a current trend worldwide. The described organisations in Auckland, Wellington and Dunedin have been expected to provide the cities with a solid asset in terms of consolidation, manipulation and negotiation within critical areas of city development, including the economy, investments, tourism and events. At the time when the research was conducted, WREDA and Enterprise Dunedin just commenced their activity, and it was impossible to track any significant achievements of these agencies. In comparison, ATEED was the oldest and more experienced organisation. From 2011 to 30 June 2017, major events supported by ATEED contributed NZ$360 million to the regional economy and generated 2,224,381 visitor nights. ATEED's successful intervention in major events may be expected to serve as a guiding example for other cities in an attempt to capitalise on their potential and maximise the return on investment from staging major events.

Inter-organisational relationships

The appearance of new players on the institutional arena of the cities leads to the formation of new or re-formation of previous relationships between key stakeholders. Well-developed relationships among different stakeholders have been considered as one of the critical elements of a successful implementation of major event strategies in Auckland, Wellington and Dunedin. It is possible to highlight at least two types of stakeholders operating in the cities: strategic and operational stakeholders.

Strategic stakeholders

A group of strategic stakeholders includes different agencies from national and city levels that have the authority to influence decision-making regarding hosting and funding major events in the cities. Apart from the economic development agencies (ATEED, WREDA, Enterprise Dunedin), this group includes city councils, Tourism New Zealand and Sport New Zealand, which are two national destination management and sporting organisations, and New Zealand Major Events, a central government division responsible for supporting major events of national importance.

Taking into account the fact that city event teams in Auckland, Wellington and Dunedin are either incorporated into the council's structure (Dunedin) or belong to relevant CCOs (Auckland and Wellington), the relationships between the councils and major event planners in general can be described as constructive. In Auckland, appropriate policies, protocols or statements of intent regulate the relationships between AC and ATEED. However, the communication between ATEED and AC was not great all the time. Although they were improving and getting better, 'it is still bit of a case of them and us'. The reason behind this contradiction lies in the fact that some responsibilities and decision-making were taken from the Council and passed on to ATEED. This transition did not always go smoothly. Some Council departments were not prepared to share or relocate authority to a new agency.

In Wellington, the head of the WCC events team met the city's mayor regularly to report on current event-related initiatives and discuss any emerged strategic issues. WCC, as a stakeholder, controlled the regulations around staging and supporting major events. The establishment of WREDA, as a new key major events player, in the city re-structures and redefines the allocation of responsibilities with regard to major events programming. However, at the time when the data were collected, the relationships between WCC and WREDA were at their immature stage without clear established structure and regulations.

In Dunedin, the merged management of events within DCC predefines a leading role of the Council in planning and developing major events strategies. As indicated in the previous sub-section, Enterprise Dunedin is not involved in major events planning. The relationship between DCC and Enterprise Dunedin were also at an immature, introductory stage without clear distribution of responsibilities in the major events sphere.

The prevailing data regarding the necessity of well-developed relationships between city event planners and national strategic stakeholders came from the case of Auckland. The city has been actively involved in different national and international bidding projects in cooperation with Tourism New Zealand, Sport New Zealand and New Zealand Major Events. ATEED usually plays the role of a key negotiator with these national organisations. The relationships between the city event planners and key national partners have been evolving since the establishment of ATEED in 2010. The concentration of all event-related strategic activities within one organisation makes it possible to build a constructive collaboration between the city and national stakeholders.

New Zealand Major Events possesses the authority to manipulate and even refuse to support some Auckland major events projects. An example is the NRL Auckland Nines, a weekend-long rugby tournament. In 2014, New Zealand Major Events declined the city's application for sponsorship, arguing that the financial support of this event may have negative impacts on another rugby-themed event, hosted in Wellington around the same time. However, in some other cases, e.g. the 2008 FIFA Women's U-17 World Cup, where the benefits for the whole country were seen as greater than for an individual city, the Auckland event's team was able to push back to central government in order to negotiate the split of financial support for the event. Another example of a collaborative relationship between Auckland event planners and national institutions, in particular, Sport New Zealand, is the World Masters Games, an event hosted in Auckland in 2017. From a very early stage, the stakeholders worked in partnership, identifying event-related opportunities and expected outcomes.

Event planners from Wellington and Dunedin also emphasise the critical role of the strategic stakeholders in the major event sector. However, the active phase of the relationship usually occurs during the national bidding projects where these cities participate. WREDA is expected to become a key negotiator with the national strategic stakeholders. A more ad-hoc approach prevailed in Dunedin. For example, city event managers relied heavily on Tourism New Zealand and their mass-media projects in promoting Dunedin as an event destination. This demonstrates a somewhat passive role of the city event planners in establishing strategic relationships with national organisations. The realisation of a new Festival and Event Plan can positively affect the stakeholders' cooperation and collaboration.

Operational stakeholders

The members of the operational stakeholder group in the cities under study vary. In general, the group includes all the organisations which are directly or indirectly involved in planning and hosting events. Auckland, for example, has established a 'Number Eight Group' which includes Auckland Transport, Waterfront Auckland, Auckland Regional Facilities, Auckland Police and some other relevant AC departments. The group meets quarterly and discusses current issues with events in the city, common objectives and operational plans. The relationships between these stakeholders have been regulated by a specific protocol that acknowledged the distinct objectives of the stakeholders and encouraged them to cooperate in order to facilitate the realisation of the events strategies in the city.

In Wellington, key operational stakeholders, including Wellington Tourism, Wellington Venues and Grow Wellington have been amalgamated into WREDA. Considering the city retail and hospitality industry as one of the critical event stakeholders, city event planners have organised meetings with the representatives of these areas of business on a monthly basis. The key purpose of such meetings is to communicate joint plans and knowledge sharing. In Dunedin, a city coordination group of the key operational stakeholders included representatives of the Police, Otago University, schools and city retail.

Overall, the relationships among city event planners and other strategic and operational stakeholders plays a critical role in planning and delivering major events in the cities under study. The ability to coordinate stakeholders through the implementation of different tactics (e.g., protocols and group meetings) provides event planners with an opportunity to purposefully communicate with the interested event-related agents and direct joint efforts to the realisation of major event projects.

Element 3: Event policy frameworks

The cities under study operate with relatively distinct bodies of official strategies and policies. In Auckland, a cluster of regulations includes documents which regulate all the main dimensions of event programming. The summary of implemented policies and strategies is presented in Table 8.2.

Table 8.2: Auckland event policy framework – key documents.

2011: Auckland Major Events Strategy 2011-2021 (AMES)
A framework for planning and development of major events. Presents a detailed typology of major events, their roles and main city's objectives with regard to hosting major events. A portfolio approach is presented and discussed. Key outcomes and measurement criteria are outlined.
2013: Auckland's Major Events Protocol (AMEP)
A guide for the key event stakeholders in the city and for a wider events industry on how the process of major events selection and support is organised. Roles and responsibilities of key actors are explained.
2013: Auckland Events Policy (AEP)
The overarching strategic document that explains the rationale for events planning\ hosting\development and justifies the involvement of AC in these activities. It explains key principles for delivering events, funding criteria and strategic objectives. Roles and responsibilities of local and regional boards, governing body and ATEED are detailed.
2018: Auckland's Major Event Strategy 2018-2025 (AMES 2018)
An update of the AMES 2011 with an updates approach to major events.

In 2010, ATEED developed Auckland Major Events Strategy. AMES 2011 emphasised the importance of major events in achieving long-term economic and social goals of the city. Events can deliver immediate economic benefits, impact on a city image, make cities more vibrant and interesting places to live and be a catalyst for change and further development (ATEED, 2011). The development of the strategy was a well-timed decision for the city that had lost several important events, turned down a free waterfront stadium and, in spite of this, envisioned itself as the best events destination and the most liveable city in the world. The strategy was of an expansionary nature, concentrating on buying, bidding, and growing major events that could bring significant economic return to Auckland and enhance its brand.

In addition to AMES 2011, an Auckland Major Events Protocol (AMEP) was announced in 2013. The key objective of AMEP was to create an event-friendly culture within AC, relevant CCOs and the wider event industry. The protocol regulated the relationships between key event stakeholders in the city, and clarified the operational procedures that drive major event selection and funding. Such processes as allocation of major events funds, event development, event operations, and event debrief and event facilitation were explained in detail.

AMEP represented a clear guide and message to the event industry on decision-making criteria, timeframes and efficient customer-driven service.

In 2013, AC released an official Auckland Events Policy (AEP). The document articulated how and why the Council was involved in events, what it aimed to achieve, the various roles the Council would play and the context within which decisions for events in the city would occur. AEP suggested a general framework that embedded city events into a wider context and strategically aligned them with Auckland's Unitary Plan and other strategies, programmes and plans (e.g., Economic Development Strategy, Arts and Culture Strategic Action Plan, Integrated Transport Programme, Sport and Recreation Strategic Action Plan). The policy became a valuable guide for city authorities, covering all important areas of event-related activities.

In 2018, a new strategy, AMES 2018 was presented (ATEED, 2018). ATEED will continue focusing on mega and major events of national and international significance. Several portfolio attributes have been introduced, including seasonality, genre, frequency, size, geography and reach of events. The ability of an event to meet the requirements of the attributes will determine the support of the event as part of the city's portfolio.

Overall, Auckland has produced a solid regulatory foundation for the realisation of a strategic approach to major events. Event policies and strategies guide this process, emphasising such aspects as delimitation of authority, distribution of funding and establishment of precise targets and outcomes in the major event sphere.

In contrast to Auckland, in Wellington and Dunedin event policy frameworks are less developed. In Wellington the first city event strategy was released in 2003 (Wellington City Council, 2003). One of the goals of the strategy was to develop a strong event support infrastructure. Thus, a single co-ordinating unit for events development in the city was established within the Council. The team produced a set of 'how to' event guides including information and advice on regulatory compliance, protocols and risk management. The strategy also coordinated the relationships between key tourism and event-related agencies in Wellington, including the City Council itself, events unit and Positively Wellington Tourism. Overall, the document was a good starting point for the development of a united official vision on events, their organisation and possible outcomes for the city.

The strategy was succeeded by the Wellington Event Policy (WEP) in 2012. It was developed within a general city development framework 'Wellington 2040 – Smart Capital'. WEP emphasised the role of major events as a key economic contributor. They attract visitors, provide jobs and help to position the city as an attractive destination. WEP identified a set of critical directions for the industry, including the development of new major events, sustainable development, strengthening of current partnerships, city profiling and construction of a balanced and diverse calendar of events (Wellington City Council, 2012).

The WCC's role was formulated in facilitating, partnering and advocating the event-related strategic initiatives in the city. With the establishment of WREDA, city event planners expected some changes in the current event policy, in particular with regard to event classification matrices and spheres of responsibility between the new entity and WCC events' team.

The first experience of event strategy making in Dunedin dated back to 2009, when a Dunedin Festivals and Events Strategy (DFES) was released. DFES outlined the general idea that events and festivals play an important role in the city development (Dunedin City Council, 2009). The key purpose of this strategy was to fill the gaps in the city attitude to public events, their funding and development. Before the release of the strategy, the decisions on the number of supported events and their genres were made during the annual planning meetings in DCC without any evaluation, market research and strategic guidelines. Although the strategy was supposed to play a fundamental role in Dunedin's public event sector, the researcher was surprised to find out that only one out of five managers, who closely worked with event planning and promotion in Dunedin, were aware of the existence of DFES. The stated targets and measures of success did not reflect the real situation in the industry, and the strategy required revision and adjustment with other city development policies.

A new Festival and Events Plan 2018-2023 was introduced in May 2018. The document emphasises the leading role of DCC in financial and governmental support of the local event sector. The vision of making Dunedin 'One of the world's great small cities' is planned to be achieved through encouraging and providing opportunities for the local community to celebrate its identity, facilitating the process of putting on major events in the city, attracting events capable of showcasing Dunedin as a vibrant place, promoting a rich calendar to locals and international visitors, strengthening the city's framework of funding and developing event-led leveraging and legacy plans.

Element 4: Applied portfolio approaches

Each of the cities under study has applied a distinct approach and incorporated diverse financial, planning and managerial strategies that result in the formation of different portfolios.

Outcomes-driven portfolio approach in Auckland

Antchak (2017) argues that the roots of the outcomes-driven portfolio approach to major events in Auckland lie in the established event-related institutional structure and event policy framework in the city. Indeed, the concentration of decision-making within one agency, ATEED, as well as the development of a pool of event policies and strategies, determines a pure investment and outcomes-oriented nature of the city's portfolio of major events.

The portfolio consists of events that have been chosen within a given financial year to achieve the current city outcomes and guarantee ROI (Return On Investment). The rationale behind portfolio creation is to establish a balance between productive and consumptive outcomes delivered by events and develop a clear vision on the outcomes the whole programme of events should achieve (ATEED, 2011). The portfolio-related objectives may vary due to the current vision and targets of the city. For example, a set of the city's strategies and policies, including events, have been clustered around the construction of Auckland's image as the world's most liveable city. This presupposes and signifies the achievement of ongoing city prosperity, the growth of the visitor economy, the enhancement of the city's status as a major event and tourist destination, as well as the development of a creative, vibrant international city. The event portfolio has been viewed as a strategic grouping of investment where the value is estimated on the basis of the sum total of the events included into this portfolio (Antchak, 2017).

This approach suggests a more strategic vision on events in the city, "'ticking all the boxes' at the programme level, rather than requiring each event to 'tick all the boxes' on a stand-alone basis" (ATEED, 2011, p. 14). Such an approach corresponds with the national major event strategy, discussed in the previous chapter, where an overall balance of the suggested major events' criteria should be planned and measured at the national portfolio level, and not for separate events which are planned to be staged in New Zealand (Ministry of Economic Development of New Zealand, 2007). The event planners from ATEED make a clear distinction between a portfolio of major events and an overall events landscape in the city, which includes events of different size, genres and scale.

Diverse minimum approach in Wellington

In contrast to Auckland's maturity phase of major event portfolio development, Wellington has entered the 'early growth' stage. The establishment of WREDA and necessity of new guidelines for major events sector have determined the slow transformation of the currently implemented 'diverse minimum' approach (Antchak & Pernecky, 2017).

Although WEP does not contain such term as 'portfolio of events' (a term 'programme' is used instead), event planners in the city actively use it. The portfolio can be described as a composition of events that the city owns or invests in. The key objectives of investment in events have been stated in WEP and cover such areas as growing the economy and making Wellington an attractive destination to visit, to invest or to live in (Wellington City Council, 2012). The portfolio of events is expected to showcase and promote the brand of the city.

As already mentioned, until recently the whole event portfolio was managed by WCC events team. That approach influenced the compositional structure of the portfolio. Compared to Auckland's focus on portfolio outcomes, Wellington event planners strived to achieve balance between different types and genres of events. This strategy was supported by WEP, where the delivery of diverse events (sport, arts, culture, music, food, and environment) was stated as one of the key policy directions (Wellington City Council, 2012). The recent establishment of WREDA, however, could significantly change this approach. The CCO would mainly focus on major events and their economic and image contribution. One of the first decisions with regard to major events was the increase of funding to attract and support major events. In the past, major events were sponsored together with other economically valued initiatives and partnerships from the Economic Development Initiatives Fund with the total value of NZ$3 million. The new WREDA plan proposed NZ$5 million investment in major events in order to achieve 1:20 economic return (Wellington City Council, 2015).

One of the fundamental characteristics of the 'diverse minimum' approach is a limitation of major events funds (Antchak & Pernecky, 2017). The reason for limited investment opportunities lies also in the fact that Wellington utilised a multi-year contracting scheme, when a sponsorship agreement with an event promoter or owner was signed for several years. This approach did not give the necessary flexibility for event planners should any other advantageous event options arise.

On the other hand, such a situation simplified the process of annual investment allocation and event marketing and promotion. In this regard, the most appropriate strategy with event funds should include the availability of miscellaneous spending that can be invested in events that might come to the attention of event planners during the course of the year.

Due to the limitations with available financial support the portfolio in Wellington is "at its capacity" (Antchak & Pernecky, 2017. p. 554). As was mentioned by the city event practitioners, the further major event programming should probably be oriented more on 'in-depth' event development, where new elements would be designed and included into the programme of already existing events. Instead of building a completely new event, the idea is to widen the offered experience and audience of available recurrent events in order to refresh their content and attract new non-targeted groups of visitors and participants.

Simplistic programming of events in Dunedin

Following Auckland's 'maturity' and Wellington's 'early growth' stages, Dunedin represents an 'introductory' stage of portfolio planning and development. This is characterised by the hereditary composition of the portfolio and a lack of strategy in major events programming. What is noticeable is an active role of the local community in major events planning and management. The absence of clear public goals and measures opens up room for the community to intervene major events sphere with new ideas and innovations (Antchak & Pernecky, 2017).

Although the concept of event portfolio was mentioned in relevant public documents (e.g., Dunedin City Council, 2012), it was not a popular term among the city event planners. Event portfolio was usually used as a synonym to a list of planned events that were supported by DCC. In other words, it was a synopsis of 'what is on' in the city. The compositional structure of this portfolio list in Dunedin was influenced by the historical legacy of the city and its traditions. Many major city events were organised in an ad-hoc manner without any clear indication of their long-term objectives and purposes.

One of the key characteristics of the simplistic programming approach was the reliance of the city event planners on hosting events with a long community history. The adherence to the hereditary composition of an annual event programme was backed up by the argument that the community supported these events and did not want them to be changed or cancelled. Such orientation lacked critical evaluation of event feasibility and practicality for current city objectives. However, events that were supported by the community seemed to be more sustainable and embedded into the city life.

Although the establishment of the DFES structured funding procedures and regulated the relationships between key industry players in Dunedin, it did not affect the programming process. Dunedin was still at the stage of an 'open market' where all the organisers, owners or promoters of different events competed with each other for the opportunity to receive some funding from the Council. The event planners, who guided this process, did not clearly express the criteria for events, or the expected outcomes from hosting these events.

A 'free for all' style also resulted in a situation when other departments of DCC organised their own city-scale events without any assistance from the Council's events team. They used their own resources and budgets, and although such events did not get any financial support from the relevant event fund, they were officially included into the city event programme.

The shortage of funds and human resources significantly limited the city events team in an attempt to create a vibrant and attractive programme of events. At the same time, such a dearth instigated the rise of community participation in the portfolio planning. The local community became a good ground for event ideas and a prospective starting point for developing interesting events. A good example is a Port Chalmers Seafood Festival, a fully community-designed event that obtained a major event status because of its embeddedness into the local context and support from the whole community.

The situation with limited financial support for large-scale events left some room for innovation and creativity with regard to other events in the city. In 2014, the city officially supported the Dundead Pop culture and Science Festival, timed to the premier of the locally made short horror film about zombies. The event was very atypical for the heritage-oriented city; however, it succeeded in covering and blending such themes as science and modern pop culture and was enthusiastically accepted by the audience. All profits from the event were donated to the New Zealand Red Cross organisation. An updated Festival and Event Plan 2018-2023 that went through two consultation phases and a feedback from community groups and individuals can facilitate the implementation of a more strategic approach to events in the city (Dunedin City Council, 2018).

Overall, each of the studied cities developed its major event portfolio approach within distinctive local conditions. Current event-related objectives, availability of funds and city capacity influenced the nature of the approach and the ways of its realisation. The scope of the approaches in the cities varied from fully out-come-oriented in Auckland to an ad-hoc simplistic programming in Dunedin. Wellington's 'diverse minimum' approach is situated somewhere in between, demonstrating an ability of city events planners to create a solid portfolio of events under the conditions of limited financial resources and less clear strategic goals.

Comparing contextual environments in the cities

The analysis demonstrates that the institutional structures, including institu-tional arrangements and event policy frameworks, influence the strategic nature of major event portfolios in the cities under study (Figure 8.2). The separate management of events by a specific agency, as was in the case of Auckland, led to the elaboration of a more strategic approach to major events programming. Events were selected and grouped in a portfolio with the purpose of achieving certain objectives and outcomes, defined within the applied event policy frame-work. This orientation on outcomes determined the distinction between a port-folio of major events and a programme of local and regional events. The applied outcomes-driven portfolio approach fitted the general city strategy to position Auckland as a national economic centre, a vibrant and liveable place to visit and to live in. A set of public strategies and event policy provides a guideline for city event planners. Recent city awards and the positive economic contribution of major events back up the rationale for this strategy and have justified the signifi-cant investment into the major event sphere made since 2010.

In Wellington, prior to WREDA, the portfolio was viewed as a composition of events, rather than a grouping of investment assets (Antchak & Pernecky, 2017). The creation of WREDA has instigated a revision of the portfolio concept towards an Auckland-like strategic approach. Relocation of major events pro-gramming under the jurisdiction of a semi-autonomous organisation could lead to the development of certain outcomes and evaluation criteria that major events would need to meet in order to be included in the portfolio.

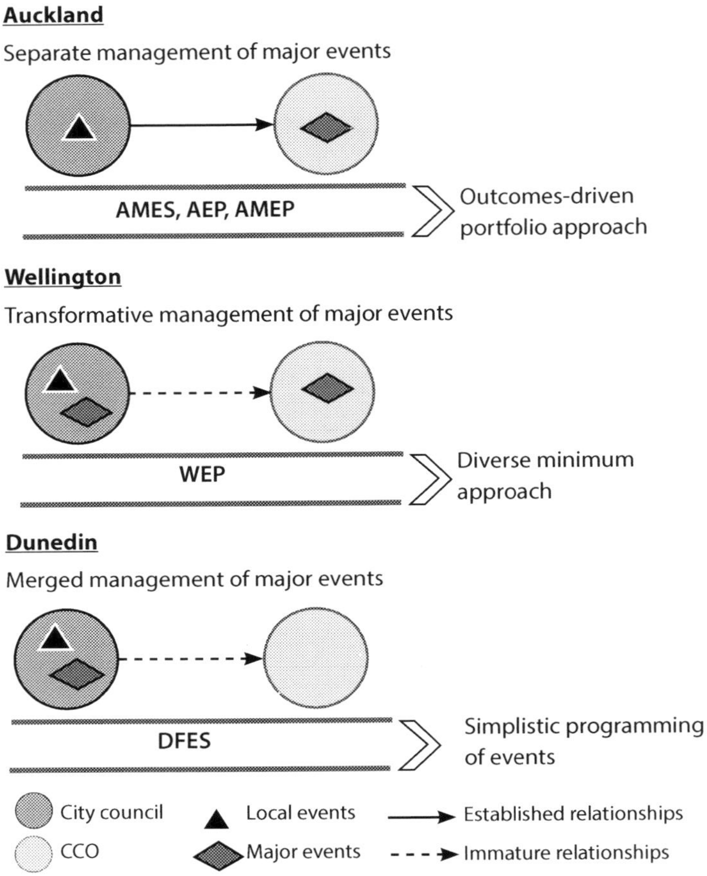

Auckland

Separate management of major events

AMES, AEP, AMEP   →   Outcomes-driven portfolio approach

Wellington

Transformative management of major events

WEP   →   Diverse minimum approach

Dunedin

Merged management of major events

DFES   →   Simplistic programming of events

City council   ▲ Local events   ——→ Established relationships
CCO   ◆ Major events   - - -→ Immature relationships

Figure 8.2: Organisational and public policy arrangements in major events sphere in Auckland, Wellington and Dunedin.

In spite of funding and other resource limitations, the city event planners were capable of constructing an original and competitive programme of major events, which covered diverse themes and met the expectations of the local community. The changes in the institutional and organisational structures of the city may affect the 'diverse minimum' approach, which was discovered in Wellington (Antchak & Pernecky, 2017). One of the benefits for the major events sector and the city's portfolio could be the creation of an Auckland-like 'one stop-shop environment' where events will be treated as an element of joint city strategies to increase the economic and tourism prosperity of the city.

In Dunedin, where major events were planned and delivered together with other local and regional events, a portfolio semantically referred to the overall programme of events (Antchak & Pernecky, 2017). Although the city event planners understood the value of the portfolio-style event programming, this concept has not yet been utilised. Enterprise Dunedin was expected to play a more active role in major events management in order to facilitate the inclusion of events into the sphere of the city economic development. The current approach to major events programming in Dunedin was an as ad-hoc strategy. A lack of sufficient funds and the reactive way of the Council's intervention into the event industry called for a revision of the current event policy and the city government's role in the process of event planning and development. A recently presented Festival and Events Plan can provide a platform for a new approach to major events in this city.

The overall process of event portfolio planning in Auckland, Wellington and Dunedin is summarised in Figure 8.3.

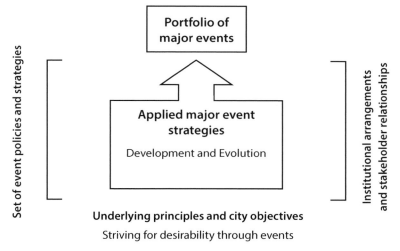

Figure 8.3: Developing a portfolio approach to major events: Key elements.

The process of strategic planning rests on the underlying principles or layers that stem from the contextual variability in the destinations. The general principle that has emerged from the discussion in this chapter is the cities' determination to enhance and promote their desirable image and competitive identity through hosting major events of national and international significance.

A clearly formulated and city vision paves the way to the process of major events legitimisation and the creation of an appropriate institutional structure in the destinations. Legitimisation is accomplished through the creation of city event strategies and policies. Strategies and policies clarify the importance of events and their contribution to the economic and socio-cultural development of the destinations. They guide the processes of major event planning, selection and development.

The existence of a general strategic vision on how capitalise on major events affects the conditions of the operational environment in the host cities. The relationship between key players in the event industry starts to take a more strategic orientation. Usually a new institution that is responsible for major events is created. The idea that lies behind the establishment of such agencies is to create a one-stop-shop for all major events. These organisations take the role of a key negotiator, regulator and partner in the local events industry.

The realisation of the portfolio approach to major events may take different forms. The spectrum of possible variations includes a strategically formulated outcome-driven approach in Auckland, a diverse minimum strategy in Wellington that guarantees the delivery of a substantial minimum of major events, and a more ad-hoc approach in Dunedin where the decision to host a major event is taken from a short-term 'easy to do' perspective. The application of the portfolio approach includes an evolutionary phase of revision.

Summary

To sum up, the contextual environment played a critical role in major events portfolio planning and managements in the cities under study. Different levels and stages of its development affected the strategic perspectives of event portfolios, the realisation of portfolio objectives and overall growth of local event industry. The degree to which the explored institutional structures and policy frameworks affect the foundation of portfolio approaches in the cities depends on the organisational arrangements and availability of written regulations, rules and protocols. Portfolio of major events can be viewed as a continually-developing product of the utilisation of different portfolio approaches in a destination. Different approaches influence the objectives of a host destination and the overall focus of the portfolio towards, for example, cultural or sporting events. They affect the nature, planning and design patterns of the current event portfolio. The change of paradigm in the approach inevitably affects the portfolio structure and expected results.

References

Antchak, V. (2017). Portfolio of major events in Auckland: characteristics, perspectives and issues. *Journal of Policy Research in Tourism, Leisure and Events*, **9** (3), 280-297. doi:10.1080/19407963.2017.1312421

Antchak, V., & Pernecky, T. (2017). Major events programming in a City: Comparing three approaches to portfolio design. *Event Management, 21* (5), 545-561. doi:10.3727/152599517X15053272359013

ATEED. (2018). *Auckland major events strategy*. Retrieved from https://www.aucklandnz.com/sites/build_auckland/files/media-library/documents/Auckland-Major-Events-Strategy-October-2018.pdf

ATEED. (2011). *Auckland's major events strategy*. Auckland, New Zealand Retrieved from http://businessaucklandnz.com/resources/MajorEventsStrategy.pdf

ATEED. (2013). *Auckland's major events protocol.* Retrieved from http://www. aucklandnz.com/images/uploads/page_images/Major_Events_Protocol_2013. pdf

ATEED. (2014). *Statement of intent for Auckland tourism events and economic development Ltd. (ATEED) 2014-2017.* Auckland, New Zealand Retrieved from http://www.aucklandcouncil.govt.nz/EN/AboutCouncil/ representativesbodies/CCO/Documents/ateedstatementofintent20142017.pdf

ATEED. (2015). *Top results for Auckland's non-stop 2014/15 year of events.* Retrieved from www.sportbusiness.com/top-results-auckland%E2%80%99s-non -stop-201415-year-events

aucklandnz.com (n.d.). *Tourism sector: Bold plans for a thriving industry.* Retrieved from http://www.aucklandnz.com/invest/tourism-sector

Dunedin City Council. (2009). Dunedin festival and events strategy, 2009- 2019. Retrieved from https://www.dunedin.govt.nz/__data/assets/pdf_ file/0004/132754/Events-Festival-Strategy-2009_11.pdf

Dunedin City Council. (2012). Dunedin economic development strategy: By Dunedin, for Dunedin and beyond 2013-2023. Retrieved from https://www. dunedin.govt.nz/__data/assets/pdf_file/0008/262997/Dunedins-Economic- Development-Strategy-2013-2023.pdf

Dunedin City Council (2018) Festivals and Events Plan 2018-2023. Retrieved from https://www.dunedin.govt.nz/__data/assets/pdf_file/0004/132754/ Dunedin-Festival-and-Events-Plan-2018-2023.pdf

Dunedin City Council (2018) Festivals and Events Plan 2018-2023. Retrieved from https://www.dunedin.govt.nz/__data/assets/pdf_file/0004/132754/ Dunedin-Festival-and-Events-Plan-2018-2023.pdf

dunedin.govt.nz (n.d). *Enterprise Dunedin taking shape.* Retrieved from http://www.dunedin.govt.nz/your-council/latest-news/june-2014/ enterprise-dunedin-taking-shape

Lonely Planet (2011). Lonely Planet's top 10 cities for 2011. Retrieved from https://www.lonelyplanet.com/travel-tips-and-articles/ lonely-planets-top-10-cities-for-2011/40625c8c-8a11-5710-a052-1479d2773094

Mercer (2014). Mercer quality of living rankings. Retrieved from https://www. uk.mercer.com/newsroom/2014-quality-of-living-survey.html

Mercer (2015). Mercer quality of living rankings. Retrieved from https://www. uk.mercer.com/newsroom/2015-quality-of-living-survey.html

Mercer (2018). Mercer quality of living rankings. Retrieved from https://www. mercer.com/newsroom/2018-quality-of-living-survey.html

Ministry of Business Innovation and Employment. (2012). *New Zealand core cities: Research summary.* Wellington, New Zealand Retrieved from http://www. med.govt.nz/sectors-industries/regions-cities/pdf-docs-library/core-cities- research/Core%20Cities%20Research%20Summary.pdf

Ministry of Economic Development of New Zealand. (2007). *Operation of the major events development fund: Evaluation report.* Retrieved from http://www. majorevents.govt.nz/pdf-library/nz-major-events/strategy-documents/ evaluation-Major-Events-development-fund-2007.pdf

Statistics New Zealand. (2013). *QuickStats about Wellington region*. Retrieved from www.stats.govt.nz/Census/2013-census/profile-and-summary-reports/quickstats-about-a-place.aspx?request_value=14322&tabname=&sc_device=pdf

Statistics New Zealand. (2014). *Regional gross domestic product: Year ended March 2014*. Retrieved from http://www.stats.govt.nz/browse_for_stats/economic_indicators/NationalAccounts/RegionalGDP_HOTPYeMar14.aspx

Wellington City Council. (2003). *Wellington city council event strategy*. Retrieved from http://wellington.govt.nz/~/media/your-council/plans-policies-and-bylaws/plans-and-policies/a-to-z/eventstrategy/files/2003events.pdf

Wellington City Council. (2012). *Wellington Events Policy*. Retrieved from http://wellington.govt.nz/~/media/your-council/plans-policies-and-bylaws/plans-and-policies/a-to-z/eventspolicy/files/2012-05events.pdf

wellingtonnz.com (n/d). *The coolest little capital in the world*. Retrieved from http://www.wellingtonnz.com/media/media-backgrounders/the-coolest-little-capital-in-the-world/

WREDA. (2015). *The Wellington Future. Statement of intent 2015-2018*. Retrieved from http://wellington.govt.nz/~/media/your-council/WREDA/wreda-soi.pdf

9 Event Portfolios and Cultural Exhibitions in Canberra and Melbourne

Valentina Gorchakova

The sustainable development of an event portfolio requires a synergy between the different types of events included in it. The pool of events that are commonly used by city event planners and destination marketers usually revolve around major sport events, cultural festivals and celebrations, and world trade expositions. Some cities, however, also attract and stage international touring exhibitions that bring together a collection of rare art works, significant cultural objects, or memorabilia to tour a limited number of destinations.

In this chapter, major events such as international touring exhibitions will be explored as key components of portfolios of events in Canberra and Melbourne. The chapter discusses the different ways event and tourism planners in Canberra and Melbourne have been approaching major touring exhibitions, and the specific roles these events can play in delivering a balanced and successful portfolio. It will be demonstrated that the decision making around events and event portfolio composition needs to be considered within a wider context, in the light of the city's geography and demographics, as well as political, social and cultural factors.

An exploratory qualitative research was conducted in Canberra and Melbourne, Australia. The primary data was collected from 12 semi-structured interviews with managers and executives in tourism and major events planning in both cities, as well as managers and curators of the cultural institutions that had hosted major touring exhibitions. The secondary data included a range of documents pertinent to the cities' tourism and major events policy and strategy, existing research about touring exhibitions, and websites and articles in the mass media. In the chapter, examples of past major exhibitions are given.

Major touring international exhibitions

Major touring exhibitions, often referred to as 'major international exhibitions' or 'blockbuster exhibitions', represent collections of art works and objects that are brought together under a specific topic or theme to travel outside of their place of permanent exhibition. These exhibitions have been hosted by many cultural institutions around the world but have not often been discussed in the events literature. The nature of major international exhibitions, however, is one of a special event (Gorchakova, 2017) – they are hosted for a limited period of time, attract tourists, raise awareness of the host city, offer a social experience and are out of the ordinary occurrences (Jago & Shaw, 1998). These events can play an important role in tourism both in the short- and long-term perspectives. As a 'must-see' attraction, they draw significant number of visitors over a relatively short period of time and can contribute to the host city's image and profile, and enhance the events portfolio of a city.

A portfolio of events can help in the achievement of synergy between otherwise unrelated events and in leveraging their benefits (Costa & Ziakas, 2011). It can also foster collaboration within a network of stakeholders and sustain the outcomes of events that singly may be short-term or ephemeral (Ziakas, 2014). Event portfolios cannot be considered outside of the wider socio-economic, political and geographical contexts of the cities where they are being developed. In fact, these considerations play an important role in the decision-making of destination marketers and major events planners, and eventually affect the composition of portfolios of major events – as will be shown in the next section: An overview of the city contexts.

There are, however, other effects on the major events portfolio in a city. These effects, which include variety, orientation, seasonality and uniqueness, are discussed further in the chapter, with examples drawn from Canberra and Melbourne where major touring exhibitions have been hosted over a number of years as part of those cities' event portfolios.

An overview of the city contexts

Australian Capital Territory (ACT) is located within the state of New South Wales, and is a self-governing internal territory in Australia. Canberra is located in this territory and is its urban centre. Canberra has been the capital city of Australia since 1913. The Australian Capital Territory Legislative Assembly acts as both a city council and territory government. The choice of a place for the capital was defined by a dispute over this role between Melbourne (the capital of the Victoria state) and Sydney (the capital of the New South Wales state). A consensus was reached, and the capital was built in New South Wales, 170 miles (280 km) away from Sydney, and 410 miles (660 km) away from Melbourne.

Canberra is close to Sydney, and relatively close to Melbourne – the two larg-est Australian cities – and these are the sources for Canberra's domestic tourism. A tourism study (Tourism Research Australia, 2017a) found that more than a half of all domestic overnight visitors to Canberra come from NSW and the state of Victoria. There are more than 15 flights daily from Melbourne to Canberra and more than 20 from Sydney, with a flight time of 55 minutes from Sydney and 1 hour 5 minutes from Melbourne. The flight connections make travelling to Canberra from the states of New South Wales and Victoria a relatively easy task, which is a favourable attribute of the geographical context. Overall, 4.7 million domestic tourists, both those staying overnight and coming on a day trip, and 249,000 international overnight visitors, visited Canberra in the year ending June 2018 (Visit Canberra, 2018).

The estimated resident population of ACT as of June 3, 2018 was over 420,902 people, which is the second strongest growth in estimated resident population of all jurisdictions in Australia (ACT Government, 2018). The average salary in the ACT is A$94,224, while the full-time earnings in Australia average A$82,436 a year (Australian Bureau of Statistics, n.d.). According to the AMP.NATSEM report (Cassells Duncan, Abello, D'Souza, & Nepal, 2012), ACT residents are highly educated – 78% of 25-43 year olds and 80% of those aged between 35-44 hold a higher education qualification, with 25% holding a bachelor's degree, above the national average of 17%; they also are twice as likely to hold a post-graduate qualification – about 9% of the total surveyed population, as opposed to the rest of Australia at 4.5%. The Australian National University in Canberra ranks second in the country and is in the top 50 in the world (Times Higher Education, n.d.) and counts six Nobel Laureates among staff and alumni – more than any other Australian university.

Many cultural and political institutions are located in Canberra, such as the Parliament, the Australian War Memorial, the National Gallery of Australia, the National Portrait Gallery, the National Library, the National Archives, the Australian National Botanic Gardens, and the National Zoo and Aquarium. As a result, there is a strong sense of the national capital role the city is destined to play. The idea of 'being of service' for the country and its residents stands out in most of the communications – both in person and in the city's strategic documents. Canberra is called 'the Home of the Australian story' (Visit Can-berra, n.d.-a), and the variety of institutions of national significance makes the city rather unique.

Melbourne is the fastest-growing city in Australia due to both internal and overseas migration (Royall, 2015). It is more than ten times bigger than Canberra – in 2018 the population hit 5 million people (Population Australia, n.d.) and the city may become the largest in the country by 2028 (Longbottom & Knight, 2018). In the year ending December 2017, Melbourne welcomed 2.7 million inter-national visitors and 9.3 million domestic overnight visitors (Destination Mel-bourne, 2018).

The population of Melbourne is ethnically diverse, with at least one parent of 58% of its residents born overseas (State Government of Victoria, 2016). Melbournians are also well-educated – 73% of those aged 25-34 and 69% of 35-44 year olds have higher education (Cassells et al., 2012). The University of Melbourne and Monash University rank first and fifth respectively in Australia's top 10 universities, and both feature in the top 100 in the Times Higher Education's World Rankings 2019, making the city a desirable place to study for both domestic and international students.

Melbourne has received numerous recognitions over the past 10 years. Melbourne was awarded the Ultimate Sports City award in 2006, 2008 and 2010. The city was the winner of 'SportBusiness Ultimate Sports City at 10 Anniversary Award', Best Large Sports City and Best Venues in 2016, having been acknowledged as the city with the greatest impact in the decade (SportBusiness Group, 2016). In 2011-2017, for a record seven years in a row, Melbourne won 'the most liveable city in the world' award, according to The Economist Intelligence Unit's (EIU) Liveability Index (The Economist, n.d.).

Melbourne is famous for its vibrant arts and cultural life, delivered across different locations in the city, including museums, theatres, and arts centres, as well as Australia's largest concentration of live music venues (Visit Victoria, n.d.). The well-known laneway culture, including bars, restaurants and street art, is also part of the city, and is now taken for granted as part of the city's modern identity (Quinn, 2017). Local residents were described by the interviewees of this study as active events-participants, those who engage with and get involved in the various types of special events run in the city.

Managing portfolios of events

Major events are well-known for their contribution to destination awareness and brand enhancement; they create an urgency to 'visit now', promoting the visitor economy of the host city. Therefore, destination marketing, or destination management, organisations (DMOs), are often in charge of portfolios of major events in a city. In both Canberra and Melbourne, their respective DMOs are involved in the creation and management of their portfolios of events. The management may involve financial or non-financial types of support in bidding, organising, and promoting events.

Canberra's DMO, Visit Canberra, creates and implements marketing and development programmes to increase the benefits from tourism (Visit Canberra, n.d.-b). Visit Canberra administers the ACT Special Event Fund (ACT SEF), which can be used to fund the marketing of an event that "has the ability to attract significant interstate and international visitation and focus positive national and international attention on the ACT" (Visit Canberra, n.d.-c). The funding is available to event organisers and local cultural institutions, provided that the amount requested from the ACT SEF is met on 'a minimum dollar for dollar' basis. This ensures an equal partnership between the DMO and the ben-efitting organisation in marketing.

Visit Canberra has recognised the potential appeal of major cultural exhibitions for the visitor economy, and continues to invest in them through the ACT SEF in order to broaden the events portfolio of the city (Visit Canberra, 2015). This marketing funding was first used to support the *Masterpieces from Paris* exhibition in the National Gallery of Australia in 2009, when it had not yet been established as a permanent fund. The number of tourists who came to see the exhibition, however, was so impressive that it was decided to keep the fund and provide grants on an annual basis to stimulate event tourism in the region. According to the ACT Government, blockbuster exhibitions "have delivered outstanding return on investment for the Canberra region. The ACT Government has invested A$1.2 m. in 5 blockbuster exhibitions since 2009 delivering A$260 m. in economic value to the city" (Visit Canberra, 2014, p. 24).

However, it is not only the economic benefits that have prompted Canberra's DMO to invest in major events. Due to housing the National Parliament and other political institutions, Canberra developed a reputation which was very much associated with politics. As the previous section outlined, the city originally played an important role as the national capital, linking it more to political decision-making and rhetoric, than to an exciting place to visit. As a result, it was not considered by Australians as an attractive destination to go to, especially not several times. Therefore, from a marketing perspective, it was critical to find ways to shift this perception. In terms of international tourists, it was important, first of all, to put Canberra on the map, as there was little awareness of the city across the world. The efforts must have been successful, as the city was named third best city in the world to visit in 2018 by Lonely Planet. Special events appear to have contributed to this highest ever listing of an Australian city in the publication: "There's a lot of events that are actually going to be staged in 2018 which makes it a perfect excuse for us to be able to highlight Canberra as a destination for people to come to", said Lonely Planet's spokesperson Chris Zeiher (Nguyen, 2017).

In Melbourne, too, major events, including major exhibitions, are conceived of by tourism marketers as important drawcards to drive visitation: "Events are a significant part of Victoria's tourism offering and will continue to be supported by the Victorian Government in Melbourne and regional Victoria" (State Government of Victoria, 2013, p. 18). In Melbourne, two organisations can be considered as DMOs: Visit Victoria, the state's tourism and major events company, and Destination Melbourne, a Greater Melbourne destination marketing organisation, that markets Melbourne across the state of Victoria. Since 2016, Visit Victoria has been an organisation that provides support to major touring exhibitions hosted in Melbourne. Previously, the Victorian Major Events Company and Tourism Victoria were involved – the former assisted a cultural institution to secure a major exhibition, and the latter to promote it outside of Melbourne.

The Melbourne Winter Masterpieces series of major touring exhibitions has been held in the city since 2004. The key objectives of this programme are associated with attracting tourists during winter months and offering local residents an opportunity "to experience exclusive art exhibitions of the highest international standards" (Creative Victoria, n.d.-a). In 2004-2017, 22 blockbuster exhibitions were organised under the Winter Masterpieces umbrella. Between 2004 and 2013, more than 4 million people were "a part of the Melbourne Winter Masterpieces story" (Victorian Major Events Company, n.d., p. 50).

In response to the 2017 award, the Victoria State Government issued a media release that praised its education, healthcare, and transportation system, but also referred to the exhibitions and other major events as contributors to the city's recognised quality of life: "There's a buzz about the city that keeps bringing the world's best to enjoy Melbourne – the biggest exhibitions, the best events, world-renowned restaurants and all night public transport to get you home safe" (Victoria State Government, 2017).

The next section shows examples of major international exhibitions hosted in both cities and looks into the various roles they have played in the respective portfolios of major events.

Contribution of major international exhibitions to a city event portfolio

There are different types of major international exhibitions that tour to one or several locations across the world. They can present collections of works of art of a particular artist or from a specific era, or various objects of cultural value and public interest, as well as memorabilia from famous 'blockbuster' movies. Major touring exhibitions contribute to a balanced portfolio of events in four directions: by adding to the variety of events; by supporting tourism in a season when additional incentives are required; by meeting the needs of both local residents and tourists; and, finally, by adding an element of uniqueness to the overall portfolio, for example by requesting exclusive rights to host an exhibition (Figure 9.1).

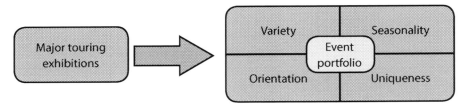

Figure 9.1: Contribution of major international exhibitions to an event portfolio.

Variety

Throughout the year, Canberra's major event portfolio comprises a wide range of events of different kinds, aimed at different audiences. There are international and local sports, arts, and community events, food and wine fests, entertainment, and events aimed at remembering the past. International touring exhibitions are some of those events in the portfolio. For example, the 2016-2017 portfolio of major events included *A History of the World in 100 Objects from the British Museum* presented at the National Museum of Australia and *Versailles: Treasures from the Palace* hosted by the National Gallery of Australia.

Whilst major international exhibitions naturally add to the variety of the overall portfolio through enhancing its cultural dimension, the diverse profiles of these exhibitions have contributed significantly to the variety of the cultural events organised, as the examples below demonstrate.

One of the long-term priorities of the National Gallery of Australia (NGA) is to present international blockbuster exhibitions of the world's finest art (National Gallery of Australia, 2015). *Masterpieces from Paris*, the most visited international exhibition at the NGA yet, brought 112 of some of the best-known post-impressionist artworks from the Musee d'Orsay in Paris, including Van Gogh, Gauguin, and Cezanne. *The Turner from the Tate* exhibition featured 110 works by Turner, including his most famous painting, as well as works never previously shown. *The Gold and the Incas: Lost Worlds of Peru* presented more than 200 works of Peruvian ancient art. *Versailles: Treasures From the Palace* featured more than 130 objects from the Versailles palace, including paintings, sculptures, tapestries, furniture, and personal items from the kings, their wives, and mistresses, with some of the objects having never previously toured outside France (Pryor, 2016).

The National Library of Australia (NLA) is a unique example of a library initiating and pursuing the hosting of international exhibitions, having created a temporary gallery for touring exhibitions. NLA first brought in a major exhibition in 2001 to mark its 100-year anniversary. *Treasures from the World's Great Libraries* presented exhibits – original manuscripts material – borrowed from 32 major libraries around the world, and it was clearly highly successful. The exhibition included such rare and highly delicate items as a Dead Sea Scroll, a Gutenberg Bible, a Beethoven manuscript, and letters written by Gandhi, Florence Nightingale, and Charles Darwin (ABC news, 2001), and it attracted 115,000 visitors, "many of whom queued around the National Library in Canberra day and night" (National Library of Australia, 2014).

NLA has hosted major international exhibitions on a two-year cycle since 2011. These included *Handwritten: Ten Centuries of Manuscript Treasures* from the Berlin State Library, *Mapping our World: Terra Incognita to Australia* – showing some rare cartographic objects from the world's map collections, and *Celestial Empire: Life in China 1644-1911,* an exhibition of some exquisite objects from the National Library of China.

The mandate of being a *national* institution is strongly taken into account by NGA and NLA when selecting a special touring exhibition. The criteria include not only featuring rare and high-quality exhibits, but the exhibitions must also fit the purpose and mission of the organisation, support its respective brand, and reflect well on the permanent collections, and support organisational objectives.

In Melbourne, the portfolio of major events is a mix of sporting and cultural events of various scales: from more locally-orientated festivals to the events attracting visitors from all over the world, such as the Australian Open and the F1 Grand Prix. Major international exhibitions, mostly presented as part of the Melbourne Winter Masterpieces series, have been part of the portfolio since 2004 and have been hosted at three cultural institutions of different profiles. These institutions are: the National Gallery of Victoria, the Melbourne Museum, and the Australian Centre for the Moving Image.

The National Gallery of Victoria (NGV) hosted a 'blockbuster' exhibition in 2013 – *Monet's Garden: The Musée Marmottan Monet, Paris*, showcasing more than 50 masterpieces by the French Impressionist Claude Monet and attracting 342,788 visitors (National Gallery of Victoria, 2014a). During 2014-2015, the Gallery hosted two major international exhibitions: *Italian Masterpieces from Spain's Royal Court, Museo del Prado*, arguably the finest collection of Italian masterpieces ever to come to Australia (National Gallery of Victoria, 2014b), and *The Fashion World of Jean Paul Gaultier: From the Sidewalk to the Catwalk,* with more than 140 garments and stage costumes – from the first dress created by the designer in 1971 to his latest collections – costumes worn by Kylie Minogue and Beyoncé, and haute couture dresses worn by Nicole Kidman.

Melbourne Museum is a multi-disciplinary public museum operated by Museums Victoria. During 2009-2011, the Museum hosted a series of major international exhibitions: *A Day in Pompeii* – an exhibition of ancient Roman artefacts, filled with interactive display and events; *Titanic: The Artefact Exhibition*, presenting the artefacts from the ship; and *Tutankhamun and the Golden Age of the Pharaohs*, a collection of artefacts from the Cairo Museum. Attendance reached unprecedented visitor numbers of 333,000, 481,000 and 796,277 people respectively (Australian Leisure Management, 2011). Since the *Tutankhamun* exhibition, there have not been any more exhibitions of that scale. One of the reasons is that the museum's image became a bit diluted by exhibitions with a stronger entertainment element rather than a scholarly account of the topics.

Australian Centre for the Moving Image (ACMI) is a unique cultural institution in Melbourne, in that it is neither a traditional type of museum, nor an art gallery, while at the same time it spans definitions of both of those. ACMI's highest attended international touring exhibition was *Tim Burton: The Exhibition* that presented over 700 works from The Museum of Modern Art (MoMA), New York, in 2010. Another major exhibition, hosted in 2013 from the Victoria and Albert Museum (London), *The Hollywood Costumes*, showcased iconic film costumes from over a century of film history, from such classics as *Gone with the Wind*, *Breakfast at Tiffany's* and *Ben-Hur* to more recent blockbusters such as *Titanic* and *Casino Royale*. In 2015, *David Bowie Is* featured objects and some of the legendary costumes of the famous artist, his handwritten lyric sheets, album artwork, rare film, video, and photographs (Premier of Victoria, 2015). These exhibitions fit the ACMI profile well, and they also contributed to the variety of cultural exhibitions in the city.

Orientation

Events may be aimed at driving visitors to the city (visitation-driver events) or may be aimed at pursuing community and social goals (community-oriented events) through bringing vibrancy and community pride. In Canberra, major touring exhibitions have an external, tourism orientation, as well as an internal, local residents, orientation.

Over a four-month period, the *Masterpieces from Paris* exhibition at the NGA welcomed 470,000 visitors, 80% of whom were tourists coming from other states or from overseas (Tourism Research Australia & Australian Capital Tourism, 2012). The ACT Government estimated that the economic impact of this exhibition was A$95 million (Tourism Research Australia & Australian Capital Tourism, 2012). *The Turner from the Tate* exhibition attracted 153,627 visitors from across Australia, with almost 70% being interstate tourists, injecting an estimated A$34 million into the ACT economy (National Gallery of Australia, 2013). Similarly, the *Gold and the Incas: Lost Worlds of Peru* exhibition was visited by 160,647 people, almost 68% of whom travelled from interstate, contributing an estimated A$33.5 million into the ACT economy (National Gallery of Australia, 2014). These figures look particularly impressive in the light of the fact that the population of Canberra has only recently exceeded 400,000 residents.

The tourism development in Canberra is to a large extent driven by those coming to visit friends and relatives (VFR) – accounting for 35% of overnights and 21% of day visitors (Tourism Research Australia, 2017b). These figures show the significance of the VFR motive for the domestic tourism in Canberra. In this regard, there are a few characteristics of the Canberra community which appear to be helpful for event planners and tourism marketers. As discussed earlier, local residents are well-educated and in high-paid jobs, overall. Therefore, they tend to have more opportunities to travel and explore different countries and cultures, which may affect their attitude towards events in their home city. Canberrans are positive about the government investing in major events in general and international touring exhibitions in particular, and often invite their friends and relatives who live in other parts of Australia to come when a major event is on.

According to the interviews conducted for this study as well as secondary data (Tourism Research Australia & Australian Capital Tourism, 2012), major touring exhibitions have proven successful both in attracting interstate tourists and in keeping the local residents entertained. Without the former, bringing in high profile exhibitions would not be financially feasible, and without the latter, the Government would not be able to provide necessary support to the cultural institutions that have hosted them. Interestingly, recent research has shown that Canberra residents are among the happiest people in the country, with a high score for community, which is rare for a metropolitan area (Brown, 2018).

In Melbourne, the support of locals encourages the tourism and events bodies to fund such events as major touring exhibitions: "Audiences are sophisticated and educated – yet highly curious and open to new experiences. They value artistic merit, cultural diversity, rich history and entertainment. Melbourne Winter Masterpieces has become a cornerstone of Melbourne's award winning major events calendar" (Victorian Major Events Company, n.d.). One of the key objectives of the Winter Masterpieces programme is to enable local residents to have access to the high calibre international cultural exhibitions, as well as attract domestic tourists and those from the nearest country, New Zealand. Many of the exhibitions have been advertised in the New Zealand mass media. The VFR factor is also prominent in domestic tourism – over 3 million visitors stayed overnight in the city visiting friends and relatives.

The 23 blockbuster exhibitions organised in Melbourne since 2004 as part of the Winter Masterpieces have attracted 5 million visitors, including local, domestic, and international tourists (Visit Victoria, n.d). Between 2004 and 2018, NGV hosted 15 of these exhibitions. The *Van Gogh and the Seasons* exhibition, hosted in 2017 at the NGV, alone generated nearly A$56 million for the Victoria state's economy, attracting 462,262 visitors, thus making it the most popular ticketed exhibition in the gallery's history. The most recent exhibition, *MoMA at NGV: 130 Years of Modern and Contemporary Art*, organised in 2018, was visited by 404,034 visitors in 4 months (NGV, 2018).

The numbers recorded at other major exhibitions are also substantial. ACMI's *David Bowie*, *Tim Burton*, and *Hollywood* costume exhibitions all attracted 200,000 or more visitors (Creative Victoria, n.d.-b; Premier of Victoria, 2015; Weller, 2013). *Italian Masterpieces* from The Prado Museum in the NGV was visited by more than 152,000 visitors, and the *Jean Paul Gaultier* exhibition was attended by more than 226,000 people (National Gallery of Victoria, 2015). The overall attendance at one of the most recent exhibitions at Melbourne Museum from the blockbusters ranks, *Jurassic World: The Exhibition*, in 2016, was 400,000 (Brundrett, 2016).

Although both cities support major international exhibitions that can both attract tourists and cater to the interests of the local residents, the importance of either orientation varies. The number of people living in Canberra is such that an exhibition must be attractive enough for the domestic tourists to come, and its economic viability depends to a large extent on the numbers of visitors from other regions. External orientation of such events is, therefore, strong in the city. Exhibitions in Melbourne, a large city with a multi-million population, are arguably less dependent upon domestic tourists. Although the external orientation is prominent in the promotion of these exhibitions, the major event planners and destination marketers are more flexible in balancing the external and internal orientation of such major events in the portfolio.

Seasonality

Both Canberra's and Melbourne's events portfolios are balanced throughout the year, so that there is something happening in any given season. In Canberra, the event portfolio is filled with major events, particularly in spring and summer. These include such flagship events as Floriade, the largest floral festival in the Southern Hemisphere, sports events, fireworks, family entertainment activities, wine festivals, and cultural events. Major international exhibitions are usually organised during the warmer seasons, too, in order to entice people to come to an inland city, when most would prefer to spend time at the seaside otherwise.

Melbourne is a coastal city, and its major events portfolio includes international events that attract tourists from all over the world, e.g. Formula 1 Australian Grand Prix, Australian Open, and the Emirates Melbourne Cup, along with the locally grown events that include an international film festival, literature festival, fashion, and jazz festivals. Admittedly, few major events of international calibre take place over winter, when it is a general downtime in the tourism sector. The Melbourne Winter Masterpieces programme was created to address this challenge in the event calendar; exhibitions are not contingent on the weather as much as sport events are, and people can stay indoors; consequently, the winter months have been identified as the best time for an annual exhibition event.

Notwithstanding the seasonal nature of tourism, visitation rates in Melbourne seems to be consistent throughout the year – in 2014, each season accounted for 22% to 26% of overnight tourists (Tourism Victoria, 2015). The Victoria State Government believes that events support the even distribution of the tourist flows, "especially during winter when visitation rates would normally decrease" (State Government of Victoria, 2013, p. 8).

Canberra and Melbourne have different seasonality challenges. Initially, for Melbourne, winter was the season that required additional attention from tourism marketers and event planners and, thus, the city set up an annual cultural programme of major international exhibitions in wintertime. Canberra focused its attention on creating pull factors to prompt Australians to come during the summer months, and most of the high profile touring exhibitions have subsequently been hosted in the warmer seasons.

Uniqueness

One of the key characteristics of a major touring exhibition, that both Canberra and Melbourne are looking for, is the exclusive rights to hosting it, being 'the only venue' – at least in Australia and New Zealand. Not only does this exclusivity generate an opportunity to tap into a wider audience through the 'only-in-this-city' message, but it also creates a sense of uniqueness of the experience and a 'must-see' status, which are both helpful in promoting an event. Melbourne was the first city in Australia to start exploring the opportunity to secure the exclusive rights for a touring exhibition with the cultural institutions that were lending their works of art. It was also the first city in Australia to create a specific brand for this type of event, adding yet another layer of uniqueness and reinforcing the event's connectedness to the host city, which resonates through the *Melbourne Winter Masterpieces* title. As a result, the programme has become recognised as "a cornerstone of Melbourne's award winning major events calendar" (Victorian Major Events Company, n.d.).

The logistics, insurance, and often environmental conditions involved in presenting major international exhibitions are very elaborate and require significant resources. Arguably, this also contributes to the uniqueness of the visitors' experience, who are thus getting an opportunity to see an exhibition with rare, fragile and precious objects. Although most touring exhibitions are normally created by the lending institutions, some cultural organisations have started demonstrating increasing interest in co-creating major exhibitions. Thus, NGV developed the *Degas: A New Vision* exhibition, hosted in June – September 2016, over several years, and the former curator of the Louvre and a renowned Degas scholar, Henri Loyrette, was invited specifically to work on this project as its principal curator. *MoMA at NGV: 130 Years of Modern and Contemporary Art* was co-organised and co-curated by the NGV and the Museum of Modern Art (New York). Therefore, some exhibitions may indeed become a one-and-only show outside the cultural institution they belong to.

The cultural institutions in both Canberra and Melbourne are well-known, with impressive collections. For example, the art collections in the NGA contain more than 160,000 works (National Gallery of Australia, n.d.). NGV, Australia's oldest and most visited gallery (National Gallery of Victoria, n.d.), has approximately 70,000 works. Museums Victoria, the country's largest public museum organisation, is looking after the state collection of nearly 17 million objects, documents, photographs and specimens (Museum Victoria, n.d.) whose value is estimated to be A$699 million (Creative Victoria, n.d.-c). Permanent collections, however, do not create an 'urgency to visit' either for tourists, or for locals, to the extent that special events do. It is the unique experiences of major international exhibitions that are capable of significantly increasing the awareness of what cultural institutions that host them have to offer. The exhibitions, in the longer term, help to raise the host institution's own profile as relevant and popular, increasing the membership base and repeat visitation. Supporting them, the host cities also seek image- or awareness-related benefits, apart from the overnight stays and tourist spending.

The role of major exhibitions in an event portfolio

A balanced event portfolio can enrich a destination's tourism product, strengthen or alter its image, and help deal with seasonality (Ziakas, 2014). Event portfolios in Canberra and Melbourne are conceived as a programme or calendar of events that are selected by city event policy planners in accordance with the city's event agenda and objectives. The portfolios of Canberra and Melbourne comprise a wide variety of events organised and hosted in these cities. Westerbeek and Linley (2012) suggest that a strong event portfolio may be important in generating long-lasting positive impressions about a city and its image. Melbourne positions itself as a city that is "always packed with arts festivals, live music, exhibitions, blockbuster theatre shows, sport and activities for kids" (City of Melbourne, n.d.). The research data demonstrate that when considering the financial support of an exhibition, destination marketers and event planners are taking into account not only the tangible economic outcomes of exhibitions – although these tend to be critical – but also, the less tangible effects, such as enhancing the city's brand image and international profile, which are regarded as significant.

In both cities, major touring exhibitions are part of these cities' portfolios of major events. The Australian Capital Territory's DMO, Visit Canberra, considers touring blockbuster exhibitions as major events that can draw domestic tourists to Canberra and encourage them to explore the city's other attractions. These exhibitions in Canberra are normally scheduled for a warmer period of the year, covering the weeks around Christmas and attracting families that travel during the Christmas holidays. At the same time, the portfolio does not offer many exciting events over the colder winter months, which may need to be addressed in due course.

The *Melbourne Winter Masterpieces* programme of major exhibitions has become an intrinsic part of the event portfolio of Melbourne. The programme is deliberately scheduled for winter months to add appeal to event tourism during the time when weather-dependent events may not be as attractive. The integrity of a portfolio of events can arguably be understood in terms of portfolio balance, scheduling, and leveraging of events (Antchak, 2016). Major sport and cultural events complement each other in Melbourne's event portfolio, and the city's so-called 'menu of experiences' seem to be carefully orchestrated. It may be suggested that the strategic and consistent policy in attracting both major cultural and sporting events has been productive and effective for the city in terms of supporting its tourism offering and image.

The case of Melbourne demonstrates that major events can not only be included in the portfolio, but also be managed as a portfolio themselves. It may be sensible to talk specifically about a portfolio of cultural events in a destination (Soldo, Arnaud, & Keramidas, 2013), and the Melbourne Masterpieces series constitutes a successful example of a portfolio of cultural events, specifically, major touring exhibitions. This 'portfolio within a portfolio' includes events that are hosted by cultural institutions with different profiles, contributing to the diversity and uniqueness of experiences that appeal to a wide range of audiences.

Managing a portfolio of major events, as well as the series of major international exhibitions, clearly requires a high level of cooperation between all the stakeholders. In regard to the major exhibitions, the research has shown that the cultural institutions are an intrinsic part of the network of stakeholders. It is important to recognise the role that various organisations, including newspapers, radio stations, television partners, the City of Melbourne Council, tourism and events bodies, and potential sponsors, played in the organisation and marketing of the first major exhibition hosted within the *Melbourne Winter Masterpieces* series in 2004. Bringing together partners from various industries and with different expertise to this major cultural event generated a productive environment for cooperation and benefitted both the event and its stakeholders, forming longer-term trust between all the parties involved.

Tourism and event planners in Canberra are looking into the possibility of establishing a more long-term planning and funding scheme for events, instead of the current one-year cycle. This would mean more opportunities for engagement with the businesses working in the tourism industry, including hotels and airlines, as well as better planning and resource allocation for the local DMO. Switching to, for example, a three- or four-year funding cycle would also mean that the institutions would be able to plan for a few years ahead, building their programmes, including major international exhibitions, on more stable and clear funding arrangements. There are clear signs that the approach of tourism and event planners in the city is shifting towards a more holistic view of events. It calls, however, for a certain degree of transparency and trust between stakeholders, which is essential for sharing plans and ideas, and in practice this has not been easy to achieve. At the time the research was conducted, it appeared that the city's cultural institutions had been somewhat cautious about revealing their projects, possibly at times seeing each other as competitors rather than partners.

Touring exhibitions can arguably be beneficial for portfolios of major events (Antchak, 2017; Gorchakova, 2017). The presence of high-profile international exhibitions in event portfolios as regular, recurrent major events can be advantageous to the cities' wider marketing, tourism, and internal agendas. The cases of Canberra and Melbourne show that major exhibitions benefit from being part of the city's portfolios, too, due to the fact that a portfolio allows synergy to be produced between events, can enhance collaboration between the stakeholders, and can sustain the outcomes that may otherwise be short-term (Costa & Ziakas, 2011; Ziakas, 2014). The event portfolio composition also reflects the thinking of policy planners and tourism marketers regarding events' roles and orientation (Antchak, 2016). It is suggested that both Australian cities have formed a vision of the role these cultural events as a phenomenon play in their agenda, rather than ad-hoc events organised by different cultural institutions.

Both cities show the value of local residents' profiles and attitudes for the success of major events. Their propensity and eagerness to participate in events encourages local institutions and organisations to deliver a variety of experiences, resulting in more high-profile exhibitions that locals invite their friends and relatives from other states of the country to attend. The vibrancy and saturation of the event portfolio with outstanding events that drive visitation appears to create more opportunities for hosting more events in the future, developing a momentum of event attendance. This has been the case with major touring exhibitions, in particular in Melbourne, where their contribution to the major events portfolio in general, and its cultural part in particular, has yielded remarkable results. In Canberra, it is acknowledged that major touring exhibitions can contribute to "a cultural feast" in the city (Visit Canberra, n.d.-a), and also facilitate friends and families to meet, relax, and connect (Visit Canberra, n.d.-d).

It is argued that city event portfolios may benefit from major international exhibitions and that a strong event portfolio contributes to generating a desirable image of the host city (Westerbeek & Linley, 2012). The collective impact of the quality event programme eventually drives visitation (Richards & Palmer, 2010), therefore contributing not only to short-term goals associated with the rise in tourist numbers, but to more long-lasting marketing effects for the host city.

Summary

The chapter discussed findings from research conducted in two Australian cities. The portfolios of major events in Canberra and Melbourne are full of events of various types and scales and are aimed at both meeting the needs of local residents and attracting tourists. There are four major ways that international exhibitions can contribute to the city portfolio of events: by adding to the variety of events in general and the variety of cultural events in particular; by attracting tourists during lower tourism seasons; by meeting the needs and responding to the interests of the local residents as well as those of city visitors; and by creating unique, once-in-a-lifetime experiences. Cultural events, such as high-profile touring exhibitions, can form and be managed as a portfolio within an overall portfolio of events in the city. This requires close collaboration between the state and city stakeholders, as well as between the cultural and the corporate sector.

References

ABC news. (2001). *Treasures at the Library*, Dec 3. Retrieved from www.abc.net. au/radionational/programs/latenightlive/treasures-at-the-library/3499726

ACT Government. (2018). *Estimated Resident Population — June Quarter 2018*. Retrieved from https://apps.treasury.act.gov.au/__data/assets/pdf_ file/0008/644813/ERP.pdf/_recache

Antchak, V. (2016). *Event portfolio design: Exploring strategic approaches to major events in New Zealand*. (Doctoral thesis), Auckland University of Technology, Auckland, New Zealand. Retrieved from http://hdl.handle.net/10292/10101 Available from EBSCOhost

Antchak, V. (2017). Portfolio of major events in Auckland: Characteristics, perspectives and issues. *Journal of Policy Research in Tourism, Leisure and Events* **9**(3), 280-297. doi:10.1080/19407963.2017.1312421

Australian Bureau of Statistics. (n.d.). Average Weekly Earnings, Australia, Nov 2018. Retrieved February 6, 2019, from http://www.abs.gov.au/ausstats/abs@. nsf/mf/6302.0

Brown, A. (2018). Canberrans are some of the happiest Aussies - and the data proves it. *The Canberra Times*, Dec 2. Retrieved from https://www. canberratimes.com.au/national/act/canberrans-are-some-of-the-happiest-aussies-and-the-data-proves-it-20181127-p50iqe.html

Brundrett, C. (2016). Jurassic World: The Exhibition closes at Melbourne Museum on Sunday. *Herald Sun*, Sept 29. Retrieved from http://www. heraldsun.com.au/news/victoria/jurassic-world-the-exhibition-closes-at-melbourne-museum-on-sunday/news-story/09f03d6efaa48aaae1929f5a51e0a edf

Cassells, R., Duncan, A., Abello, A., D'Souza, G., & Nepal, B. (2012). *Smart Australians: Education and innovation in Australia*. AMP. NATSEM Income and Wealth Report, Issue 32, Melbourne.

City of Melbourne. (n.d.). *Events*. Retrieved from http://www.thatsmelbourne. com.au/Whatson/Pages/Whatson.aspx

Costa, C. A., & Ziakas, V. (2011). Event portfolio and multi-purpose development: Establishing the conceptual grounds. *Sport Management Review,* **14**(4), 409-423. doi:10.1016/j.smr.2010.09.003

Creative Victoria. (n.d.-a). *Melbourne winter masterpieces*. Retrieved from http://www.arts.vic.gov.au/Projects_Initiatives/Events_and_artworks/ Melbourne_Winter_Masterpieces

Creative Victoria. (n.d.-b). *2010 arts portfolio leadership awards – winners announced*. Retrieved from http://creative.vic.gov.au/News/News/ Archive/Media_Releases/2010/2010_Arts_Portfolio_Leadership_ Awards_%E2%80%93_winners_announced

Creative Victoria. (n.d.-c). *Museums Victoria*. Retrieved from http://creative.vic. gov.au/research/data/state-cultural-organisations/museum-victoria

Destination Melbourne. (2018). *Melbourne tourism summary*. Retrieved from destination.melbourne/news/2018/melbourne-tourism-summary-ye-dec-2017

Gorchakova, V. (2017). *Touring blockbuster exhibitions: Their contribution to the marketing of a city to tourists.* (PhD Doctoral dissertation), AUT University, Auckland, New Zealand.

Jago, L., & Shaw, R. (1998). Special events: A conceptual and definitional framework. *Festival Management & Event Tourism, 5*(1-2), 21-32. doi:10.3727/106527098792186775

Longbottom, J., & Knight, B. (2018). Melbourne's population explosion threatens to create a 'Bangkok situation'. *ABC News*, October 16. Retrieved from www.abc.net.au/news/2018-10-15/melbourne-will -be-australias-biggest-city-which-party-has-policy/10358988

Museum Victoria. (n.d.). *About Museum Victoria.* Retrieved from https:// museumvictoria.com.au/about/

National Gallery of Australia. (2013). *Turner from the Tate: The Making of a Master.* Retrieved from http://nga.gov.au/AboutUs/press/RTF/Turner_MR.rtf

National Gallery of Australia. (2014). *Gold and the Incas: Lost Worlds of Peru.* Retrieved from http://nga.gov.au/AboutUs/press/RTF/Incas_FinalRelease.rtf

National Gallery of Australia. (2015). *NGA Annual Report 2014-2015.* Retrieved from http://nga.gov.au/AboutUs/Reports/NGA_AR_14-15.pdf

National Gallery of Australia. (n.d.). *National Gallery of Australia: Permanent collection.* Retrieved from http://nga.gov.au/Collections/

National Gallery of Victoria. (2014a). *NGV Annual Report 2013/14.* Retrieved from http://www.ngv.vic.gov.au/__data/assets/pdf_file/0004/695038/NGV_ AR_2013_14_ONLINE.pdf

National Gallery of Victoria. (2014b). *Melbourne Winter Masterpieces: Italian Masterpieces from Spain's Royal Court, Museo del Prado.* Retrieved from http:// www.ngv.vic.gov.au/media_release/melbourne-winter-masterpieces-italian- masterpieces-from-spains-royal-court-museo-del-prado/

National Gallery of Victoria. (2015). *NGV Annual Report 2014/15.* Retrieved from https://www.ngv.vic.gov.au/wp-content/uploads/2015/10/NGV-2014-15- Annual-Report.pdf

National Gallery of Victoria. (n.d.). *About the NGV.* Retrieved from http://www. ngv.vic.gov.au/about/

National Library of Australia. (2014). *Mapping our World exhibition breaks NLA record.* Retrieved from https://www.nla.gov.au/media-releases/2014/03/11/ mapping-our-world-exhibition-breaks-nla-record

Nguyen, H. (2017). Canberra named Lonely Planet's third best city in the world to visit in 2018. *The Canberra Times.* Retrieved from https://www. canberratimes.com.au/national/act/canberra-named-lonely-planets-third- best-city-in-the-world-to-visit-in-2018-20171024-gz6xji.html

NGV. (2018). *More than 400,000 visit MoMA at NGV.* Retrieved from https:// www.ngv.vic.gov.au/media_release/more-than-400000-visit-moma-at-ngv/

Population Australia. (n.d.). *Melbourne population 2019.* Retrieved from http:// www.population.net.au/melbourne-population/

Premier of Victoria. (2015). *David Bowie stardust for Victoria's visitor economy*. Retrieved from http://www.premier.vic.gov.au/david-bowie-stardust-for-victorias-visitor-economy-2/

Pryor, S. (2016). Versailles will be on show for the National Gallery of Australia's next summer blockbuster in Canberra. *The Canberra Times*, July 18. Retrieved from http://www.canberratimes.com.au/act-news/canberra-life/the-opulence-and-luxury-of-versailles-will-be-on-show-for-the-national-gallery-of-australias-next-summer-blockbuster-in-canberra-20160718-gq884p.html

Quinn, K. (2017). Laneway culture is the beating heart of Melbourne. But it wasn't always like this. *The Sydney Morning Herald*, March 30. Retrieved from https://www.smh.com.au/opinion/out-of-the-way-industrial-a-little-shabby-how-very-melbourne-20170330-gv9z8f.html

Richards, G., & Palmer, R. (2010). *Eventful Cities: Cultural management and urban revitalisation*. Oxford: Butterworth-Heinemann.

Royall, I. (2015). Booming Melbourne population on track to overtake Sydney. *Herald Sun*, Dec 3. Retrieved from http://www.heraldsun.com.au

Soldo, E., Arnaud, C., & Keramidas, O. (2013). Direct control of cultural events as a means of leveraging the sustainable attractiveness of the territory? Analysis of the managerial conditions for success. *International Review of Administrative Sciences*, **79**(4), 725-746. doi:10.1177/0020852313502154

SportBusiness Group. (2016). *Ultimate sports city 2016*. Retrieved from http://www.sportbusiness.com/sportbusiness-ultimate-sports-cities-awards-2016-new-york-city-triumphs-sportaccord-convention

State Government of Victoria. (2013). *Victoria's 2020 Tourism Strategy*. Retrieved from http://www.tourism.vic.gov.au/component/edocman/?view=document&task=document.download&id=500

State Government of Victoria. (2016). *Greater Melbourne demographics*. Retrieved from http://www.invest.vic.gov.au/resources/statistics/greater-melbourne-demographics

The Economist. (n.d.). *The Global Liveability Index*. Retrieved from https://www.eiu.com/topic/liveability

Times Higher Education. (n.d.). *World University Rankings 2019*. Retrieved from https://www.timeshighereducation.com/world-university-rankings/2019/world-ranking

Tourism Research Australia. (2017a). *Travel by Australians: Results of the National Visitor Survey for year ending March 2017*. Retrieved from https://www.tra.gov.au/tra/nvs/nvs_mar_2017.html#MainFindings

Tourism Research Australia. (2017b). *Australian capital territory tourism audit*. Retrieved from https://www.tra.gov.au/Archive-TRA-Old-site/Research/View-all-publications/All-Publications/Destination-Visitor-Survey-results/Strategic-regional-research-reports/act-tourism-audit

Tourism Research Australia, & Australian Capital Tourism. (2012). *Destination visitor survey - Australian Capital Territory: Major blockbuster events in the ACT*. Retrieved from https://tourism.act.gov.au/wp-content/uploads/2017/05/SRR_ACT_Major_Blockbuster_Events.pdf

Tourism Victoria. (2015). *Melbourne Market Profile: Year ending December 2014*. Retrieved from http://www.tourism.vic.gov.au/component/edocman/?view=document&task=document.download&id=918

Victoria State Government. (2017). *Seventh heaven for the world's most liveable city*. Retrieved from https://www.premier.vic.gov.au/wp-content/uploads/2017/08/170816-Seventh-Heaven-For-The-World%E2%80%99s-Most-Liveable-City.pdf

Victorian Major Events Company. (n.d.). *Melbourne Winter Masterpieces*. Retrieved from http://www.melbournetourism.com/events/arts-and-culture/melbourne-winter-masterpieces/

Visit Canberra. (2014). *2020 Tourism Strategy: Growing the visitor economy 2014-2020*. Retrieved from https://tourism.act.gov.au/wp-content/uploads/2017/05/2020_strategy_disscussion_paper_march_2015.pdf

Visit Canberra. (2015). Destination marketing strategy 2015-2020. Retrieved from https://tourism.act.gov.au/wp-content/uploads/2017/05/Marketing_Strategy_15-20.pdf

Visit Canberra. (2018). *Tourism in the ACT: Year ending June 2018*. Retrieved from https://tourism.act.gov.au/wp-content/uploads/2016/10/Tourism-Snapshot_June2018.pdf

Visit Canberra. (n.d.-a). *Brand Book*. Retrieved from http://www.tourism.act.gov.au/images/documents/corporate/strategic_reports/VisitCanberra_BrandBook.pdf

Visit Canberra. (n.d.-b). *VisitCanberra*. Retrieved from http://www.tourism.act.gov.au/

Visit Canberra. (n.d.-c). *Special Event Fund*. Retrieved from http://tourism.act.gov.au/industry-services/special-event-fund

Visit Canberra. (n.d.-d). *Domestic marketing strategy 2013-2015*. Retrieved from http://tourism.act.gov.au/images/documents/corporate/strategic_reports/Marketing_Strategy_2013-15.pdf

Visit Victoria. (n.d.). *Melbourne – Entertainment*. Retrieved from https://www.visitvictoria.com/regions/melbourne/things-to-do/entertainment

Weller, T. (2013). *Hollywood Costume a star for ACMI*. Retrieved from http://www.artshub.com.au/news-article/news/all-arts/tammy-weller/hollywood-costume-a-star-for-acmi-196360

Westerbeek, H., & Linley, M. (2012). Building city brands through sport events: Theoretical and empirical perspectives. *Journal of Brand Strategy, 1*(2), 193-205.

Ziakas, V. (2014). Planning and leveraging event portfolios: Towards a holistic theory. *Journal of Hospitality Marketing & Management, 23*(3), 327-356. doi:10.1080/19368623.2013.796868

10 Sector-focused Approach to Business Events in Manchester

Zuzana Vokacova and Vladimir Antchak

This chapter explores the development and planning of a portfolio of business events in Manchester, UK. The portfolio approach combines a strong focus on the city's key industry sectors with a 'quality-orientated' way of event strategy development and implementation. Rather than aiming at filling the event venues with a quantity of random business events, Manchester has successfully secured a number of large-scale conferences with a strong international profile that are aligned with the city's key industry sectors such as Biomedicine, Healthcare, Sport, IT and Social Science. The city also aims at creating its own business events to fill the gaps in the calendar and prioritise specific areas, Digital or Advanced Materials, for example.

The chapter also analyses the nature of the inter-organisational collaboration and joint decision-making in Manchester in relation to the business event sector development and destination promotion. The overall realisation of the business event strategy is guided by Marketing Manchester (MM), a local DMO, and Manchester Convention Bureau (MCB), responsible for event bidding and collaboration with the local, national and international partners and clients.

This chapter draws on primary research in the form of document analysis and interviews conducted by the authors with several industry experts, responsible for business event strategy development and destination marketing in Manchester.

The value of business events

In tourism and event sectors, the significance of business events has been proven by the fact that almost all major cities have been investing extensively into convention and exhibition centres and facilities (Getz & Page, 2016; Rogers

& Davidson, 2016) alongside the increasing number of companies operating or selling these facilities and securing international conferences (Kim, Yoon, & Kim, 2011).

The business events industry is often referred to a 'MICE' sector which stands for Meetings, Incentives, Conferences and Exhibitions (Getz, 2013). The major value of business events has been seen in their economic contribution to the host destination (Deng & Li, 2014; Getz, 2013; Raj, Walters, & Rashid, 2017). Statistically, international business-event travellers tend to spend more at a destination than leisure tourists (Getz & Page, 2016). Therefore, business events' delegates are considered to be higher-yield tourists than travellers with leisure motives (Rogers & Davidson, 2016).

In addition to the direct economic value, a more general social and economic legacy of business events has been also recognised (Getz & Page, 2016). Such events can be seen as 'communication vehicles' with internal audience (personnel training, board and sales meetings, annual congresses, etc.) as well as with external audience (product launches, press briefing, general meetings or conferences). In broader sense, they represent "a diverse mix of communications events" (Rogers, 2013, p. 3).

The UK Conference and Meeting Survey (2018), reveals an estimated £18.1 billion of direct expenditure generated by conference and meeting delegates in venues and in wider destination spend in 2017. There were an estimated 92.8 million delegates accounting for approximately 147.4 million delegate days.

To maintain and maximise the benefits of business events, a long-term strategising is required. Many cities across the globe has shifted their ad-hoc approach to business events to the strategic planning of portfolios of events which requires consolidation and collaboration from different institutional organisations, commercial sector and local community.

Manchester as a business event destination

The city of Manchester is an industrial national hub located in the northern part of England in the United Kingdom. It is a central city within a metropolitan county of Greater Manchester (GM), which also comprises Bolton, Bury, Oldham, Rochdale, Salford, Stockport, Tameside, Trafford and Wigan. As of 2013, the GM economy generated £48 billion GVA (Gross Value Added) which is a 4% share of the national economy (GM Integrated Support Team, 2013). In 2017, Manchester was ranked the 3rd most visited city in the UK. It was included in the Top 10 most intriguing places to visit in 2017. It was number one European city for FDI (Foreign Direct Investment) and the fastest growing city and most economically productive in the UK (Marketing Manchester, 2017a).

One of the city's strategic objectives is to promote Manchester as a leading business event destination. In the city strategies, launched recently (Table 10.1), business events have been described as one of the four strategic aims for overall destination development, alongside the positioning of Manchester as a leading international destination, improving the quality of visitor experience and maximising the overall capacity for growth.

Table 10.1: Destination development in Manchester. Key documents.

Documents	Year	Brief summary
Greater Manchester Destination Management Plan (GDMP)	2017	The action plan for the visitor economy for Greater Manchester that is connected to the tourism strategy for 3 years. It states what has been achieved, where the city is positioned now and its aims & targets for 2020.
Conference Value & Volume	2016	The biennial report on business tourism activity in the Greater Manchester.
The Greater Manchester Strategy 2014-2020 'Stronger Together'	2013	Overall strategy for the Greater Manchester development.
Manchester City Council Report for Resolution	2016	Marketing Manchester's report – overview of the Manchester's visitor economy.
Marketing Manchester Visit. Meet. Invest. Study.	2017	Report on collaboration of Manchester's stakeholders and its priorities and strategies.
Greater Manchester Strategy for the Visitor Economy 2014-2020	2014	Sets out strategic directions for the visitors' economy in Greater Manchester.
The Greater Manchester Internationalisation Strategy	2017	Manchester's strategy for reaching international markets

Indeed, the value of business events is rather significant. The MICE sector generates around 5 million delegates a year, contributing £823 million annually to the Greater Manchester economy. In total, 40,100 direct and indirect jobs have been generated by the corporate event sector in the city (Marketing Manchester, 2017b).

The planning and implementation of all city event and destination related strategies is operated by the two key agencies, Marketing Manchester (MM) and Manchester Convention Bureau (MCB). MM is the agency responsible for promoting Greater Manchester on the international and national level. The MCB team is part of the MM and works proactively in identifying international and national conferences; it also facilitates event bid proposals. In 2016/17, MCB won 38 bids to host major international business events, and over 15,000 delegates were welcomed to the city (Marketing Manchester, 2017c). Such results contributed positively to the brand of the city and allows Manchester to compete against cities such as Frankfurt, Prague and Barcelona (Manchester City Council, 2017).

Overall, the value of business events in Manchester can be summarised in two ways. First, business events have been viewed as economic contributors to the city prosperity. Second, business events enhanced the city's profile by increasing the awareness of Manchester as a leading business tourism destination.

Sector-oriented approach to business events

The sector-oriented approach to business events in Manchester is based on a strategic selection of events which "resonate with the brand values of Manchester, seeking out conferences that highlight and support our academic, business sector and industry strengths…" (Marketing Manchester, 2017d, p. 32). The business event strategy in Manchester aligns with the key city's industry sectors, including Manufacturing and Advanced Engineering, Life Science, Energy and Environment, Financial, Professional and Business services (See Table 10.2).

Table 10.2: Key sectors of economy in Manchester. Source: Greater Manchester Combined Authority (2017).

Sector	Job generation	Gross Value Added (GVA)
Manufacturing and Advanced Engineering	114,000	£7.7bn
Life Science	157,000	£4bn
Energy and Environment	114,000	£5.4bn
Financial, Professional & Business services	266,900	£15.5bn

In addition, a vibrant visitor economy sector supports 99,000 jobs and generates £2.1bn GVA. The sector is crucial in pursuing Manchester's ambition to be a top 20 global city by 2020 (Greater Manchester Combined Authority, 2017).

A common way of securing business events in Manchester is via a bidding process. The owners of a biddable event accept proposals from temporary or one-off hosts and make decisions through a competitive bidding process often several years in advance. The active work on the international event market has resulted in securing 38 international conferences worth around £25 million in 2016/17. Key conferences and their contribution to the city economy are presented in Table 10.3.

Table 10.3: Key business conferences and their contribution to the city economy in Manchester in 2016/17. Source: Marketing Manchester (2017c).

Event	Contribution to the local economy
Annual Conference of Particle Therapy	1,500 delegates, worth £2.5m
Society for Molecular Biology and Evolution Conference	1,300 delegates, worth £2.7m
Guidelines for International Network	500 delegates, worth £1m

As a result of such positive achievements Manchester was included in Top 10 Emerging International Meeting Cities in 2016 and was ranked 21st meeting destination in Europe, Middle East and Africa in 2017 (Marketing Manchester, 2017a).

Chapter 5 explains potential difficulties with regard to composing business event portfolios as this is usually a process with high investment and high risks. Development of one's own business events is a more sustainable and proactive strategy. Such events can obtain the status of anchor or hallmark events and generate sustainable and accumulating benefits. However, it requires long-term planning and marketing expenses.

In Manchester, the creation of new business events has been seen as a rather innovative strategy to fill the gaps in the annual calendar: "The development of new conferences is an original approach few other destinations are undertaking. It seeks to identify gaps in the conference offer for specific sectors, in which Manchester has a particular strength" (Marketing Manchester, 2017b, p. 13).

Creating business events and owning them is highly valuable in terms of consistent economic impacts and long-team sustainable development for the city. Some, already existing events can be supported with a perspective to grow and obtain a major event status. For example, Digital Summit, a rather low scale event has the potential because of the rapid growth of the digital sector. It is expected that it could attract more international delegates to Manchester in the future if it is supported in marketing and international promotion.

The realisation of the sector-orientated approach has been facilitated by government financial and marketing support. For example, the 'Business Events Growth Programme', operated by the country's official tourist board, Visit Britain, has been designed to provide support for event bids and conference planning. There are three key types of support through this programme. The objective of the first, Bidding & Enhancement Support, is to facilitate the winning of new high-profile international business events. The second, International Delegate Growth, aims at supporting the growth of already existing events. The third, Government Advocacy, refers to general 'soft power' support of the national business event industry in a form of letters of support, ambassador programmes and keynote speeches. Grant funding is available of up to £20,000 per event.

In the past two years, two business event projects, initiated by Marketing Manchester, have been supported via the 'Business Events Growth Programme'. For the 2016 EuroScience Open Forum a billboard campaign was launched in the arrivals area at Manchester Airport, as well as the distribution of event brochures was organised at Manchester Piccadilly train station. The event was attended by 3,500 delegates. The promotion campaign helped to raise the profile of Manchester and the North-West of the country as a leading region for scientific research. The 2019 World Healthcare Congress Europe is supported through the realisation of an extensive international marketing campaign to attract attention and increase the number of international delegates.

On a city level, business events in Manchester have been supported through the local government's subventions. Subvention is a financial grant issued by the Manchester City Council and operated by Marketing Manchester. The city subvention assists mainly in reducing venue costs or free promotion campaigns. The subvention can be obtained through the Subvention Framework Assessment which contains criteria such as contribution to GVA, the growth of the city's key industry and academic sectors, overall sustainability of the event, and its impacts on the local community and businesses. The city subventions are due to end by March 2020 and that might be one of the challenges for the business event sector in Manchester in the upcoming years.

Collaboration and inter-organisational relationships

Ziakas (2014) and Ziakas and Costa (2011) acknowledge that the effective implementation of an event policy requires coordinated collaboration and partnership among stakeholders. These partnerships create a policy network (Weed, 2001; Ziakas, 2014). The key actors of the inter-organisational network in Manchester are presented in Figure 10.1.

Figure 10.1: Key stakeholders in the Manchester's business events sector.

MM and MCB play a central coordinating role within the business events network in Manchester, supporting other stakeholders and sharing information at destination level. Both organisations play a vital part in positioning and promoting Manchester as a leading events destination. As a national tourism board, Visit Britain acts as 'an over-looking' partner providing support and assistance in the business events area. The City Council provides legislation and financial support.

Three main city universities, including the University of Manchester, Manchester Metropolitan University and the University of Salford provide academic research and business opportunities for the Manchester's key sectors. With their international expertise and networks, the universities play an important role in city image formation and promotion. They also host international academic and business conferences.

Manchester Central is the largest convention venue in the city. Its facilities include the purpose-built 804-seat Exchange Auditorium; the 1800m² exhibition, conference or 1200-capacity dining space Exchange Hall; the 10,000m² column-free and divisible Central Hall and a range of smaller meeting rooms.

Manchester Airport Group collaborates through opening new routes and thus, providing new potential markets for business events. The Group is also a member of an executive board of Manchester Central. Transport for Greater Manchester facilitates other means of transportation within the city. Manchester Hoteliers Association represents large city hotels and assists with accommodation booking for the business events' delegates. It also acts as a provider of additional venues for hosting business events. Other venues comprise, for example, Manchester's football and cricket stadiums, Fringe venues and theatres with meeting space for smaller events or as venues for openings and gala dinners of the larger conferences.

The nature of a collaborative approach in Manchester can be described through a set of joint activities and processes taking place within the stakeholder network. These include cooperation in securing business events on the international market, regular meetings, knowledge exchange and an ambassador programme launched in 2016 (Figure 10.2).

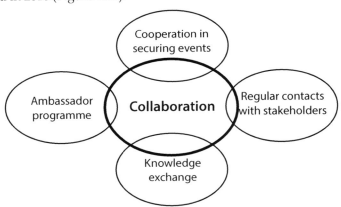

Figure 10.2: Collaborative networking in Manchester.

As it was mentioned earlier in the chapter, the process of securing business events for Manchester is coordinated by MM and MCB. Their responsibility is to customise bids, locate appropriate venues, prepare budgets and conduct feasibility studies as well as communicates with all relevant stakeholders. For example, Manchester Central and Manchester University and Manchester Metropolitan University, which are capable of accommodating large international and national events in the city, are the ones who are directly involved in the preparation of bid documentation. Collaboration in bidding is important in terms of a unified promotion message about the destination, which is a vital part of every successful event bid.

In terms of knowledge exchange, Visit Britain has launched a series of workshops for event professionals to introduce and discuss the aspects and requirements of international bidding, marketing and PR campaign's design and ambassador programme development. A great emphasis has been put recently in explaining and communicating the value of International Congress and Convention Association (ICCA) ranking. The rationale for the importance of ICCA ranking lies in the promotional potential and worldwide recognition it brings. The annual ICCA country and city ranking have been widely used to promote a destination, venue or service to the international corporate clients, business event promoters and right holders. The 2017 annual ICCA report ranked Manchester 47th among European business event destinations with 32 international association events hosted (ICCA, 2018).

Another aim of knowledge exchange is to work closer with the city hotels and event venues and explain the nature of the business events sector, with the requirements to book facilities several years in advance and secure and block, for example, accommodation as part of a bid book preparation. Marketing Manchester also collaborates with the academic institutions and organisations in order to strengthen research areas, which are capable of attracting major international and national business events.

A vital part of stakeholder collaboration in Manchester is the Manchester Conference Ambassador Programme. It offers support and partnerships to inspire high-profile business leaders and academics to host prestigious business events in Manchester. It is believed that ambassador-led conferences are capable of generating substantial economic benefits for the city as well as positively affecting its international profile. For example, in 2015, Manchester Metropolitan University hosted EuroCHRIE Conference 2015, a big conference for hospitality and tourism educators. Manchester ambassador, Associate Dean for Knowledge Exchange at MMU, Dr Steven Rhoden and his team were supported by Marketing Manchester's Convention Bureau team, including assistance with the bidding process, which culminated in a presentation to the EuroCHRIE delegation in Dubai in October 2014.

Regular meetings with the involved stakeholders is an essential requirement for a productive stakeholder collaboration. Marketing Manchester and MCB organise regular meetings with all relevant city actors to facilitate the process of communication and cooperation. Periodic meetings take place with the universities and ambassadors with regard to the selected conferences. A new Conference Initiative's series of meetings have been set up with the Hoteliers Association. Quarterly meetings have been held with Manchester Central to discuss potential conferences suitable for Manchester's sectors and also for the venue itself. Biannual meetings are held by MCB with Transport for Greater Manchester and Manchester Airport, regarding new routes and new markets.

Overall, the existence of a stakeholder collaborative network in Manchester proves to be critical for the operational success of business event sector development. Regular contacts between stakeholders, knowledge exchange, operational collaboration in bidding and complementary 'ambassador' initiatives facilitate a quality-orientated and sector-focused development of business events in Manchester.

Challenges and issues

The uncertainty of the consequences of the results of the United Kingdom European Union membership referendum in 2016 has been recognised as an issue that is likely to cause significant impacts on the business event sector and affect the entire destination strategy in the future. For example, it is unclear whether new visa regulations will be introduced and, if so, how this could affect the willingness of international conference right holders to choose cities in the UK as event hosts. However, the industry also sees Brexit as a new opportunity for Manchester as a business event destination. For example, the devaluation of the national currency caused by the political and economic instability could open new conference markets, as Manchester can be seen as a more affordable destination.

The direct challenge for the business event sector lies in the ending of the city's subventions in March 2020. Therefore, MM and MCB will need to design and implement new support mechanisms to maintain and further develop attractive business event offers.

Summary

The city of Manchester provides an interesting case for this book. A portfolio approach to business events is an underdeveloped area in event management studies. Until recently, the research and academic publications have been exploring a generic portfolio of events as a conglomeration of events of different genres. This chapter provides an overview of a focused portfolio (Getz, 2013) which has the potential to generate sustainable competitive advantages for a host destination. The sector-focused portfolio of business events in Manchester has been designed with the emphasis on the 'quality' of events rather than their 'quantity'. Economic and reputational benefits have been expected, however, mainly from those business events that align with Manchester's brand and key industry sectors. Manchester's quality-driven approach is characterised by a 'slow and steady' development of the business event sector. Although a bidding strategy have been implemented to a certain extent, the city's business event planners have understand the necessity of applying more sustainable portfolio composing strategies as owning and developing 'organic events' with the purpose to also offer such events to other destinations.

The inter-organisational relationships in Manchester are characterised by a highly collaborative environment within the stakeholder network. The cooperation offers stakeholders an access to shared resources and information, which is essential to achieve mutual objectives. The findings from the Manchester case study emphasise the importance of knowledge, information, and resource sharing, especially in the bidding process. The stakeholder collaboration is a crucial part of the quality-driven and sector-focused approach to business events in Manchester.

References

Deng, Q., & Li, M. (2014) A model of event-destination image transfer. *Journal of Travel Research*, **53**(1), 69-82, doi:10.1177/0047287513491331

Getz, D. (2013) *Event Tourism: Concepts, international case studies, and research*. New York: Cognizant Communication Corporation.

Getz, D. & Page, S. (2016) Progress and prospects for event tourism research, *Tourism Management*, **52**, 593-631, doi:10.1016/j.tourman.2015.03.007

GM Integrated Support Team (2013) Stronger together: Greater Manchester Strategy. Summary. Available at: https://www.growthco.uk/media/1077/gm_strategy_stronger_together_summary3.pdf

Greater Manchester Combined Authority (2017) The Greater Manchester Internationalisation Strategy 2017 — 2020. Available at: http://www.marketingmanchester.com/wp-content/uploads/2017/07/GM-Internationalistion-Strategy.pdf

IICCA (2018) ICCA Statistics Report 2017. Country and City Rankings: Public Abstract. Amsterdam: International Congress and Convention Association. Available at: https://iccadata.iccaworld.com/statstool2017/ (Accessed: 12th June 2018)

Kim, S. S., Yoon, S., & Kim, Y. (2011) Competitive positioning among international convention cities in the East Asian region, *Journal of Convention & Event Tourism*, **12**(2), 86-105, doi:10.1080/15470148.2011.566760

Manchester City Council (2017). Report for resolution, 8 November 2017. Available at: https://secure.manchester.gov.uk/download/meetings/id/23839/11_overview_report

Marketing Manchester (2017a), Manchester Accolades. Available at: http://www.marketingmanchester.com/wp-content/uploads/2017/02/MM-Accolades-2017.pdf (Accessed: 17th October 2018)

Marketing Manchester (2017b) Marketing Manchester: Visit. Meet. Invest. Study (2017-2020). Available at: http://www.marketingmanchester.com/wp-content/uploads/2017/07/Marketing-Manchester-Strategic-Priorities.pdf (Accessed: 17th October 2018)

Marketing Manchester (2017c) Review 2016-2017, Available at: http://www.marketingmanchester.com/wp-content/uploads/2017/07/Marketing-Mcr-Look-Book.pdf

Marketing Manchester (2017d) Greater Manchester Destination Development Plan 2017-2020. Available at: http://www.marketingmanchester.com/wp-content/uploads/2017/02/DMP-2017_2020-FINAL.pdf

Raj, R., Walters, P., and Rashid, T. (2017) *Events Management: Principles and practice*. London: Sage Publications.

Rogers, T. (2013) *Conferences and Conventions: A global Industry*. (3rd Ed.). Oxon: Routledge.

Rogers, T. & Davidson, R. (2016) *Marketing Destinations and Venues for Conferences, Conventions and Business Events*. (2nd Ed.). Oxon: Routledge.

UK Conference and Meeting Survey (2017) News. Available at: http://ukcams.org.uk/news%20about%20ukcams.html. (Accessed 4th March 2018)

Weed, M. (2001) Organizational culture and the leisure policy process in Britain: How structure affects strategy in sport–tourism policy development. *Tourism Culture & Communication*, **3**(3), 147-163, doi:10.3727/109830401108750751

Ziakas, V. (2014) Event *Portfolio Planning and Management: A holistic approach*. Abingdon: Routledge.

Ziakas, V. & Costa, C. A. (2011) Event portfolio and multi-purpose development: Establishing the conceptual grounds. *Sport Management Review*, **14**(4),409–423, doi:10.1016/j.smr.2010.09.003.

11 Edinburgh, a Festival City

Edinburgh has long been recognized as a global model for "festival cities", and is often cited as a leader in the planning and evaluation of events. In 2010 Edinburgh won the World Festival and Event City award from the International Festival and Event Association (IFEA) and was declared the most outstanding global entry.

According to Visit Scotland's 2015 visitor survey (cited in BOP Consulting 2018, p. 8), "Edinburgh's Festivals each year deliver over 3,000 events, reaching audiences of more than 4.5 million and creating the equivalent of approximately 6,000 full time jobs. 32% of the 14 million+ annual visitors to Scotland are motivated by the nation's cultural and heritage offer, in which the Festivals play a defining role."

The city is frequently cited in the events literature, and its generous posting of material online is a boon to scholars and practitioners alike. The companion book in this series, *Event Impact Assessment* (Getz, 2019), presents highlights from a succession of impact studies that Festivals Edinburgh has placed online, while in this book we examine portfolio management through a review of published documents (all available online) and input from Festivals Edinburgh.

Permanent, formal stakeholder collaboration, and strategic planning supported by research is in large part what distinguishes Edinburgh's event portfolio. The Festivals Forum (established in 2007 following the first *Thundering Hooves* report) facilitates stakeholder collaboration, particularly by bringing major funders to the table with events and venues. Festivals Edinburgh is a formal, staffed association of the eleven major, permanent festivals that contribute most to the city's image and to event-tourism impacts. Leadership is shared, not concentrated in one organization. As well, the city and Scottish Government work closely together, facilitated by the explicit portfolio strategy followed by EventScotland.

Innovation in programming the festivals is matched by leadership in environmental sustainability and social responsibility. Engagement with residents is considered to be a high priority, and this includes demonstrating benefits through regular and comprehensive impact studies that cover cultural, social, economic and environmental impacts. Investment in venues and infrastructure has also been a priority for the city.

The success of Edinburgh illustrates several important points for event portfolio creation, management, and strategy:

♦ Edinburgh and Scotland demonstrate that portfolio management is being implemented at three levels: nation, city, and festival programming; the Edinburgh arrangements have been referred to as a 'festival ecosystem'.

♦ The 11 major Edinburgh festivals have a formal organization and can be considered a managed portfolio.

♦ Integration of vision, policy, strategy and funding between festivals, city and national agencies works well in Scotland; there are common goals and integrated actions.

♦ Collaboration of key stakeholders is both formal and informal; networking procedures are well established.

♦ Strategic planning and research have facilitated innovation and competitiveness.

♦ Synergies are fostered with regard to achieving desired benefits in the fields of branding, communications, financing, venues and the engagement of residents.

Festivals Edinburgh

The formal organization Festivals Edinburgh can be considered the focal organization from a portfolio perspective. Few cities have this level of institutionalized collaboration among festivals or events, complete with full-time and part-time staff. It is noteworthy that the initiative to form Festivals Edinburgh was taken by the festivals themselves rather than the city. Figure 11.1 describes this organisation's mission, objectives, priorities, governance and 'insight'.

Figure 11.1: Festivals Edinburgh. Source: edinburghfestivalcity.com.

Edinburgh International Children's Festival

Imaginate Festival School (Credit: Kat Gollock)

Edinburgh International Book Festival

Book Festival Village (Credit: The Festival)

Edinburgh Film Festival

Opening Gala (Credit: The Festival)

Edinburgh's Hogmany

Torchlight Procession (Credit: David Cheskin)

Scottish Storytelling Festival

Open Heart (Credit: Ludovic Farine)

Edinburgh International Festival

Virgin Money Fireworks Concert (Credit: Dave Stewart)

The Royal Edinburgh Military Tattoo

Tattoo Fireworks Finale (Credit: The Tattoo)

Edinburgh International Science Festival

GastroFest (Credit: The Festival)

Edinburgh Art Festival

Art Late at Talbot Rice Gallery (Credit: The Festival)

Edinburgh Festival Fringe

Street Performance (Credit: Dave Monteith-Hodge)

Edinburgh Jazz and Blues Festival

Mr Sipp (Credit: The Festival)

Figure 11.2: The eleven members of Festivals Edinburgh (as of 2019).

Four working groups are supported: programming, the environment (greening/sustainability initiatives), joint marketing, and innovation. Note that this is an organization of independent festival organisations and it does not produce events. Rather, it exists to foster collaboration and progress for all 11 members (Figure 11.2).

Membership criteria of the joint company Festivals Edinburgh are specified. Members must "...commit to contributing to joint initiatives of the Company members and have the financial and/or human resources to do so." Members should make "...a positive contribution to the mix on offer of Festivals Edinburgh". In 2016, the Edinburgh Mela was deleted from the organisation after its sudden cancellation and the loss of funding, so membership is not permanent. Since this is a membership organisation, it constitutes a unique kind of event portfolio. It is not 'managed' from outside, and each member is independent and values control of its own destiny. Many of the events are legal charities.

External influence is brought to bear on occasion, and funding applications must show delivery against set criteria, but these never amount to being 'managed'. Indeed, as with much of the UK arts sector, there is a scrupulous adherence to the 'arms length' principle. City councillors do sit on the governing boards, so the links to city hall are generally strong.

As with any portfolio, the creation of mutually beneficial synergies is a high priority. Festivals Edinburgh deliberately and professionally creates synergies in several key areas. This begins with what the organisation describe as a "singularity of mission", whereby the festivals agree that working together makes more sense than working alone and this principle is enshrined within an agreed business plan. The festivals do not work together on all matters, but rather only on those areas that they have a common interest in such as brand positioning, marketing, and environmental sustainability. The second key area is advocacy, and by association the research on impacts that provides the foundation for evidenced-based advocacy, whereby the festivals speak with one voice on a range of issues aligned to their common business interests.

Festivals Forum

Two strategic planning projects, called Thundering Hooves (discussed later) have led to establishing of a broad Festivals Forum that extends networking beyond the eleven festivals to government and independent experts. A Thundering Hooves Steering Group monitors implementation of the strategy and action plan. Established in 2007, The Festivals Forum "...is a high-level strategic commission bringing together representatives of those with a stake in maintaining the future success of the Edinburgh festivals. Its main purpose is:

◆ To ensure that Edinburgh maintains its position as the pre-eminent Festival City delivering cultural, social and economic benefit to the city, the region and the country;

- To agree the long term strategic development of the Edinburgh Festivals, working closely with the festivals, Festivals Edinburgh and the Thundering Hooves Steering Group;

- To articulate and oversee the investment strategy required to sustain Edinburgh's position as the world's leading Festival City;

- To support and encourage a positive working relationship between the festivals and their stakeholders;

- To monitor and ensure the delivery of this [Thundering Hooves] Strategy and Action Plan" (Festivals Forum, n.d).

Sometimes it is suggested that the Festivals Forum 'manages' the festivals but this misinterprets their role: rather than 'managing' the festivals, they seek to influence the wider environment within which the festivals operate. Synergies pursued by Festivals Forum start with a sense of collective ownership, whereby the stakeholders that support the festivals feel a common desire to aid their long term development. This is represented in a collective agenda, whereby the stakeholders have worked with the festivals to identify key challenges and opportunities over the next decade – as enshrined in the Thundering Hooves 2.0 document – and use this as the basis for agendas at their meetings (BOP Consulting and Festivals & Events International, 2015).

City of Edinburgh Council supports festivals and events to achieve social, cultural and economic goals. There is a formal City of Edinburgh Councils Festivals Strategy, an Events Planning and Operations Group, and within staff there are the Events Team, Arts and Learning Team, Public Safety Team, the Licensing Division, the Culture and Sport Division, the Economic Development Division – and a number of other officers across environmental health, parks and libraries. Council officials sit as board members or trustees of festivals. The City is a partner in festival funding and venue and infrastructure development.

Funding

Tourism, festivals and events are important to the national identity and to the economy, with strategy and funding coming from several agencies. Scottish Government's Festivals Expo Fund supports a wide range of Scotland's productions and artists through the Edinburgh festivals. Visit Scotland is the national tourism organization and it encompasses EventScotland and Business Events Scotland. EventScotland has a number of funding programmes, outlined online at: (http://www.eventscotland.org/funding/). The national events strategy is outlined later. Creative Scotland (formerly Scottish Arts Council) has funding programmes for international festivals and for taking festivals and the arts throughout the country.

To mark the 70th anniversary of the founding of the festival city, the Festivals came together with the Scottish Government and the City of Edinburgh Council to create a three-way funding programming called PLACE (Platforms for Creative Excellence). It provides five years of funding for creative and community projects, which will renew the Festivals' ambition and purpose after the defining moment of their 70th anniversary.

The Programme is funded by the Scottish Government, the City of Edinburgh Council, and the Edinburgh Festivals, and supported and administered by Creative Scotland. …The introduction of the five-year commitment of the Platforms for Creative Excellence Programme creates a strategic approach to evolving the future direction of the festivals through long-term developments and collaborations with global as well as Scottish partners." (https://www.edinburghfestivalcity.com/about/unique-funding-partnership-backs-festivals-ambitions-for-wider-reach). When it comes to funding, other stakeholders include planned 'giving' by corporations and trusts, formal sponsorships, and ticket sales to residents and tourists.

Strategy

The Thundering Hooves analysis and resulting strategy for Edinburgh festivals came about through collaboration by the Scottish Government, EventScotland, Scottish Enterprise, Creative Scotland, and City of Edinburgh Council. The first report was in 2006 and the second in 2015. The 2006 Thundering Hooves led directly to establishment of the Festivals Forum, and action intended to maintain the city's global competitive advantage related to its festivals. The reports can be found at: (https://www.edinburghfestivalcity.com/about/documents/196-thundering-hooves).

From the 2006 report:

This study was commissioned by the Scottish Arts Council in partnership with Festivals Edinburgh (formerly, the Association of Edinburgh Festivals), the City of Edinburgh Council (CEC), the Scottish Executive, EventScotland and Scottish Enterprise Edinburgh and Lothian. Its purpose is to examine the competitive position of the eleven festivals belonging to Festivals Edinburgh and the extent to which that position is likely to be affected by:

-the burgeoning number of festivals, both in the United Kingdom and overseas, that are competing for artists, audiences and funding;

-the increasing use of cultural programming (festivals and events) as strategic devices to promote tourism and to build the brand-identity of the cities or regions where they are located; and /or

-any other factors.

Edinburgh's festivals were established in a less competitive environment than the current one, and most developed in an organic rather than a 'top-down' fashion. Their evolution has served as a model for many of the world's leading international festivals. However, the client group is concerned about the gradual attrition of Edinburgh's competitive position and, with it, a long term decline in its status as a cultural city in the eyes of artists, promoters, audience and media, disadvantaging both the festivals and Edinburgh alike.

There were three main dimensions to the 2006 study: "consultation with stakeholders and review of festival literature; benchmarking of Edinburgh against other festival cities in order to gauge the present state of the competition and find examples of good practice; and involvement of the client group in a scenario planning process designed to facilitate long-term strategic thinking in the light of global trends".

EventScotland's Strategic Plan: Scotland The Perfect Stage

Scotland is a nation that takes events very seriously, and its event strategy explicitly recognizes the portfolio concept and related planning and management issues. The current plan (building on a 2008 version) drew on wide stakeholder consultations and research, as indicated in the following quote from the document Scotland The Perfect Stage, Scotland's Events Strategy 2015-2025 (Visit Scotland, 2015) (p. 8):

Wide consultation has informed the development of this strategy. Input has been drawn from across the industry, from industry representative groups including the Scottish Events and Festivals Association (SEFA), the National Outdoor Events Association (Scotland) (NOEA Scotland) and the Edinburgh Festivals Forum to the organisers of individual events of all types and sizes, from visitor attractions to suppliers and from national sports associations and governing bodies to destination management organisations. The Scottish Government, its agencies and non-departmental public bodies along with Scotland's local authorities have also contributed to the strategy's production. A list of those consulted is included at the back of the document. Significant research was also undertaken to benchmark Scotland's performance against other countries and to analyse global demographic and technological trends, this was supported by the input of expert advice from Professor Donald Getz of the University of Calgary who is recognised internationally as an expert in event-led tourism.

Scotland's events portfolio will provide:

-core of events each year which are unique to Scotland and are embedded in Scottish culture covering sport, the arts and heritage as well as a wide range of business events;

-high profile one-off and recurring events, including 'mega events', which complement the core portfolio and have been attracted to Scotland by its unique appeal as a destination and international reputation as a country which delivers high quality events; and

-entertainment, opportunities, experiences and education for all the people of Scotland and visitors ensuring that impact and legacy are delivered on an on-going basis.

As part of the Festivals' on-going programme of impact analysis, The Network Effect (BOP Consulting, 2018), looked at a different aspect of festivals, namely their synergistic effects. The report was supported by EventScotland and Creative Scotland. Here are some quotes, and they refer to "sectorial lead bodies" which are the organisations devoted to specific arts and cultural fields.

Edinburgh's identity as a festival city has been built over the past 70 years to its current position as an acknowledged world leader. Its individual festivals are leading cultural brands in their respective fields; collectively, they attract audiences in excess of 4.5 million and have an economic impact of £313 million annually. Their pioneering collaborative approach has enabled them to plan certain aspects of their work collectively and has led to the production of a series of major impact studies to support the Festivals' continuing growth and development (p. 3).

The Edinburgh Festivals are visioned, designed and funded as festivals. They are not in themselves sectorial lead bodies, but they are valued by these bodies and in some cases embedded within organisations that take on sector development roles. Their key stories to date have been of the international, economic and city-wide benefits they bring – and these are the stories that interviewees found easiest to tell. But in addition to these impacts, the Festivals play an important role in the Scottish creative and cultural sectors at strategic level – as hubs, networks, key players, lighting rods, collaborators, colleagues. Some of this is formalised, much of it is delivered informally through personal contacts or as offshoots of other initiatives, and the Festivals provide an important forum for debate, not through specific initiatives but through the critical mass of attendees. The Festivals are therefore valued by sectorial lead bodies as important supports in sustaining and developing Scottish arts and events (p. 11).

The Edinburgh Festivals, as 'signature events' within the national portfolio, play an important role in delivering on the strategy: they provide employment, enhance Scotland's reputation, attract visitors and play a supportive role in the events industry. It is this latter role – the Festivals' support to the Scottish event ecosystem – that has been explored in more depth through this research (p. 19).

Issues and future directions

Festivals Edinburgh does not actively pursue growth, nor changes in its composition. Rather, they are concerned with the performance of the member events, singly and collectively. They use their brand as a lens through which to see such issues, with four in particular being of current interest.

The first issue pertains to global forces, such as trends towards the closing of borders and restricting of travel, as these threaten their competitive position. The organisation therefore works hard to deal with the issue of obtaining visas for artists and other participants.

The second relates to innovation and current changes in the ways in which audiences and visitors discover, plan, travel and share experiences. Festivals Edinburgh believes they need to seize digital opportunities, particularly in partnership with the university sector. The University of Edinburgh has established the Edinburgh Futures Institute, committed to data-driven innovation and digital cultures, with particular relevance to festivals.

At the level of individual festivals there is an on-going issue with investment, leading to the need to explore changing business models and discover additional investment channels, particularly those focussed on identifying and 'exploiting' unique festival assets.

Regarding relationships with the City, there is the commitment to inclusion. Specifically, there is a strong desire to ensure that the citizens of Edinburgh feel ownership and engagement with the festivals. Levels of support and engagement are good (e.g., 67% of residents in the 2017 Edinburgh People's Survey reported that they had been to one or more festivals in the last two years, compared to 62% in 2016) but it is recognized that complacency is unacceptable.

Summary

In reading the Edinburgh case study it should be stressed that this is a rather unique portfolio, being a formal consortium of independent festivals that manage their collaboration in the spirit of mutual advantage. Festivals Edinburgh exists within a world-class festival city and the country of Scotland where events are prominent in both the tourism and cultural-policy spheres. Many cities around the world have looked to Edinburgh for guidance and they find not only important lessons on how festivals (or other event organisations) can collaborate, but also how the city, country and other stakeholders all share in the process of maintaining their competitiveness and leadership roles.

Key lessons are highlighted in the Introduction to this chapter, listed as success factors, but one additional point should be added. Festivals Edinburgh is a voluntary collaboration, complete with staff and shared resources, but all the festivals remain independent. This portfolio is not managed from outside, although the City and Scottish governments clearly do assist and support its efforts. In this regard it is a model of what can be done when all stakeholders find common cause.

References

AEA Consultants, London (2006). *Thundering Hooves: Maintaining the Global Competitive Edge of Edinburgh's Festivals.* https://aeaconsulting.com/insights/thundering_hooves_maintaining_the_global_competitive_edge_of_edinburghs_festivals

BOP Consulting (2011). *Edinburgh Festivals Impact Study - Research and Knowledge Exchange in the Creative Economy: Impact and Effect.* Prepared for Festivals Edinburgh. https://www.st-andrews.ac.uk/media/icc/newwebsite/documents/Edinburgh%20Festivals%20presentation%20BOP%20v1.pdf

BOP Consulting (2016). *Edinburgh Festivals 2015 Impact Study Final Report.* Prepared for Festivals Edinburgh. https://www.edinburghfestivalcity.com/assets/000/001/964/Edinburgh_Festivals_-_2015_Impact_Study_Final_Report_original.pdf?1469537463

BOP Consulting (2018). *Edinburgh Festivals The Network Effect: The role of the Edinburgh Festivals in the national culture and events sectors.* https://www.edinburghfestivalcity.com/assets/000/003/791/The_Network_Effect__July_2018__original.pdf?1531301203

BOP Consulting and Festivals & Events International (2015). *Edinburgh Festivals: Thundering Hooves 2.0. A Ten Year Strategy to Sustain the Success of Edinburgh's Festivals.* https://www.edinburghfestivalcity.com/about/thundering-hooves

Festivals Forum (n.d) www.edinburghfestivalcity.com/about/core-partners

Getz, D. (2019). *Event Impact Assessment.* Oxford: Goodfellow Publishers.

Visit Scotland. (2015). Scotland the perfect stage: Scotland's events strategy 2015-2025. Retrieved from http://www.eventscotland.org/assets/show/4658

12 International Comparison of Festival and Event Cities and their Portfolios

In this chapter a systematic comparison of 23 eventful cities has been conducted to gain insights on event portfolio development and management. All the selected cities are the recipients of the IEFA (International Festivals and Events Association) World Festival and Event City Award (https://www.ifea.com/p/industryawards/worldfestivalandeventcityaward).

The application documents were downloaded from the IFEA website, covering awards from 2014-2018. These submissions by cities are available to members only. Some cities have received the award multiple times; only their most recent submission has been reviewed.

This data collection method has limitations, as the geographic representation is weak (See Figure 12.1) which limits opportunities for generalisation. Another limitation is that the application documents follow a pro-forma set by the IFEA that does not specifically pertain to portfolios and their design and management.

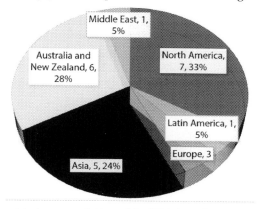

Figure 12.1: Geographical representation of the IFEA Award winners.

Award criteria and requirements

The IFEA website provides award criteria, and these can be interpreted as the association's perspective on what a city should be doing to be supportive of events and maximise their positive contribution across economic, social and cultural domains:

♦ Adding to the quality of life for local residents;

♦ Driving tourism;

♦ Showcasing a positive community brand and image to the media, business community, and visitors;

♦ Creating economic impact that translates into jobs, tax revenues and enhanced infrastructure improvements;

♦ Providing enhanced exposure opportunities for the arts, not-for-profit causes and other community programmes and venues;

♦ Promoting volunteerism and bonding the many elements of the community together;

♦ Encouraging community investment, participation, creativity and vision; and

♦ Building irreplaceable 'community capital' for the future.

IFEA selects an international panel to review applicants each year. Applicants pay a fee and follow a pro-forma procedure. This is not a contest, so there are no 'winners'. Because the submissions follow a prescribed format and details are specified by IFEA, the material cannot be assumed to reflect all the policies and actions by cities related to festivals and events. The entry requirements consist of six sections, including:

♦ Community Overview to provide a better understanding of the community and the infrastructure in place to host events and support event industry;

♦ Community Festivals and Events to provide an understanding of the diversity and success of current festivals and events in a city;

♦ City Governmental Support of Festivals and Events. This section describes the strength and depth by the applicant city and other area governmental bodies (County, State, taxing districts, etc.);

♦ Non-Governmental Community Support to understand the commitment to festivals and events and direct support provided by community individuals and non-governmental organisations;

♦ Leveraging and Community Capital should provide information how the City and its non-governmental partners maximise the 'community capital' created by festivals and events in your market;

♦ Extra Credit to highlight any other programmes, services, resources, activities around public event planning and management.

Comparative analysis of the 23 cities

The results of the comparative analysis are presented in Table 12.1. For each city the year of award is given, plus the population indicated in the document - sometimes for both a city and a metropolitan area. Addresses are listed for one or two websites for each city, enabling the reader to find out more about the city and its events.

In Column 1, is an indication of whether the words 'portfolio' and 'strategy' are mentioned, and what that means in context. Some quotations are provided to illustrate these points, but there can be a portfolio strategy without use of these terms. Also shown are examples of the events the document highlights, as the emphasis does differ, especially between sports and festivals. Business events are mentioned in most, but emphasized only in a few. This is likely owing to the fact that in many jurisdictions there are one or more convention bureaus attached to venues that attract conventions and exhibitions (usually through a mix of sales and competitive bidding) and these operate rather independent of DMOs and government agencies. Key stakeholders and their roles are noted, with the city government being the most common focal organisation, and tourism or a DMO the next most frequent. In Column 2, specific points about the events strategy or plans, and major goals where available have been summarised.

Table 12.1: Comparison of award cities.

PORTFOLIO MANAGEMENT -including stakeholders, funding & synergies	STRATEGY & MAJOR GOALS
Greater Palm Springs California (2018) Area population: 500,000	
http://www.visitgreaterpalmsprings.com	
No explicit mention of 'portfolio' The area hosts 200+ events in 9 constituent cities Events highlighted: festivals, golf, tennis "All of the sponsors, departments, agencies, schools, bureaus and cooperatives mentioned in the preceding sections are heavily involved in the local and regional event, tourism and hospitality industries. This team effort enables the local and regional event industry to thrive. Also, through networking events, including those organized by chambers of commerce, companies are encouraged to be actively involved in the events community. The Greater Palm Springs Convention and Tourism Bureau ensures that the Palm Springs Convention Center is booked with exciting meetings and conferences throughout the year, and local event service and equipment providers keep event producers and meeting planners supplied with the essential tools of the trade." Direct funding and support for events provided by cities	Events are core to tourism, the top industry Destination Development Plan provides the strategy "Recognizing the value and unlimited potential of events as both a tool of economic diversification as well as a driver of social cohesion, Greater Palm Springs leadership works closely with public and private sectors to put events on the forefront of Greater Palm Springs' growth and brand development strategies." Not clear if there is direct government ownership of events (if there is it is minor)

Tuscon, Arizona with Pima County (2017) Population: City 50,000; SMA 1 million	
https://www.visittucson.org/	
https://www.visittucson.org/visit/events-festivals this website contains the IFEA award video	
No explicit mention of 'portfolio' The report describes an 'event ecosystem' involving media, sponsors, volunteers, professionals, businesses and residents as supporting the events sector Events highlighted: festivals; parade/procession; trade fair; sports; conference; street fairs; rodeo Civic Event Committee under City Manager is the regulatory body Funding: a bed tax enables Visit Tucson to support events, based on (a) room-nights generated and (b) national or international exposure City and County also fund events No direct government ownership of events	"The General Plan is the City's long-term strategic plan developed through numerous community workshops. …There are numerous goals related directly to embracing arts, culture and events: 1. A community whose economic stability and sense of place reflects its commitment to arts and culture and its care for the natural environment; 2. A community whose vibrant economy and quality of life benefits residents and attracts visitors; 3. Encourage community and neighborhood events and ensure their safety through accessible City permitting and coordination; 4. Improve the quality of life and livability of the community through the arts by supporting avenues for expression and creativity that strengthen and enhance the social, civic and cultural participation of citizens; 5. Promote heritage destinations and annual heritage events regionally, nationally, and internationally.
Des Moines, Iowa (2017) Population: City: 219,000; region: 500,000	
https://www.catchdesmoines.com/about/	
No explicit mention of 'portfolio' Events highlighted: state fair, festivals, markets, concerts, golf, track and field, agriculture expo, parade Data indicate that visiting events is one of the top three reasons to visit the city Funding: portions of hotel tax go to Bravo and to the Visitor and Convention Bureau to support events Bravo Greater Des Moines is a partnership of 22 municipalities: "Arts and culture mean business in Des Moines. Not only is the sector a $185 million industry, but through a unique regional partnership, public investment in Bravo Greater Des Moines pumps more than $3.5 million in hotel/motel tax dollars into more than 70 arts and culture non-profits annually, from festivals to live theater, architecture to Broadway."	No clear strategy or goals Recognition that events contribute to quality of life "The success of festivals and events in Des Moines is due to the community's attendance, involvement, financial support and volunteerism." From their website: "The Greater Des Moines Convention & Visitors Bureau and the Des Moines Area Sports Commission, collectively known as Catch Des Moines, market the region as a visitor destination increasing economic growth and enhancing the visitor experience." Apparently no city ownership of events

Philadelphia, Pennsylvania (2018) Population: City: 1.6 million, region: 6 million	
https://phlevents.org/ this website contains the IFEA award video	
No explicit mention of 'portfolio'	No clear strategy or goals
No documentation of an events strategy	The document refers to over 1,600 'man-aged events', but this is regulation
The only policy relates to regulations	
Two lead agencies are city's Office of Special Events and the Parks and Recreation Special Events Office	"These impressive figures speak to the overall health and vibrancy of Philadelphia's event landscape and hospitality industry as a whole."
Events highlighted: parades, running events, regatta, festivals, consumer/trade shows, track meet	
Funding: two 'signature' running events are directly operated by city, plus funding assistance is available to others	Benefits are identified as economic impact, lasting image and bringing people together.
A portion of bed taxes goes to attracting conventions and events	

Dublin, Ohio (2014) Population: 43,000 Region: it is a suburb of Columbus	
https://dublinohiousa.gov/events/; https://www.visitdublinohio.com/	
No explicit mention of 'portfolio' or 'strategy'	Resident surveys show a high value attached to events
Events highlighted: Irish festival; St. Patrick's Day Parade, golf (home of annual PGA's Heritage Classic)	Event strategy is not explicit, but clearly linked to the Irish theme
Bed tax supports CVB and in turn it supports events financially; the bed tax also pays for a CVB special events coordinator	Economic impact of events is documented
The City has an Events Administration Department with and Event Manager and A Volunteer Coordinator; funds are available to assist events	Formal goals for the City apply to events: health and wellness; broad economic development - especially tourism; fostering partnerships
The City produces several events directly	

Winnipeg, Canada (2018) Population: 750,000	
https://www.tourismwinnipeg.com; https://winnipeg.ca/filmandspecialevents/	
No mention of 'portfolio'	Goals are contained in the city's 25-year development plan
No specific events plan	
The IFEA submission was made by Tourism Winnipeg, a division of the City's Economic Development department	Strong emphasis on tourism and on being a winter city
	Promotion of arts and culture is also important
Funding is through a "special event tourism fund" managed by Tourism Winnipeg using accommodation tax revenue	Sports-event and convention bidding are part of Tourism Winnipeg's mandate
Also available: grants from Winnipeg Arts Council	
Events highlighted: festivals, exhibition, marathon native Pow Wow, Pride fest	"Enabling strategies" include promoting the city as a world-class event venue
Regulations administered by the City's Film and Special Events Office; a 45 member special events committee co-ordinates city departments	

Ottawa, Canada (2018) Population: 1 million metro area	
https://www.ottawafestivals.ca/; https://www.ottawatourism.ca/	
No mention of 'portfolio' Events highlighted: Winterlude, running events, festivals Ottawa Tourism is also a sport tourism agency and bids on events The city encourages partnerships and networking, including Ottawa Festival Network, Arts Council and Music Industry Coalition Funding: events can receive funds from the National Capital Commission, Heritage Canada (a federal agency) and the City (cultural funding) The festival network receives financial support	Strategy: a collaboration of Ottawa Tourism and the City aims to "bid more, win more, host more" events Local festivals and events are part of the City's PR strategy Being the nation's capital there is always a federal involvement in development and major events 2017 was Canada's 150th anniversary and Ottawa hosted a complete year of special events, many one-time only
Rotterdam, Netherlands (2015) Population: City 600,000; region: 1.2 million	
https://zakelijk.rotterdamfestivals.nl/about-rotterdam-festivals	
No mention of 'portfolio' Festivals supported by the city attract 3.9 million visitors a year Events highlighted: festivals, architecture biennale, arts fair, tennis, marathon Rotterdam Festivals operates on behalf of the city in a coordination role, knowledge centre (does research), and funder of festivals Top Sport acts in the sports field for the city Not a producer of events	The city claims to have a "cohesive program of events" and a "consistent and innovative event policy" Is the "Dutch city of sports" Festivals are supported for the aims of "bonding and identity" "The festival infrastructure plays a vital role in the economic life of the city" From their website: "Rotterdam Festivals coordinates Rotterdams events policy and encourages culture participation of the citizens of Rotterdam. We realise a distinctive festival programme with events that are embraced by Rotterdammers, that reflect the themes of the city and deeply penetrates throughout the city and into the world. Under the umbrella of Uitagenda Rotterdam and in collaboration with the cultural institutions we aim to reach a wide and divers public as possible for culture in Rotterdam. The knowledge we gain during our activities we share actively with the sector. Our activities range from financial support for festivals to collaborative marketing, and from developing festival programmes to distributing cultural information about Rotterdam."

Krakow, Poland (2016) Population: 800,000 (plus 200,000 students)	
http://www.krakow.travel/en/	
No mention of "portfolio" Only festivals are highlighted The Krakow Festival Office operates the convention centre and city arena, and works with the Department of Culture and National Heritage The city has an Alliance of Independent Festivals which is an "advocate for sustainable festival development and the health of the festival ecosystem" See a Prezi on Krakow Festival Office at: https://prezi.com/vcxoytg12jhq/krakow-festival-office/	The document demonstrates a culture-led tourism and economic development strategy Krakow Festival Office is a city agency; it implements the city's "cultural and creative strategy" and produces 12 of its "flagship events" Was a previous European Capital of Culture (2000) Belongs to UNESCO Creative Cities Network and to the Festivals City Network
Moscow, Russia (2018) Population: 12.5 million	
https://moscowseasons.com/en/about	
No mention of 'portfolio'", but it is clear that the application pertains to a managed set of city-produced events called 'Moscow Seasons' Events highlighted: Journey to Christmas, Pancake Week, festivals, re-enactments (sports are feature within some of the street festivals) Funding: "an open tender is held once a year to determine the organizers of the festivals. The winners receive funding to organize, put on, and promote city festivals." The City's Dept. of Trade and Services selects participants (e.g. vendors) and co-ordinates activities; all services provided free Also involved is Moscow Fairs Agency, Moscow City Investment Agency, and Dept of Culture	"Moscow Seasons are part of the City's strategy to develop event tourism and provide residents with quality entertainment" On the website it is described as a "project" of the City All events in this portfolio are free to enter and participate, making the events popular with residents
Sao Paulo, Brazil (2014) Population: City: 11.3 million, region: 20million	
http://www.spturis.com; http://www.cidadedesaopaulo.com	
No mention of 'portfolio' or 'strategy' A joint application by Sao Paolo Tourism and the city Sao Paolo Tourism is an official tourism and events company that produces events, promotes and regulates, and funds events Claims 90,000 events annually in the city Events highlighted: trade fairs, carnival, World Cup, festivals, Pride parade, Formula 1, sports fest, fashion week	Claims to be the 'Brazilian Capital of Events'" as well as a 'capital of culture'

Taichung City, Taiwan (2018) Population: 1.1 million	
https://english.taichung.gov.tw/	
No mention of 'portfolio' or 'strategy'	"Festivals are iconic symbols that represent a city's culture. They have meanings and hold memories for local residents but also act as a great access point for visitors to learn about and experience a city."
The City's role is not clear when it comes to producing or support events	
The document mentions various city agencies including tourism, sports, culture, industrial development, economic development and a council for the affairs of a local ethnic group	Festivals provide a city with a platform to showcase its creative and vibrant energy and give the city a unique brand. Festivals bolster a city's cultural economy and help develop citizens' pride and a sense of positive identification toward their city. As a result, festivalization has become a global trend of city development.
Events highlighted: festivals, pilgrimage, bike-week fair/sport, mini marathon	
Funding is available to events by city agencies "To assess the public benefit, the government will consider the review system, activity type, the level of risk, and location into the management policy."	
The city directly produces events:	Taichung, too, has been dedicatedly promoting festivalization. Dubbed as the "event city," the city hosts featured activities all year round with a glamorous variety throughout the four seasons."
"Taichung City is known for its multiple colorful events held throughout the year, with the government being the hosting organizer for many of them, including: the New Year Concert, the Central Taiwan Lantern Festival, Taichung Children's Art Festival, Daan Sand Sculpture Music Festival, Taichung Jazz Festival, Taichung International Dance and Parade Festival, and Taichung Arts Festival. The government considers an event's scale and type to decide whether or not to commission an event planning company to run it with the government still being the head organizer."	
Jinju, South Korea (2015) Population: 350,000	
http://english.jinju.go.kr/main/	
No mention of 'portfolio' or 'strategy'	Goals expressed: enhance image of city, foster growth of culture, promote tourism through world-famous festivals and to promote local products
"The city has overall responsibilities from the festival planning to setting up of budgets to their approvals".	
"Culture and Tourism Department" is lead agency	
Funding from three levels of government	
Events highlighted: commemorative and arts festivals	
New Taipei City Taiwan (2017) Population: 3.9 million	
https://foreigner.ntpc.gov.tw/	
'Portfolio' not mentioned; no strategy evident	Tourism and culture are both emphasized
Events highlighted: rituals, festivals pilgrimage, marathon	
The city sports office produces the marathon	
The city agriculture departments produces events	

Hadong-Gun, South Korea (2017) Population: 50,000	
http://www.hadong.go.kr/english.web	
No mention of 'portfolio' or 'strategy'	This is a thin document; few details
The County has a Local Festival Committee within the Office of Culture and Tourism	It features festivals that 'represent' the region, evidently within a national approach to developing regional identity
Festivals promote "local specialties and environmental factors, including tea, flowers, fish, fruit, mineral water, cherry blossoms, kimchi; there is also a literary festival mentioned	It is an official "slow city"

The document states: "activation of local economy through festivals" |
| Direct government funding of festivals, with the 'tea festival' receiving the most | It is implied that the County plans and produces the main festivals |

Boryeong-Si, Chungcheongnam-Do, South Korea (2018)	
http://www.brcn.go.kr/eng.do	
The application is not available	
Coastal city, famous for its annual mud festival	

Dubai, Emirates (2016) Population: 2.5 million	
https://www.visitdubai.com/en	
This document explicitly refers to and describes their event portfolio: "We have experienced tremendous growth in both our business and leisure event portfolios…"

The document claims there were over 2,000 events held in the previous 12 months including 950 leisure events and over 1,000 business events

Dubai Tourism is evidently the lead agency

"Specific Dubai Tourism units responsible for the Emirate's ever-growing events portfolio include…"

Partnerships are emphasized: "…each of these new concepts or partnerships were developed to further amplify Dubai's portfolio of events and showcase our diverse capabilities in both developing new events and encouraging new interests and trends"

Key Agencies:

Dubai Business Events and Dubai Festivals and Retail Establishment (DFRE) are responsible within Visit Dubai

Dubai Culture and Arts Authority also supports events

Dubai Design District supports events

Dubai Sports Council

Dubai World Trade Centre (convention and exhibition) | Their strategy is to use events to achieve ambitious tourism and economic development goals

Boasts of being a "leading cultural and events capital"

The ambition to be a "global city" is clear

Events are said to be a "showcase" for growing expertise in a range of economic activities

There is an emphasis in their events to present the Emirates culture and distinct brand

A number of major events are produced by the FFRE

Probably no other city has invested more in special events venues and districts - for culture, arts, sport, and design

"Events and festivals have become a way of life in Dubai, with residents, regional visitors and, increasingly, international tourists aware that at any time throughout the year there is an abundance of activities to keep them engaged, entertained and excited." |

Taupo, New Zealand (2016) Population: 36,000	
https://www.taupodc.govt.nz/our-district/events/Pages/default.aspx	
Makes explicit references to event portfolios	Uses "events capital" as a brand
Events highlighted: Ironman, concert, cycling, festivals, swimming, rugby street art, hunting show	"The district's overall events portfolio continues to grow…"
Council's "events team" has specific goals and roles: "prospecting" for new events, capacity building, building a calendar of events, partnerships, infrastructure, marketing, maximizing economic benefits	"A balanced portfolio of diverse festivals and events spread evenly throughout the year, in keeping with the seasonal climate, ensures our district is a great and vibrant place to live."
The Council has an "events shed" with equipment for events, and a event trailer to move stuff	"with a well-developed sporting portfolio…"
	No direct government production/ownership of events

Gold Coast, Australia (2018) Population: 600,000	
http://www.goldcoast.qld.gov.au/thegoldcoast/events-118.html	
Their events strategy: http://www.goldcoast.qld.gov.au/documents/ps/Gold-Coast-City-Events-Strategic-Plan-2011-2015.pdf	
Follows an explicit event portfolio strategy	The award submission was a joint initiative between City of Gold Coast, Destination Gold Coast and Tourism Events Queensland.
Events highlighted: Commonwealth Games, golf, festivals, marathon, car racing, triathlon, surfing, TV awards	
The City Events Unit has the explicit role of "event investment and the development of a strategic citywide events portfolio"	The City has an 'Events Strategic Plan' to position Gold Coast "a global events destination" and an "elite sport city"
Several "controlled entities" (e.g., Cultural Precinct") within the City administration each "develop and deliver a portfolio of events funded by the city, and coordinate with private event producers".	"The city's events portfolio is integral to the city's reputation…"
Funding for events, and for bidding, is from the city and the State of Queensland	A heavy emphasis has been placed on the 2018 Commonwealth Games and legacy of venues and infrastructure
"Events play a significant role in the liveability, lifestyle, and image of the Gold Coast and provide benefits to the city's economy, add to residents' lifestyle opportunities and enhance the experience of visitors.	"The City understands the cultural, social and economic benefits of events and has a strong event community that works together to ensure the continued success of this important industry on the Gold Coast."
	"In short 32% of domestic Gold Coast visitors said that festivals/community events, theatre or concert events, major events or live sports events were the reason they chose to come to Gold Coast."

Newcastle, Australia (2016) Population:160,000	
http://www.newcastle.nsw.gov.au/home	
http://www.newcastle.nsw.gov.au/Newcastle/media/Documents/Strategies, Plans and Policies/Plans/2355-Events-Plan-2016-19-WEB_v2.pdf	
'Portfolio' is mentioned once as the city is "building on its existing event portfolio" Events highlighted: hockey, motorbiking, surfing, mountain biking, Anzac Day, skateboarding, writers' festival, music festival, conference Notes that in 2013 in peak holiday season 20% of visitors "reported coming to Newcastle to attend an event or festival" The city and Destination New South Wales (state) are in partnership regarding events development and promotion	Emphasizes how this 'steel city' has been repositioning into "a thriving cultural and events city" Support strategy is clear, with 3 criteria: 1: local economic impact generated 2: strategic and marketing value 3: community benefits Newcastle Business Events is the convention bureau, also there is an "Inter-agency Events Coordinating Group" An events strategy is mentioned, but was not complete; see the website to download the 2016-2019 plan
Coffs Harbour, Australia (2018) Population: 75,000	
https://www.coffsharbour.nsw.gov.au/; https://www.coffscoastevents.com.au/	
Their events strategy: https://www.coffsharbour.nsw.gov.au/Business/Documents/ATT1 Coffs Harbour Event Strategy 2020 %282%29.pdf	
Explicitly recognizes the portfolio management concept "Developing a successful event portfolio is a complex task…" "sports tourism events portfolio" is identified Events highlighted: car rally, cricket, festivals, triathlon, touch football The City is involved in direct ownership of events plus financial support "Depending on the type of event, Council may act as an owner/organiser, facilitator, sponsor, supporter or venue manager. Council as the event organiser, undertakes a number of festivals and events of all sizes including major events at the C.ex Coffs International Stadium, Coffs Harbour International Buskers and Comedy Festival, Multicultural Harmony Festival, Japanese Festival of Children's Day as well as regular events such as the weekly Coffs Coast Growers Markets held in the City Centre. Council also acts as an investor for events, providing financial and in-kind support Criteria for funding are specified: economic development; community development; branding and marketing; sustainability New South Wales State also provides support for events throughout the state	The City has both Events and Tourism strategies "These two plans have developed the pathway for the attraction and retention of a variety of events to position the Coffs Coast as the foremost regional destination for festivals and events, leisure and nature-based tourism and cultural experiences." Events strategy covers: spreading events all year; balancing major events with community events; appeal to varied audiences

Port Macquarie Hastings, NSW, Australia (2017) Population: 50,000

https://www.pmhc.nsw.gov.au/Home; https://portmacquarieinfo.com.au/host-your-event

The city has an "exciting events portfolio"

"The events portfolio will also bring growth to place-making outcomes."

Events highlighted: Ironman, touch football, market, theatre, festivals, surfing, youth week, Australia Day

"Council plays several roles in the event space. It acts as a government regulatory body, as well as an events advocate , supporter, sponsor, and for some events - organizer and owner".

There are two event teams: Community Participation Team operates resident-oriented events and Major Events, which bids; they will also "seed and establish major events".The Port "Macquarie Hastings Council runs and coordinates numerous events and festivals across the region. Hosting one of the largest events on the region's calendar (Tastings on Hastings), Council's Community Participation team deliver key community driven outcomes for the region, resulting in strong economic growth and community capacity building. Council has budgeted and invested in some of the region's largest and most diverse events including Tastings on Hastings, Australia Day, NAIDOC Week, Heritage Festival, Youth Week, Seniors Week, Countdown to Christmas and ArtWalk, enabling access, inclusion and participation in festival and events for all members of the community.

Council's Community Participation team actively encourages and collaborates with community groups to enable community driven events to develop and grow. Working closely with organisations, they foster growth of skills within the community, and facilitate the development and processes within the government system to enable events and programs to proceed. This is supported by a community grants program, designed to support community programs and events."

The city's Destination Management Plan recognizes event tourism benefits to the community, environment and local economy

The City's Economic Development Portfolio encompasses event tourism

11% of total visitation is attributed to "events or event-related activities".

Three key actions to implement strategy: collaboration, proactive engagement and 'place vibrancy'

"The Major Events Strategic Action Plan seeks to achieve three major outcomes:

• A successful regional events destination: Greater Port Macquarie is recognised as a premier regional event destination due to social, economic and place-making benefits, and Council and the community are seen to be supportive and welcoming of major events;

• Supporting Self- sustainable events: Council works with key stakeholders to create an environment that is conducive to growing self-sustainable major signature events, facilitating good place-making, social and economic outcomes; and

• An increased return on investment: The economic impact from major events sponsored and supported by Council will increase by 5% annually with events placed in off-peak tourist seasons being a priority. The events portfolio will also bring growth to place-making outcomes."

Sydney, Australia (2018) Population:5 million (metropolitan)	
https://int.sydney.com/; https://www.businesseventssydney.com.au/	
Submitted by Destination NSW (a State agency)	Aims to be 'world class' and branded as 'Australia's Events Capital' and a 'Business Events City'
Event portfolio is only mentioned once, referring to the State of NSW and its "creative industries events portfolio"	"With its role as an events city so firmly embedded in city planning…"
Events highlighted: running festival/marathon, fashion week, festivals, musical shows, exhibitions, parade, tennis, football, golf, opera	City and Destination NSW are a "strategic partnership"
Both the City and State of NSW fund events	The State's Visitor Economy Action Plan applies
The City produces the New Year's Eve spectacular	
Business Events City is the convention bureau	

Major observations

The size of cities and regions is a critical factor to consider. City/regional populations in the sampling range from small (for example, under 100,000 in Tuscon, Hadong-Gun, Dublin, Ohio) to very large (20 million in the San Paulo region in Brazil). 'World cities' compete aggressively to host the biggest and most prestigious events, build the largest and most attractive venues, and engage in sophisticated branding and place marketing. In contrast, some of the smaller cities follow a 'place-making' strategy in which events are used to advance the community in a triple-bottom-line or balanced-scorecard manner. Some Australian cities, for example, have separate policies for tourism-oriented 'major events' and for 'community events'.

There is widespread recognition of the multiple values derived from events, including economic, social, and cultural. Tourism and economic development seem to dominate overall, but in many cities economic and social/cultural goals appear to be equally important. Newcastle in Australia is a city employing culture, tourism and events for re-positioning, in their case departing from a 'steel city' reputation.

A strategy that takes a long-term perspective is 'sustainability'. The usual use of this term in the documents is related to the 'greening' of events. For example, Gold Coast's City Events Unit "…is an active participant of the citywide Events Sustainability Working Group, tasked with developing and implementing sustainability measures at all Gold Coast events." Another example: "The City of Philadelphia is dedicated to providing event producers and organizers with the necessary resources and information to encourage sustainable and ethical organized events." Newcastle has the vision of being a "smart, livable and sustainable city" and provides pertinent social/cultural, environmental and economic goals.

The term 'sustainable' is also used in the context of ensuring viable and resilient events, and for sustainable development or economic growth. The two usages were combined in a description from Dubai of its Dubai International Kite Festival (DIKF): " Keeping in line with the sustainable development vision of Dubai, the event was designed as a green event focusing on consideration for the environment and respect for natural resources." Dubai also emphasizes sustainable development of the event sector as a goal.

Coffs Harbour has a Sustainable Living Festival. "This is held in November each year and showcases the natural beauty and wonder of the region and focuses on all areas of sustainable living including healthy food & lifestyles, saving energy & water, growing your own food, backyard biodiversity, supporting local food, reducing waste and ethical choices." The city employ a Sustainable Living and Community Programs Coordinator who manages a number of community events.

Event-specific plans or strategies are not the norm, except in Australia, and in many cases the strategy and goals for events are subsumed under tourism and economic development, and sometimes in partnership with community culture and leisure. Newcastle, Australia has developed a full event strategy. Port Macquarie, Australia is another small city with a well-developed events strategy, featuring both major events (tourism oriented) and community events. The city is both producer and funding agency, regulator and bidder. Australian cities and states in general are probably the most sophisticated in developing and managing event portfolios, with a long history of both city and state-level event development agencies going back to the 1980s.

Newcastle, Australia is the only one of these award cities that mentioned an events plan. The Newcastle City Council Events Plan 2016-2019 implements in part the vision set by the city's general strategic plan, and reflects triple-bottom-line thinking. The plan identifies three categories of event, including community events, flagship events, and major events.

A majority of the cities do not use the term 'legacy'. In Newcastle's funding criteria both legacy and sustainability points are given, with sustainability referring to the likelihood the event can endure, whereas legacy refers to measurable outputs. Neither of these connotations embodies the principles of theory of change, wherein an event (or events in concert) might be conceived as agents of change for lasting (i.e legacy) outcomes/impacts such as social integration, economic prosperity, cultural transformation, or a sustainable environment. These high-end outcome goals are generally mentioned, but with no pathways identified.

Evidence of portfolio management

'Event portfolio' is a term in widespread use in Australia and New Zealand, but not elsewhere. Sometimes 'portfolio' was used in a way that indicates recognition that there is more than one event, but does not imply a portfolio strategy or management. Nevertheless, there are clear indications of strategy when goals, policies, plans and funding priorities are stated.

As it was discussed in Chapter 5, there are four trajectories of event portfolio development, namely symmetrisation, specialisation, multi-constellation, and macro-expansion. The evidence from the explored cases demonstrates that the multi-constellation strategy appears to be the most widespread and easiest to manage approach.

The multi-constellation trajectory with a variety of different genres of events, incorporated in a city portfolio, has been portrayed in most of the analysed documents. A multiplicity of event-related goals are being pursued, mostly economic and social/cultural. Some cities produce their own events, but most do not. A minority have explicit portfolio strategies or event-specific plans. In other words, the majority engage in limited portfolio management, and no doubt they arrived at this status of being 'eventful cities' in an organic manner rather than by a clear event strategy. The adjective 'eclectic' applies, as the cities pursue their own goals and policies towards events in a manner that suits their history, culture and politics. Only in Australia and New Zealand, plus Dubai, is there a pattern of explicit event portfolio development and management. Dubai is in a class of its own, being a world city that has invested enormous sums of money in venues and events, and in attractions and tourism in general. Dubai, and other cities in the Gulf, went very quickly from under-developed to major players on the world economic and tourism stage.

Symmetrisation or a proportional clustering of events based on their type or scale was not explicitly used or mentioned by the IFEA award cities, but it is implicit in the hierarchy described earlier in the Newcastle events plan. It also reveals itself implicitly in the ways in which event populations and event calendars were presented. Most cities boasted of numerous events (mostly festivals and sports) in their calendar, but highlighted a selection that they believed reflected their strengths and accomplishments. While the vast majority of noted festivals and cultural celebrations were permanent (many being hallmark events with institutional status), sport events were both permanent (i.e., 'owned' by the city/destination) and one-time, being won through competitive bidding. For example, Gold Coast featured its hosting of the 2018 Commonwealth Games and a substantial legacy, but this occurred in the context of an existing strategy to use events comprehensively as catalysts and attractions, and for place marketing and image making.

The Moscow Seasons is an example of specialisation which refers to a destination focused on a particular type of event and associated purposes. Moscow Season project is in reality a well-defined, city-owned and tightly managed portfolio of tourism-oriented events, also designed to provide free entertainment to residents (Figure 12.2). The city agency, Moscow Seasons, determines who will receive city funds through competitive bidding. This is the only case of a sub-set of the event population being the focus of the application. It might be considered a very limited portfolio strategy, but there is obviously some merit in confining event portfolios to a group that can be efficiently managed to achieve priority goals. Not only are the events in this portfolio funded and regulated, but city-driven goals prevail.

None of the other award cities appears to focus on a specific type of events, with sports and cultural events figuring prominently in all of them, and business events being mentioned but not featured. In Australian cities it is now normal to have event plans, and a common strategy can be termed "dualism": separate policies and goals for major, tourism-oriented events and for community events.

A Macro-expansion strategy is quite evident in New South Wales and Queensland Australia where the states have their own event development agencies that work closely with local and regional authorities to develop events and tourism. The Australia documents made it clear that city - state collaboration was critical and that local event portfolios benefitted from, and fitted into state strategies.

Goals
- Develop event tourism
- Provide free, quality entertainment for residents

An open tender annually to determine the organisers of city-funded festivals

Figure 12.2: Moscow Seasons portfolio.

Focal organisations and stakeholders

The 'focal organisations' are those with management responsibilities for events, the main one by far being city government. In other cases, the tourism agency or DMO takes the lead, generally because (in the USA at least) it has money to invest, derived primarily from locally-imposed accommodation taxes. Sport commissions, arts and culture bodies, and economic development authorities are also lead agencies when it comes to funding events, but most of these are an integral part of local government and they do not assume regulatory functions. In some cases, the state level is involved, notably in Australia. The number and diversity of stakeholders mentioned in the documents is quite revealing. As noted in two documents (Tuscon and Krakow) this network constitutes an 'event ecosystem', and this suggests another research question: what is the optimal network for collaboration and for management of an event portfolio? Comparative social network analysis could reveal how focal organisations can maximize efficient links and have the greatest impact on the portfolio, or even an entire population of events.

Numerous stakeholders are involved (see Figure 12.3), through formal and informal links. Three broad categories of stakeholders are illustrated below, with details extracted from all the reviewed documents. These are venues, business sector and civil society.

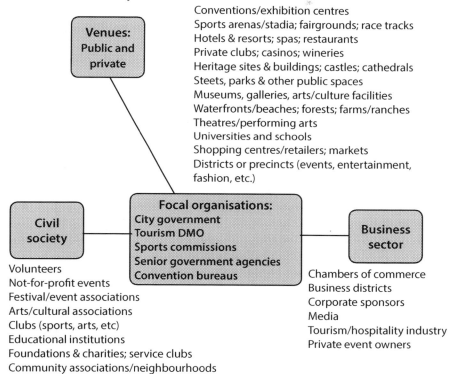

Conventions/exhibition centres
Sports arenas/stadia; fairgrounds; race tracks
Hotels & resorts; spas; restaurants
Private clubs; casinos; wineries
Heritage sites & buildings; castles; cathedrals
Steets, parks & other public spaces
Museums, galleries, arts/culture facilities
Waterfronts/beaches; forests; farms/ranches
Theatres/performing arts
Universities and schools
Shopping centres/retailers; markets
Districts or precincts (events, entertainment, fashion, etc.)

Venues: Public and private

Civil society

Focal organisations:
City government
Tourism DMO
Sports commissions
Senior government agencies
Convention bureaus

Business sector

Volunteers
Not-for-profit events
Festival/event associations
Arts/cultural associations
Clubs (sports, arts, etc)
Educational institutions
Foundations & charities; service clubs
Community associations/neighbourhoods

Chambers of commerce
Business districts
Corporate sponsors
Media
Tourism/hospitality industry
Private event owners

Figure 12.3: Three main stakeholder groups and specific examples.

The critical importance of 'venues' is evident, with an impressive array of venue types holding importance in the event sectors of these cities. Note that both public and private venues are listed together. It is clear from the documentation that major investments in event venues constitutes either: (a) an essential element of event portfolio management, or (b) is a precursor to becoming an eventful city. A research question follows: which comes first, venues or event portfolio management? This chicken or egg question is more serious than it seems, because there could be a slow evolution of venue development leading to more and more events needing management, or a city could develop its event strategy and then build the necessary venues. Perhaps it does not make much of a difference, but a retrospective assessment of the evolution of events, venues and policy or strategy across a diverse range of cities would be informative.

It is natural that volunteers constitute an important stakeholder group, but the analysis reveals a much broader category, labelled 'civil society' and defined for our purposes as non-governmental, voluntary institutions, plus the collective actions of citizens and groups that contribute to the event sector. In contrast is the business sector, with the tourism and hospitality sector being the biggest category. Tourism is the driving force in many of the cities, and it is fair to say that in North America destination development through events and venues is generally accepted as business as usual.

Taking both perspectives, civil society and business, it can be said that the 'legitimation' of events has become universal. It is impossible to imagine a modern city without a range of venues and events catering to many interests, both for community value and economic development.

The role of government

Local authorities, or the city and other agencies in collaboration, have multiple roles to play. Some cities directly produce their own events, and while this suggests a high level of portfolio management it does not define event portfolio management. Many cities have professional event staff in a number of departments, or in a dedicated events unit, and they play a variety of roles: direct event production; reviewing funding requests; co-ordination, such as producing event calendars; marketing and communications; event and venue planning; provision of in-kind services, and regulation. The regulatory function is generic, as all cities have rules and regulations governing events and venues.

Three generic models could be identified. **Model 1** is the city (local government) being the focal organisation, but with portfolio management taking the form of regulation, funding, and perhaps co-ordination. **Model 2** has the city as the driving force, engaged in a much higher level of portfolio management, including the ownership and production of events, and a clear events strategy or plan. Newcastle is an example, and they have developed comprehensive funding criteria. Moscow is a special case of this, as their application was concerned with a sub-set of city-owned but privately produced festivals (Figure 12.3). **Model 3** places events under tourism, the DMO or an economic development agency of the city, in which case events primarily serve those interests. The city of Des Moines is an example of this model (Figure 12.4). It demonstrates a common North American strategy in which a tourism agency or a DMO (in this case a convention and visitor bureau) is the central agency because it has funds to support events secured through accommodation or other service-industry taxes.

In the case of Des Moines there is also a consortium of local authorities (the metropolitan area) supporting arts and culture through an agency called Bravo. Their portfolio of events could be defined by those receiving money, some of which will be permanent beneficiaries (e.g., the state fair, as Des Moines is state capital). This tri-partite network of tourism/economic development, arts and culture, and community quality of life demonstrates the necessity of managing overlapping event portfolios, a complex task that can only be implemented through formal collaboration.

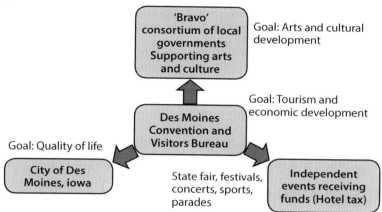

Figure 12.4: The example of Des Moines, Iowa (DMO as the focal organisation).

Evaluation strategies

It is quite evident that evaluation and impact assessment is either not being done or is very basic in nature. None of the submissions provided data on "dedicated event tourists", being the numbers attracted to the city specifically by events. Therefore, they could not provide an estimate of the economic impact of events. Many relied upon very general estimates of visitor numbers and economic impact, usually derived from tourism agencies at a higher level (e.g., state/province or nation). The Australians have better data on event tourism than most other countries.

A notable absence in all documents is consideration of events as 'assets' with individual value, and value towards the portfolio as a whole. However, specific goals and benefits of events are generally listed, and the Newcastle plan provides specific guidance to determining event value, starting with overall values and goals, and including a weighting system to determine which events to support. The sustainability of individual events is considered in the Newcastle plan, and in other documents there is discussion of sustainability from the perspective of greening events.

To advance portfolio management it will be necessary to develop concepts, measures and methods appropriate for large numbers of events, at least those receiving funds and other forms of support. For entire populations of events there are even greater challenges.

Summary

The purpose of this chapter was to compare 23 destinations which obtained an IFEA international award as best festival and event cities. The criterion for comparison was the level of event industry development on a city level, including stakeholder networks, city event policies and strategies and the extent of event portfolio development and implementation. The results of the analysis demonstrate, that although all the cities under study realise the economic and socio-cultural value of public events, the implementation of strategic portfolio approaches is still at an embryonic stage, with a lack of destination vision and established procedures. Some of the cities implement so called 'portfolio-like' approaches (Moscow, for example), however, evaluation and long-term legacy and leveraging strategies are not developed.

13 Conclusions

In this concluding chapter we summarize the major theoretical and practical contributions of the book, and suggest a research agenda to further the understanding and praxis of event portfolio management. An ontological map is first presented (Figure 13.1) that identifies and inter-connects the main concepts and terms used in this book – which we believe reflect the state of art in event portfolio studies. These terms and concepts are categorized as follows: (a) core definition and propositions (being the basis for event portfolio studies); (b) theoretical foundations, and (c) major themes explored in this book that pertain to the planning and management of event portfolios. The ensuing discussion leads to our proposed research agenda and concluding thoughts.

'Event portfolio' defined

There are two main origins of the term 'portfolio' that we draw upon, namely product portfolios within marketing, and financial portfolios that are managed by and for investors. Both are strategic in nature and give rise to the holistic definition used in this book, which also integrates the socio-cultural grounds of events:

> An event portfolio is the strategic patterning of disparate but interrelated events taking place during the course of the year in a host community that as a whole is intended to achieve multiple outcomes through the implementation of joint event strategies (Ziakas, 2014, p. 14).

The management of event portfolios can take many forms, embodying different values and strategies, programming and degrees of control, but in all cases 'portfolio management' implies a goals-oriented approach to the creation and control of multiple events to achieve their synergistic potential.

Core definition & propositions

An event portfolio is the strategic patterning of disparate but interrelated events taking place during the course of the year in a host community that as a whole is intended to achieve multiple outcomes through the implementation of joint strategies.

> **P1:** A paradigm shift has occurred (i.e., the legitimation of events in multiple roles; from single events to portfolios; emphasis on long-term sustainability)
>
> **P2:** 'Eventful cities' depend upon portfolio management
>
> **P3:** Event portfolios maximise the potential for beneficial leveraging and synergistic interactions
>
> **P4:** Overlapping event portfolios are a frequent complication necessitating coordination
>
> **P5:** Governance and management can take many forms reflecting unique circumstances, but a focal organisation will usually be required.

Foundation theories

> Marketing: product life cycle and product portfolios
>
> Financial portfolio management
>
> Event tourism
>
> Organisation ecology
>
> Inter-organisational relationships; stakeholder theory; networks; collaboration
>
> Systems theory
>
> Evaluation and impact assessment
>
> Competitive and comparative advantage
>
> Governance, ownership and decision making

Event portfolio management (themes, concepts, models and tools)

> Leveraging strategies & tactics for tourism & social leveraging
>
> Roles for hallmark, iconic, mega, community, and one-time vs. periodic events
>
> Relatedness and multiplicity
>
> Critical portfolio design factors
>
> Pyramid, matrix & process models
>
> Governance models & development strategies (symmetrisation, specialisation, multi-constellation, macro-expansion)
>
> Evaluation and impact assessment tools: Logic and Theory of Change models

Figure 13.1: Ontological map of Event Portfolio Studies.

Core propositions

These are the main claims to knowledge that have shaped our approach to the study and management of event portfolios. Each proposition is derived from research, the available literature, and reflection by the authors. The nature of propositions is that they can be turned into hypotheses for further testing and theory development.

P1: A paradigm shift has occurred

Event portfolios and their management have emerged as a logical outcome of continued increases in the number and significance of planned events in communities, cities and destinations around the world. In turn, this reflects the **legitimation** of planned events as instruments of public policy and corporate strategy, leading to the situation in which diverse events are an expected element in contemporary lifestyles and in liveable and attractive cities and destinations. Taking a more diverse and strategic approach to event planning, and thereby changing the focus of research and management from single events to portfolios of events, constitutes a major paradigm shift. This shift has occurred parallel to a growing interest in triple-bottom-line or balanced-scorecard management and to **sustainability** in general, all of which focus on taking a long-term perspective on desired change as opposed to a preoccupation with immediate outputs.

P2: 'Eventful cities' depend upon portfolio management

Place-making and place marketing go together in the Eventful City, a concept that is linked to 'creative cities', 'event tourism', 'competitive destinations' and other terms describing place-making and place marketing/branding in which events figure prominently. The positioning and re-positioning of cities through a 'culture-led strategy' is a related phenomenon. Event portfolio management provides essential ingredients and processes.

P3: Event portfolios maximise the potential for beneficial leveraging and synergistic interactions

The major synergies made feasible through event portfolio management include the following:

◆ The leveraging of multiple events for social, cultural, economic, ecological and built- environment benefits;

◆ Efficiencies gained through resource and intelligence sharing, joint marketing, multi-use venues, and the pursuit of major goals through strategic planning;

◆ Greater public acceptance of events, venues and interventions through the demonstration of benefits and transparent accountability.

P4: Overlapping event portfolios are the norm

With event portfolios being developed to reflect diverse policy aims, in particular culture, social and community development, economic development, environmental sustainability, tourism, and corporate strategy, there is a pressing need for co-ordination, collaboration, and the fostering of value co-creation networks. A laissez-faire approach will ensure redundancies, inefficiencies and potential conflicts.

P5: Governance and management can take many forms reflecting unique circumstances

Many styles and forms of portfolio governance and management exist, reflecting the unique history, politics and environments of cities and destinations; there is no single level or style of management that fits all. For governance of the collaboration necessary to make event portfolio management effective, deliberate stakeholder management (or relationship marketing) is essential.

Theoretical foundations

The study and management of event portfolios draws upon foundation theories from traditional disciplines, mainstream management and closely-connected fields such as tourism. We include models, concepts and frameworks. These are the main theoretical foundations.

Marketing and the product life cycle

In terms of the evolution of our thinking about event portfolios (see Chapters 1 and 2) there is a clear link to the product life-cycle concept (which is not prescriptive, but intended to shape strategic thinking), and the Boston Consulting Group Matrix (circa 1970) which links relative market share in a competitive environment to market growth when making decisions about the future of products in a company's portfolio. While that approach is informative, it is argued in this book that events cannot be treated like normal consumer-oriented 'products'.

Financial portfolio theory

Several key concepts are derived from financial portfolio management (see Chapter 2), beginning with Markowitz in 1952 who examined the relationships between risks and uncertainty on the one hand and financial returns (or ROI) on the other, when creating a portfolio of assets. Several principles from financial portfolio management can be adapted to event portfolios, including the need for diversification and balance. Event portfolios, however, must meet a multiplicity of goals, not all of which are financial or economic in nature, and such portfolios will have multiple meanings to communities, businesses and other interest groups.

Event tourism

The multiple roles of events in developing tourism and in place-making and place marketing have informed our theorising about event portfolios. Early research on events focused on their economic impacts as tourist attractions and their potential to counteract seasonality of demand, with subsequent attention given to their roles as animators of places and venues, identity builders and co-branding tools. The distinction between the forms and functions of events led to conceptualisation of hallmark events as permanent institutions and iconic events as attractions for special interests, and these are important elements in event portfolios. Mega events have received a great deal of attention and sparked much controversy over their relative costs and benefits, and in particular the equity issues that must be faced. Numerous local and regional events, primarily for and by residents, constitute the base for most event portfolios, both in terms of numbers and social value. More recently attention has been given to the concepts of 'eventful cities' and 'destination capitals', both of which rest upon event portfolio management to some degree.

From a tourism and place-marketing perspective, event-portfolio designers need to consider comparative advantages (such as location and climate), competitive advantages (often linked to investment and professionalism) when strategising and designing event portfolios. In either case, the history, culture and values of the city or destination will shape strategic choices.

Organisational ecology

This set of theory fragments pertains to the reasons why types of organisations exist (i.e., events have become 'legitimized' in their multiple roles) and related population dynamics. Regarding portfolios, there are implications for how events and portfolios of events interact with the wider environment, including the fact that event portfolios exist within whole populations of events (which defy management and are often undocumented) so that competition for resources is a major issue. Births and deaths are normal within all populations of organisms and organisations, and adaptation to changes in the environment is always important, so event portfolio managers must consider how change in a portfolio's composition can be both inevitable and desirable.

Inter-organisational relationships (stakeholder networks and collaboration)

Stakeholders involved in event portfolios must be linked in deliberate collaborations, constituting a network in which embeddedness is nurtured. Embeddedness is defined by multiple, close links to other institutions or events, and especially ties to the governance mechanisms (such as a coordinating group) and the focal organisation that manages the event portfolio. Networks are potential sources of innovation, and have been conceived as instruments for the co-creation of value – these being the primary benefits of event portfolio management. Major synergies, as exemplified by the case studies, include information and resource sharing, joint strategy making and evaluation, lobbying and problem solving. Major networking considerations are the exercise of power (with democratic decision-making preferred) and the building of trust through purposeful collaboration and shared commitment. The 'political market square' is a concept appropriate for the complex collaborations needed to create and manage event portfolios. In this model are negotiations, the formation of alliances, the exercise of power, and gatekeepers who determine who has a legitimate role to play. In true collaborations each member sacrifices some degree of autonomy in pursuit of common goals, much like the process of events become permanent institutions by maintaining committed stakeholders.

Systems theory: Single events can be conceptualized as a transforming process in which inputs are transformed to create desired outputs, but portfolios of events are much more complex open systems. A learning or adaptive system integrates evaluation, continuous improvement, and fostering innovation. Open-systems must interact constantly with their environment to secure resources and support, necessitating stakeholder management. One strategy employed by some events is that of 'institutionalisation', that is securing permanent support and resources by sacrificing a degree of independence; in this process local government is often the key stakeholder, although the focal organization for supporting an event portfolio can be a consortium – as illustrated in the case studies.

Evaluation and impact assessment

Of greatest relevance to portfolio management is the need for 'logic models' to guide planning for outputs, and 'theory of change models' (both discussed in Chapter 6) for longer-term, more complex processes. Since event portfolios are potentially powerful agents of systemic change, whether it be economic, environmental or social in nature, they have to be designed with the evaluation and impact assessment methods and measures built in. While much of this management function entails routine data collection and analysis, requiring key performance indicators, the establishment of an event or event portfolios worth (or value) is a difficult challenge involving, of necessity, different perspectives on value creation. Some stakeholders will need quantitative measures of ROI while others view events as having intrinsic worth. 'Cumulative impact assessment' describes the process by which interactions and synergies are examined, and includes the possibilities of generating unexpected and negative consequences. Uncertainty is always present in longer-term planning, so it must be accompanied by risk assessments and management of risks.

Comparative and competitive advantage

Not all event portfolio goals pertain to tourism, economic development or place marketing, but these have been and will remain major considerations – alongside community-oriented benefits. In this context, events have long been identified as important tourism attractions, image makers, catalysts for development, animators of places, and contributors to place marketing. To some extent these roles depend upon comparative advantages, being a city's or destination's endowments such as accessibility, climate and culture. The creation and effective management of event portfolios is an important element in attaining competitive advantage, as it reflects strategies, professionalism and investments.

Governance, ownership and decision making

We consider the establishment and roles of focal organisations. Their first mandate is to foster inter-organisational collaboration and develop the network synergies important to portfolio management. Second, focal organisations (or some other form of institutional arrangement) engage in multi-stakeholder governance wherein decisions can be made democratically, reflecting the varying goals and priorities of all parties involved in portfolio management and the co-ordination of overlapping event portfolios.

Case studies documented a range of focal organisations, with local government and tourist organisations (CVBs or DMOs) predominant. Sport commissions, arts and culture bodies, and economic development authorities are also lead agencies when it comes to funding events, but most of these are an integral part of local government and they do not assume regulatory functions. In some cases, the state level is involved, notably in Australia. Those who can provide funding to events, collaborations and research have leverage and possibly legitimacy in portfolio creation and management.

Urban or community regimes consist of those stakeholders who form alliances, including between public and private organisations, to achieve common goals. Case studies revealed three crucial categories of stakeholders who have to be brought into portfolio: venues, civil society and the business sector. Venues are often part of the public sector.

The political market square is an analogy for describing how alliances form, power is exerted, and collaborations achieved. The ownership of events is an issue to consider in portfolios, distinguishing between legal ownership (i.e., who owns the asset?) and perceived communal ownership by stakeholders and residents.

A number of governance models were identified in the case studies, for example, Festivals Edinburgh as a consortium of independent events and Moscow Seasons as a portfolio of city-owned but privately managed events.

Portfolio management themes, concepts, models and tools

These themes, concepts, models and tools all pertain to praxis, being the creation and management of event portfolios.

Strategies

Event portfolios do arise organically from the need for co-ordination or sharing among existing events and event-producing organisations, or strategically and top-down, involving conscious policy development and a focal organization. Four main strategies have been examined: symmetrisation, specialisation, multi-constellation, and macro-expansion. The event portfolio pyramid model suggests symmetry, with many small, community-oriented events at the base and a few major or mega-events at the pinnacle. This tends to evolve naturally, but is pursued by some focal organisations – especially in Australian cities (see the case studies) that have separate community and tourism-oriented event strategies. There are portfolios of this type based on tourism and economic development that pursue short-term ROI, such as maximizing tourist bed-nights and spending, and others that are more community-oriented with a longer-term and TBL perspective on symmetries and benefits.

Specialisation is evident when one type of event or target market is prominent, while multi-constellation implies large numbers and a high variety of events to reach broad markets. Macro-expansion is practiced in countries like Scotland that have national, regional and local event portfolio strategies (see the Edinburgh case study) and multiple portfolios are co-ordinated.

Laissez-faire is another option, simply leaving the population of events in an area to exist without interventions such as the direct production of events, grants and subsidies, sponsorship, or coordination. According to the various threads of organisational ecology and theory, the absence of intervention (however unlikely, since even simple public-sector regulations impose constraints and opportunities) might result in intense competition for support and resources, numerous event births and deaths, and the absence of synergies that can produce city or destination-level benefits.

Principles for portfolio design

Decisions about events that are part of a managed portfolio should consider formality, intentionality, directionality and rhythmicity. *Formality* refers to the level of standardisation of portfolios, operating procedures, protocols and rules. The opposing values of formality are 'standardised' and 'amorphous'. *Intentionality* determines to what extent portfolio approaches and initiatives are strategic and intended to achieve certain outcomes. The opposing values are 'purposive' and 'unintended'. *Directionality* describes the orientation of the approaches, either on the supply-side market-led initiatives or demand-side community engagement in portfolio design. *Rhythmicity* refers to the ability of city event managers to modify their approach due to the context changes and revision of objectives, with values being 'intensive' and 'passive'.

Figure 5.3 provides a model. 'Composing' includes a set of tactics to construct a competitive and diverse portfolio of major events. It entails strategic decisions with regard to the selection of events, event roles and factors that influence the process. Synergising focuses on the development of the overall portfolio value, its unity. Portfolio synergy provides event managers with an opportunity to balance events and their outcomes, to manage the portfolio calendar and proactively plan any leveraging strategies. In a synergetic portfolio, events complement one another and produce an integrative network of objectives, resources, stakeholders and expertise.

Leveraging (see Chapter 3)

Smith (2014) distinguishes between *event-led* and *event-themed* leveraging. Event-led leverage projects are closely linked to events and try to expand positive impacts that are normally expected from staging events; event-themed leveraging consists of general initiatives planned to capitalise on and maximise the opportunities derived from hosting an event. In the latter case, an event is used as a hook to achieve more benefits which are not related directly to its hosting.

The Chalip (2004) leveraging model for events identifies the potential to leverage media coverage and attendance through a number of actions including those designed to increase visitor stays and spending. Ziakas (2014a) identified other leveraging techniques focused on tourism: amplify visitation; diversify tourism product; schedule selected events off-season; rejuvenate destinations; consolidate destination assets, and bolster the destination's authenticity. Cross-leveraging among events requires that portfolio managers know how events complement each other and, in turn, how they can be complemented by the attractions, amenities, products, and services of a host community.

Social leveraging occurs when people find communitas in a liminal environment, making events suitable instruments for social marketing and, in concert through portfolios, as agents of systemic change. This process can be facilitated through the application of 'dramaturgy' and symbolism.

Conceptual portfolio models

The *pyramid model* (Figure 5.1), with a broad base of local events having little tourism value and one-off mega-events at the pinnacle, was based on observations about the population of events in many communities and destinations. Research within the frame of organisational ecology (see Chapter 2) has tended to confirm that this structure evolves naturally, but it is not prescriptive. A modified portfolio model for community goals (Figure 5.2), as opposed to tourism, economic development and place marketing, stresses occasional major events and an emphasis on permanent, locally 'owned' events.

Matrix models pertain to portfolio composition, with the matrix (Figure 6.4) based on the original Boston Consulting Group's product portfolio suggesting that permanent hallmark events provide the highest asset value against risk and cost, and one-time mega events generating the highest costs with the highest risks.

Portfolio design model

Figure 5.3 provides a process model for portfolio design, the main elements of which are: Composing (strategies, event roles and design factors) and Synergising (balancing, leveraging and scheduling).

Evaluation and impact assessment tools (Figures 6.1 and 6.2)

To integrate evaluation into the event planning and management process the *logic model* is appropriate, with its clear statements about intended outputs (short-term) and how they are to be measured (specifying methods and key performance indicators). When events and event portfolios are conceived as agents of change, it is necessary to specify the preconditions, external factors, assumptions, planned actions that should logically achieve goals, short-term outputs to be measured, and long-term systemic changes to be evaluated through key impact indicators. This more elaborate process is called a *theory of change model*, and it is based on the premise that theory exists to predict outcomes. If not, the process becomes an experiment based on propositions or faith.

Evaluation tools

Figure 6.5 provides a process model for event evaluation that starts with antecedents (stakeholder collaboration is foremost), employing logic and theory of change models, methods and indicators, and finally adaptation and revision.

A research agenda

Throughout the book we have identified theory and research needed to support event portfolio management, giving rise to the following priorities. The aim is to both advance understanding of event portfolios as a contemporary phenomenon and to assist praxis, being the professional management of event portfolios.

Research related to the core-propositions

♦   Examine and prioritise factors affecting the legitimation and growth of events and event portfolios in different economic, environmental and cultural contexts.

♦   Determine the degree to which long-term sustainability is being sought and achieved through event portfolio management, as opposed to an emphasis on short-term outputs.

♦   Compare and contrast 'eventful cities' as to their event portfolio strategies, institutional arrangements, evaluation and success.

♦   Experiment with different strategies and leveraging tools to evaluate best practices in fostering portfolio synergies.

♦   Evaluate different focal organisations and other institutional arrangements as to their governance and relative effectiveness in creating and managing event portfolios – both for cities and destinations or countries.

♦   Examine overlapping portfolios and how they can be co-ordinated. How are conflicts resolved in this context?

Research related to the theoretical foundations

♦   What is the life-cycle of events as 'assets' or 'products' within a managed portfolio, assuming either/or extrinsic and intrinsic measures of performance and value? Are tourism/economic development or place marketing goals compatible with community or social/cultural goals within portfolios and within overlapping portfolios?

♦   Can event portfolios be managed for long-term self-sufficiency and/or growth? As opposed to requiring constant injections of capital and revisions to the composition of events.

♦ What inter-organisational governance mechanisms work best for event portfolio management?

♦ What degree of centralized control is optimal for the governance of event networks? Is a loose confederation more resilient?

♦ When evaluating event portfolio performance, how is asset value to be determined? What are the appropriate methods for valuing and comparing short-term outputs and longer-term outcomes/impacts?

♦ To what extent do event portfolios compensate for comparative disadvantages, or augment comparative advantages?

♦ How can 'balance' and 'health' be measured in whole populations of events?

Research related to the management of event portfolios

♦ Through action research develop more effective ways of implementing social marketing and social leveraging within portfolios.

♦ Compare the contributions of one-off and periodic events, and mega events to community events, to portfolio effectiveness and sustainability.

♦ Consult residents and other stakeholders on perceived impacts of events, particularly community-oriented versus tourism-oriented, and determine how this affects attitudes towards events and resulting political decisions.

♦ Examine organic portfolio development and laissez-faire approaches to event portfolios to learn how various environmental conditions affect portfolio formation and effectiveness.

♦ Within a population-ecology frame, compare cities and regions as to the evolution of events and portfolios with a view to determining the key environmental factors and how to manage them for portfolio effectiveness and sustainability.

♦ Apply logic and theory of change models to event portfolio planning as action research; what can be learned about the planning and design process through this type of evaluation?

♦ Expand the research conducted for this book by undertaking systematic, cross-case analysis.

♦ Is there a critical mass in the number and/or types of events to make portfolios efficient or sustainable?

♦ What exactly defines a balanced event portfolio, including an equitable spreading of risks among stakeholders?

♦ How do professionals and politicians evaluate risk and uncertainty versus value (from all perspectives) for single events, biddable events and event portfolios?

♦ What information is needed, and how will this be obtained, to establish benchmarks for the evaluation of long-term and cumulative event impacts?

♦ Conduct longitudinal research on event portfolio formation, evolution and effectiveness.

♦ Event portfolio managers need reliable, comparable data on event impacts, with standard measures of social and cultural impacts, ecological and built-environment impacts, dedicated event tourists, direct economic contribution, and other key performance and impact indicators.

♦ Compare focused (or specialized) event portfolios with diverse (or mixed) portfolios in terms of efficiency and effectiveness; consider how various portfolio design strategies might be complimentary.

♦ What is the optimal network for collaboration and for management of an event portfolio? (comparative social network analysis could reveal how focal organisations can maximize efficient links and have the greatest impact on the portfolio, or even an entire population of events) .

♦ In terms of creating and managing a portfolio, which comes first: venues or events? Is there an optimal development strategy for events and venues?

Final words

The authors have all been engaged in scholarly research concerning event portfolios, both to increase our understanding of this important phenomenon and to advance portfolio planning and management. It is an exciting line of research that should be expanded, and augmented by contributions from various disciplines and related fields of study. It is hoped that this book, which explores theoretical foundations and practical applications, will stimulate an active discourse and concerted research efforts to answer the many questions that have been identified.

Vladimir Antchak, Vassilios Ziakas, and Donald Getz

May, 2019

References

Chalip, L. (2004). Beyond impact: A general model for sport event leverage. In B. W. Ritchie & A. Daryl (Eds.), *Sport Tourism: Interrelationships, impacts and issues* (pp. 226-252). Clevedon: Channel View.

Smith, A. (2014). Leveraging sport mega-events: new model or convenient justification? *Journal of Policy Research in Tourism, Leisure and Events,* **6**(1), 15-30. doi:10.1080/19407963.2013.823976

Ziakas, V. (2014). *Event Portfolio Planning and Management: A holistic approach.* Abingdon, England: Routledge.

Index

Printed in the United States
By Bookmasters